Things Can Only Get Worse?

www.**penguin**.co.uk

Things Can Only Get Worse?

Twenty Confusing Years in the Life of a Labour Supporter 1997–2017

John O'Farrell

Doubleday

LONDON · TORONTO · SYDNEY · AUCKLAND · JOHANNESBURG

TRANSWORLD PUBLISHERS
61–63 Uxbridge Road, London W5 5SA
www.penguin.co.uk

Transworld is part of the Penguin Random House group of companies
whose addresses can be found at global.penguinrandomhouse.com

First published in Great Britain in 2017 by Doubleday
an imprint of Transworld Publishers

A CIP catalogue record for this book
is available from the British Library.

ISBNs 9780857524744 (hb)
9780857525338 (tpb)

Typeset in 11¼/16pt Sabon by Falcon Oast Graphic Art Ltd.
Printed and bound by Clays Ltd, Bungay, Suffolk

Penguin Random House is committed to a sustainable
future for our business, our readers and our planet. This book
is made from Forest Stewardship Council® certified paper.

1 3 5 7 9 10 8 6 4 2

For Alf Dubs.
Who never gives up.

Quite Left-Wing

General Election – 1 May 1997

I was walking my dog down by the river in Oxfordshire not so long ago and a well-spoken old man stopped me. 'I recognize you! You're that writer chappie!'

'Er, yes, I am a writer, yes.'

'O'Farrell!' he declared, sounding like one of my teachers at school.

'That's right . . .'

'Yes, but *what* O'Farrell? What's your first name?'

'Oh. It's John.'

'John O'Farrell!' he said to himself, finally satisfied. 'That's right! *Very* left wing!'

I told this to my family when I got home, and they fell about laughing. 'You?! *Very left wing!*' mocked my grown-up kids.

'Well, I'm *quite* left wing.' I said, feeling a bit hurt. 'I mean, Labour Party and all that . . .'

'Exactly! You're *soooo* moderate.' And my wife and kids laughed some more as they repeated the phrase '*Very left wing!*' to each other for their continued amusement. I tried to think of an example of a political stand I had recently taken to reassert my radical credentials. 'I boycotted the free Waitrose magazine – when it started having a column by Pippa Middleton.' No, they still weren't convinced.

What was revealing about this was that I cared. I liked the idea that I might be considered 'very left wing'. It's cool to be left wing; it's not cool to appear moderate or ready to compromise. Any way you look at it, Che Guevara makes for a better student poster than David Miliband. Attending a school governors' meeting is less thrilling than putting on a Vendetta mask and smashing the windows of Fortnum and Mason. (Personally, I think it's pointless looting their windows; all their best stuff is way back inside the shop, sort of on the right as you pass the preserves.) It's so simple to be against authority. It's so much harder to represent authority yourself.

And so, when Labour at last came to power after eighteen miserable years, people like me suddenly found themselves feeling confused and disorientated. We were hard-wired for opposition. I'd been in political prison too long, I couldn't cope with all this freedom and responsibility. I hankered for the easy certainties back inside. So even back in May 1997, I knew I was going to find it hard. But Tony, you didn't have to make it quite *that* hard.

After Labour's landslide victory, I bought the BBC video of Election Night so I could enjoy that euphoric evening over and over again. And nineteen years on, I found that I still had it, the only VHS I never gave to the charity shop. There it is in a box in my loft, a film of dust over the New Labour leader as he waves to me on our greatest night. I have to rig up an old video-player to watch it again, the very format emphasizing that this is politics from another age.

Looking at that recording of our honeymoon, Tony, now, I

try not to feel too much anger, too much bitterness; I just try to remember how happy we were together back then. We had the world at our feet; it seemed like there was nothing we couldn't do. I was so giddy with the excitement of it all, I never stopped to think that it was obvious it would end up leaving me so conflicted. 'Sticking to the Conservative spending plans for two years' – that should have been a clue. *Why did I just let that pass?* I ask myself now; how come you even had those spending plans in your jacket pocket? Who gave them to you? Who'd you been talking to? You were supposed to delete all those phone numbers from your mobile the day we got hitched; Rupert, Silvio, Cliff – I'd thought you were through with mixing with those guys; this was about us now, this was supposed to be a new start. Did you ever stop to think about the compromises I made? It wasn't easy for me, you know. I took your name, though 'New Labour' never sat easily with me. Waving plastic Union flags was not really my thing either, and then when you said you wanted us to do it The Third Way, I was shocked, I was embarrassed, I felt used, Tony. I leafleted for you, I canvassed for you, and now you are over there in America with Rupert and here I am, right back where I was in the mid-1980s, Labour in opposition and another pile of undelivered leaflets in my hallway.

When New Labour came to power I was in my mid-thirties; married with two small children in a semi-detached house in the London borough of Lambeth. Once considered as 'loony lefty' but now reformed and sensible, Lambeth and I were a good fit. I had grudgingly accepted the changes Tony Blair had made to the Labour Party – after so many political defeats and my growing realization that we were not going to get the Tories out simply by suggesting it loudly on marches. I didn't wear left-wing badges any more; I had transferred them to the lapels of the full-size Maggie

Thatcher *Spitting Image* puppet I'd inherited from my time on the show and which now stared at me from beside my desk. This grotesque latex model traumatized my poor little daughter every time I forgot to close my office door. I tried to put it into some sort of context for her, explaining who Mrs Thatcher was and what she'd done as a politician, but still my daughter woke in the night crying from her nightmares about Maggie.

'What exactly are you frightened of, darling?'

'I'm scared that . . . that . . . she's going to take all the milk from the little children.'

When my son was four I'd overheard him playing with his plastic dinosaurs: 'And then the T. Wex smashed it all up and then . . . and then joined – the *Labour Party*!' My poor kids never stood a chance. We were a Labour family: our front door was red, our cereal selection was Nestlé-free and our new kitchen extension made it perfect for the Labour Party Committee Rooms on Election Day. Even my shoes were 'a bit left wing', according to one posh writer I knew. *How can my shoes have political attributes?* I thought. *That's ridiculous!* And then I looked from my plain Doc Martens across to his expensive tan brogues and thought, *Urgh! I could never wear Tory shoes like those . . .*

My parents were both Labour supporters, and a casual observer might have said that, when it came to the issues, my dad was more left wing than my mum. Rather refreshingly, he moved to the left as he got older; when I was a student, we had argued over his support for the Falklands conflict. But twenty years later, father and son bonded over our mutual opposition to the coming war in Iraq. My mum wasn't in the pub for this conversation. She was writing letters to foreign dictators for Amnesty International, or she was securing the lease for the Oxfam shop in King Street, or she was shaking a tin by Cookham station for causes she believed in. So, who was the most left wing out of any of us?

Tony Blair may have been the most right-wing Labour leader I could remember, but he alone was going to *effect change*, which also made him the most left-wing leader I could remember. Power – that's the central purpose of political parties, and ours had generally been second best at winning it. Rediscovering that VHS of *Election '97* was like watching the climactic last episode of a very long box set in which all the many villains are finally brought down one by one in lingering and imaginative detail. We watched this tape as a family at a time when Britain had just voted to leave Europe, when politics had turned particularly nasty, while Labour were rock bottom in the polls, drifting and divided and looking like they might disappear altogether. I tried to explain to my kids what a Labour landslide felt like: our incredulity at the scale of our win, when we had not dared to presume we would ever see a Labour victory in the rest of our lifetime. Picture a whole evening's television with little red bars constantly flashing across the bottom 'Lab gain Hove . . . Lab Gain Stroud . . . Lab Gain Another Implausibly Posh Place in the South . . .' The Tories lost more seats than they retained – can you even imagine how happy that made us feel? After so many agonizing defeats, after that mirage of victory in 1992 had evaporated at the very moment we reached out to embrace it, after being knocked down all through the '80s and '90s . . . at long last, it was we who were standing on chairs cheering and the Tories who were utterly defeated and dejected.

There is Battersea turning red, the place where I had become consumed by the local Labour Party when I'd first moved there, aged twenty-two. I had spent 1 May 1997 back in my old stamping ground; I delivered 'Vote Today' leaflets, I sat on a polling station collecting voters' numbers and giving a very clipped and unsmiling 'Good morning' when the Tory MP visited. He would be the first minister to lose his seat that night, but that was just to warm us up: the evening's viewing seemed carefully scripted so that the villains were decapitated in a particularly satisfying order. There goes ex-Chancellor Norman Lamont; he would later use his free time for good causes like helping the torturing mass-murderer General Pinochet escape prosecution. And there's David Mellor, shouting his defiance in defeat, with all the charm and dignity of Gollum with road rage. Then, how utterly satisfying to see the disgraced Tory MP Neil Hamilton losing the fourth-safest Conservative seat in Britain. *Well, he'll never be elected to public office again,* we all thought.

At 3 a.m. we cut to Enfield Southgate, impregnable seat of Michael Portillo, the Tories' leader-in-waiting. 'No one is saying he could actually lose,' the commentators say in the build-up to this result, 'but it looks like it could be much closer than expected!' The surprise winner, Stephen Twigg, later revealed how the returning officer had privately shared the shock result with the candidates before leading them up on to the stage. 'Everyone happy?' he had checked. 'Ecstatic!' came Portillo's sarcastic reply. In his speech, Portillo said he would do everything he could to help rebuild the Conservative Party, which apparently involved doing a series on great railway journeys wearing brightly coloured trousers.

But returning to this historic night in the summer of 2016 when Labour was in its darkest hour didn't make me happy, it made me depressed. It was like watching the happy wedding video of your bitterly divorced parents. My dear wife kept groaning, 'Oh God . . .' at every fantastic result; the more the Labour supporters on our screen celebrated, the deeper the gloom in our front room. In this political fantasy's climactic scene, as the Labour activists await the new Prime Minister outside the Royal Festival Hall,

I can just make out my own head in the crowd; freeze-frame –
look, that's me; see, kids, that's your dad – cheering and jumping
up and down to 'Things Can Only Get Better' in the light of the
new dawn. I wish we could have freeze-framed that day in British
history, freeze-framed all that optimism and hope. Look at my
expression; I can't quite believe it. *That's it!* I'm thinking. *The
Tories are banished for ever!*

The eventual Labour majority was 179; bigger than Labour's
landslide in 1945, a greater margin than anything Thatcher had
achieved and the Tories' heaviest defeat since 1832. We thought
this was it; we would never have a Conservative government ever
again. Deep down, I did worry about this new government lacking the socialist stomach to change the country fundamentally
and for ever. But I am not going to pretend I was opposed to Tony
Blair. In May 1997, I just felt this enormous sense of gratitude
towards him: he had utterly destroyed the Tories, the House of
Commons suddenly seemed fresh and progressive – we had MPs
of different genders, of different skin colours, openly gay
MPs, we had a Minister for Culture not a Minister for Heritage,
the twenty-first century felt like it started on 1 May 1997.

And then, on the Saturday night, we won another bonus landslide as the United Kingdom overwhelmingly won the Eurovision
Song Contest. There could be no clearer message from our
comrades all across the continent: 'Welcome back, Britain!' After
all those years of petty xenophobia and the embarrassment of
Thatcher hectoring foreigners, or weird, inbred-looking Tories
wanting us to quit the European Union altogether, finally we
were fully committed European partners: Tony Blair, Gordon
Brown and Katrina and the Waves.

The grand issue of Europe had dogged the Tories right to
the very end. Just to add to their miseries at the 1997 General

Election, they were undermined on the right by the creation of something called the 'Referendum Party'. This was the private project of dodgy billionaire Sir James Goldsmith, who spent a fortune during the election campaign as the Tories lost five hundred deposits and distributed 5 million videotapes presented by Gavin Campbell from the popular TV show *That's Life*. Voters were disappointed to discover that Gavin's sombre message on the EU was not followed by a dog saying 'sausages' or Esther Rantzen holding up a carrot that looked like a penis.

At the time, I regarded the Referendum Party as an irrelevant novelty sideshow. In July, Sir James Goldsmith died, his party was disbanded and I think we all presumed that the idea of a referendum on Britain's membership of the European Union would be buried along with him. But, by spending millions on one eccentric idea, he had succeeded in purchasing a slot in the national debate. 'A Referendum on Britain's membership of the European Union' – that was now, officially, a thing. A notion. Little did we know it at the time, but Goldsmith had successfully planted a time-bomb in the British political system. His supporters' slightly fascistic chanting at Putney Leisure Centre on Election Night in May 1997 was a portent of an uglier politics that would be unleashed long after he had shuffled off the stage.

But for now, shouting at your political opponents was out of fashion. In fact, so big was Tony's 'big tent' that, shortly after taking occupation of Downing Street, he even invited Margaret bloody Thatcher round for a friendly chat. I remember feeling shocked and betrayed to see that terrible woman invited into our HQ, even if I understood the audacious symbolism of it all. Blair was made of more forgiving stuff than I was. As far as I was concerned, he might as well have invited Darth Vader to Number Ten to discuss how the Jedi could adopt Dark Side reforms in order to appeal to voters from the *Death Star*. It was the shocking reveal at the end of the first New Labour episode. Young Tony was not Darth Thatcher's enemy. He was her son.

Pretty soon, being a Labour supporter would make me a total pariah again, only this time to people on the left of me instead of people on the right. My party allegiance throughout the past four decades helps me to understand what it must feel like to be a shirt-maker from Paisley. 'You'll never believe this, but there was actually one very brief moment in history when we were *really* fashionable.'

As I packed away that grainy VHS tape of *Election '97* and returned it to the loft, it felt like we could never be popular again. I thought about those final scenes: the ecstatic Labour supporters smiling and waving their Labour banners and Union flags, the map of Britain turning from blue to red, and me somewhere in that crowd at the Royal Festival Hall celebrating the greatest-ever moment to be a Labour supporter. And it was hard not to ask, *What the hell happened?* How had we allowed Labour to slide from being this media-savvy, landslide-winning machine, full of confidence and optimism, to become an angry, divided, low-polling opposition, letting down the very people the party was founded to help?

And how had we let the UK mutate from being that hopeful and outward-looking country welcomed back into the heart of Europe, a kingdom genuinely united – England voting Labour, Scotland voting Labour, Wales voting Labour, Northern Ireland voting; well, we never pretended to understand any of that – but where did it all go? How did the tolerance and hope of May 1997 and that 'new dawn' lead to the dark night of bigotry and fear of June 2016?

What is the right place for the Labour Party on the political spectrum? In seeking that balance between socialist idealism and effective election-winning popularity, who can name any point in our lifetime when Labour definitely got it just right? Do I want it to be 'very left wing', like that man in Oxford thought I was? Or should it be '*soooo* moderate', like my wife and kids think I am?

I had remained a member of the Labour Party, whether it was led by Michael Foot, Tony Blair or Jeremy Corbyn. I never would have predicted that the last could win a vote to be Labour leader; I would have laughed if you'd said Donald Trump could become the American President, and I placed a bet on Remain to win the 2016 Euro Referendum by a much larger margin than everyone was predicting.

It felt like I knew nothing any more. It had taken me two whole decades to learn it . . .

'Something of the Night About Him'

Conservative Party Leadership Election –
19 June 1997

As a writer, one is occasionally asked, 'Which book changed your life?', and you are supposed to answer *Ulysses* by James Joyce or Proust's *À la recherche du temps perdus*, casually mentioning how much more lyrical it is if you read it in the original French. But, for me, the honest answer to 'Which book changed your life?' is *my* book. The one written by *me*.

My writing career had first begun a decade or so earlier, when I had plucked up the courage to walk through the doors of Broadcasting House in London for the open meetings they had for Radio 4's long-running topical satire show *Week Ending*. It had taken me a few years of doing dead-end jobs before I even heard of the existence of this secret portal into the world of comedy-writing, and I remember I was shaking slightly as I walked into a room full of confident young men, who all seemed to know the form. But shortly after that, I had a sketch broadcast. It was like some unbelievable magic trick, that the exact words I had typed into my Amstrad 8256 should now be read out on the radio in my kitchen. And then they actually said my name in the credits at the end, and I was inspired to keep going back and give in more material. For months after that, my entire weekends were passed either in giddy elation because I'd had a sketch broadcast on Friday night or abject depression because my efforts had been rejected. Even now, when I hear the show's old theme tune ('Party Fears Two' by The Associates), I get this Pavlovian shiver of anxiety which used to herald either triumph or disaster.

I met another aspiring writer there and we started working together, discovering that being in a partnership more than doubled the quality and quantity of our material. Mark brought a whole new perspective; he came from a different Thames-side village to myself. Pretty soon, we were granted the hallowed weekly commission, and then we became the lead writers on the show and my mum could tell people that her son was a professional comedy writer, which I think she probably did even when she was just queuing in the post office.

One particular production assistant, whose job included timing my sketches for payment purposes, always seemed to log them at just over two minutes rather than just under, which meant I always got paid more. So I married her. Jackie also worked on *I'm Sorry I Haven't a Clue*, and blushed on stage at all the innuendo aimed at Humphrey's assistant, but if I met fans of that show I was able to tell them 'I married the lovely Samantha.'

After a decade of writing TV and radio comedy, I suddenly had an idea for a book, a political memoir tracking my life as a Labour activist from the day Thatcher was elected in 1979 to Labour's landslide victory in 1997. I wrote a first chapter and an outline of my thrilling bodice-ripper about inquorate ward meetings, and soon I was telling a Tory parent in the school playground how amazed I was to have various publishers bidding against each other for my lefty life story. 'Yes, John, it's called *capitalism*,' he explained.

I had thought that a book about how I helped the Labour Party lose elections at every level might be of minor interest to a few political anoraks but would soon be gathering dust in the back rooms of second-hand bookshops. However, it turned out that lots of people had been attending poorly attended meetings just like I had. All over the country, thousands of Labour Party members had sat there in draughty tenants' halls and passed ten-point resolutions calling on Margaret Thatcher to cease her programme of privatization immediately, despite our lurking suspicion that she might not always read these motions right to the end. I had correctly guessed that all Labour Party meetings were just like the ones I'd been to. It was probably the same at the very top. When Tony Blair was sitting there waiting to start a Cabinet meeting, I bet he looked at his watch and said, 'Well, let's give it a few more minutes, and see if anyone else turns up?' When Gordon Brown gave his Treasurer's Report, did the rest of them simply stare at their agendas, colouring in all the letter Os?

I got hundreds of letters from people telling me that I had written their life story, which I think they meant in the broadest sense, because not all of them could have married Jackie. So many people wrote to me to say that they, too, had been out knocking on doors for Labour in the 1980s that I was amazed we had lost so many bloody elections. I got a letter from the *New Statesman*. It read: 'Dear John O'Farrell, Subscribe now and get a free copy of *Things Can Only Get Better* by John O'Farrell.' The book went to number one and stayed there for over a month, eventually being knocked off the top spot by *Stalingrad* by Antony Beevor.

I think what happened was that people read my account of being a Labour activist during the Thatcher years and then bought *Stalingrad* to cheer themselves up a bit.

So, life under the New Labour government definitely improved for this particular voter. Under the Tories, I had been a back-room gag writer. When Labour came to power, I became an author, centre stage and suddenly getting all the credit, and this hadn't even been one of Labour's five pledges. Writing a hit book transformed me to some sort of novelty Labour mascot and occasional political commentator. Now when I went into Broadcasting House, it was to do an interview down the line with BBC Radio Three Counties.

'So, John, are you doing any book events in the Three Counties area?'

(Thinks: *Three counties? Could be anywhere.*) 'Oh yeah, in a couple of the counties, here and there. Love those counties . . .'

I was invited on to *Newsnight* and *Question Time*, I got my own weekly newspaper column; I was thoroughly enjoying all the attention. 'Tell me,' I asked, 'how long does this Flavour of the Month thing generally last?'

I got an invitation to a drinks reception at 11 Downing Street for 'people in the creative industries', which apparently included writers who spent forty hours a week playing Tetris. I presented it to the policemen on the gate and it seemed they hadn't changed their mind and I felt secretly thrilled to be doing that same walk that I'd watched ministers do a thousand times on the news. However, in my head, I had always imagined that 11 Downing Street was the first door, with Number Ten just beyond it. So I strode confidently right up to the wrong door and it was only then that I saw the famous number 10 and heard myself say to the policeman, 'Oh! Is this 10 Downing Street?'

He gave me a look as if I was an idiot alien from the Planet Stupid.

'Er, yesssss!'

'Right, so number 11 would be next door, then?'

'Yessss.'

As I walked away, I could almost hear him thinking, *Blimey, and I thought the last lot were a waste of bloody space.*

I had expected the inside of Downing Street to be old-fashioned and stuffy, but on the walls of the big reception room there were enormous modern paintings that had recently been chosen from the cellars of the national collection. Later, I got a sneak nose-around the flat above Number Ten and saw the woolly boiled-egg warmers that John and Norma Major had left behind. The stairway was lined with pictures of former prime ministers and I thought, *There's no way I would put up with that in my home!* First thing every morning, last thing at night, there's a photo of Maggie Thatcher staring right at you.

It was around this time that I heard a tantalizing new phrase which spoke of an exclusive secret cabal that intrigued me. William Hague warned the nation of the existence of the so-called 'liberal élite'. *Who are these people?* I wondered. *Do they really exist? Is there any chance I might gain admittance into this shady, well-meaning mafia?*

I have to report that the initiation ceremony to the liberal élite is brutal and testing. I was summoned to a large house in Hampstead, slightly scruffier than those around it, a copy of the *London Review of Books* on top of the recycling pile by the gate. Inside, I was subjected to three hours of intensive interrogation, including heavily loaded questions such as 'Chablis or Malbec?' and 'More raspberry coulis?' Around me were tell-tale signs that I was in the HQ of this *bien-pensant* cult; there were Fabian pamphlets on the coffee table that had actually been read, theatre programmes from the Royal Court, a rental brochure for villas in Tuscany. All of us applying to join the liberal élite were carefully monitored for our level of outrage about Tory xenophobia and the price of organic avocados. They casually referred to the great and the good by only their first names, and I tried not to let on that I didn't know who they meant when they just said 'Alan'. Yentob, maybe, or Johnson? – just don't say, 'Shearer,' whatever you do. The final test was a group discussion on second homes and selective education in which we had to affirm the correct moral stance but leave enough wiggle-room to make an exception for ourselves: 'Oh, well, it's so difficult, isn't it? One wants to do the right thing, but one doesn't want to force one's politics upon one's children.' A few more equivocations and a vague commitment to buying a Toyota Prius, and I was in. I'll never forget the euphoria I felt on the way home as I chatted in an overly friendly manner to the mini-cab driver about how well Nigeria had done in the World Cup.

For me, 'the establishment' had always meant old right-wing men who knew each other from the top private schools and Oxbridge; the phrase summoned up images of judges, generals and financiers dining with Tory MPs in the Carlton Club. But there was a new establishment and, though I can't say I ever felt particularly powerful or influential, it was important to recognize that I was now on the inside. I had my own weekly column in the *Guardian*, for God's sake! How privileged can you get? When my dad left school in Manchester aged fifteen, he went into the offices of the *Guardian* to see if there might be any entry-level jobs for an Irish boy with no qualifications. He told me the door-man nearly threw him down the stairs. And sixty years later, he was ringing up his son to say that his column was 'Absolutely marvellous!' 'Your best yet!' he would tell me every week. My mum kept a collection of them by the bed. 'Whenever I can't get to sleep, I just read a couple of your newspaper columns and I'm out like a light!'

Writing 850 words every week in the op-ed pages meant that I was now supposed to have an informed opinion on *everything*; from economics to human cloning to wind farms or whether Railtrack should run the ley lines. 'I can't work out your politics, John,' said the new comment editor Seumas Milne to me on a rare trip into the *Guardian* offices for a drinks reception.

'Well, I suppose I want the Labour Party to be as radical and as redistributive as it's possible to be,' I began, to his obvious approval, 'while still managing to win elections.' I'm sure his smile dropped a little after that. Maybe that emphasis made me a Blairite in his book; maybe even suggesting that the two were not automatically compatible marked me down as a sell-out woolly Menshevik. I didn't wait to find out; I thought, *I'm not going to stand here and be accused of being a middle-class New Labour-type. I'll go and chat to Polly Toynbee about nice restaurants in Clapham . . .*

It had been much easier doing political satire when the despised Tories had been in power; it was so much harder to be rude about a government for which I had campaigned. So, even now, I kept finding myself writing about the problems of the opposition rather than mocking the party that was actually in power.

In the aftermath of their heaviest defeat since the Second Ice Age, the Conservative Party had to find a new leader. This once-unbeatable party had become something of an irrelevant sideshow, and few people were even watching the shabby parade of the lower-ranking officers who had only been obeying orders under the previous regime. To see how pathetic they looked now, this procession of former bullies and bigots, reduced to sniping at one another in the hope of a few seconds of media attention, well, it warmed my socialist heart.

A 'dream ticket' was announced of Michael Howard standing to be Conservative leader, with William Hague running as his deputy. Then young William obviously got home to Ffion, to find her waiting in the hallway for him with a face like thunder. 'You agreed *what*? You said you'd work under that slimeball? What the hell were you thinking?! Get back out there and tell them that you're running for the leadership yourself, you idiot!'

Howard's candidacy received a second torpedo from one of the ministers who had worked with him at the Home Office. Ann Widdecombe said of her former boss that there was 'something of the night' about him. It was a wonderfully suggestive description which crystallized that creepy, sinister aspect that we'd all felt but had never quite put into words before. I know that in politics we are supposed to concentrate on policy not personalities, but it was hard to ignore the fact that Michael Howard couldn't abide sunlight and had the ability to transform himself into a bat.

Howard tried to restore his reputation by appearing on *Newsnight*; being as it was conveniently scheduled after sundown. When Jeremy Paxman asked a direct question about Howard threatening to overrule the Director of the Prison Service, the former Home Secretary didn't answer the question. So Paxman asked the question again. Twelve times. There was something almost heroic about Howard's dogged refusal to answer this simple, direct question, his inability to change tack or realize that he was being made to look ridiculous. It was like he'd got into the groove now; like Donna Summer repeating 'I Feel Love' over and over again, he was just going to keep riffing his prepared line until the synthesizers faded out and everyone stopped dancing.

So the Tory leadership was eventually won by William Hague, but nobody really cared. The Conservative Party was like *Neighbours*; apparently, it was still going, even though all the big stars had left and no one watched it any more. Young William seemed to lack a certain gravitas, which he now attempted to acquire by wearing a baseball cap and riding the log flume at Alton Towers.

The adversarial nature of politics and the constant search for short-term advantage makes it so tempting to focus your attack on the personalities of the leading players or one-off crass mistakes made by Cabinet ministers – and with the Tories in the mid-1990s, this was the gift that kept on giving. But as Labour went from opposition to government, it became clear that this was a losing game because, eventually, it comes back to bite you. One minute you're attacking leading Tories for whatever they've done in their private lives, and the next minute Robin Cook is leaving Margaret for Gaynor or Ron Davies is trying to pretend it's completely normal to be getting a bit of fresh air in the woods at half past two in the morning. And then you try to claim, 'Now, look here, it's policy that matters, not individuals! Judge us on our results in government, not on silly tabloid tittle-tattle like the taxpayers' bill for Lord Irvine's wallpaper.' (And then you glance at that story again and think, *Shit, sixty grand? That is some seriously expensive wallpaper . . .*)

Political discourse had become gentler after 1997. Under Tony Blair, our tribal colours were painted in pastel shades; now, politics was easy-listening, not punk. My youthful hatred of the Tories seemed slightly passé now that they were such an irrelevance, so perhaps it wasn't a coincidence that I was moving on from the binary world of TV satire into the more nuanced world of books.

As well as losing elections throughout the Thatcher and Major years, I had also established a pretty consistent track record for losing at awards ceremonies. We would turn up to the BAFTAs or the British Comedy Awards and notice that our table was definitely not the one closest to the stage; in fact, it was generally out in the hallway and down a flight of stairs. I seemed to spend a whole decade losing to either Margaret Thatcher or Armando Ianucci. We could never seem to beat the Wandsworth Conservatives or *Drop the Dead Donkey*.

But now, under a Labour government, I felt confident that things were going to change. Everything was more optimistic. Even my hopeless football team had turned it around: Fulham were promoted from the bottom division in 1997 and by the end of Labour's first term would be promoted to the Premiership; such was life under this new Labour government. In this positive environment of hope and justice, I had high hopes when *Things Can Only Get Better* was nominated for a very important award that no one had ever heard of before.

Channel 4 had just launched a new programme called *The Political Awards*, perhaps unaware of the old adage that 'politics is show business for ugly people'. 'Who will win the coveted award for Best Select Committee Chairman?' asked none of the tabloids. However, my opinion of Channel 4's *Political Awards* obviously went up a great deal the moment I was nominated for one. The last prize I had received for my prose was a smiley sticker for neatly joined-up letters. I was up for 'Political Book of the Year'. (Who can forget Karl Marx's tearful speech when he won in 1867?) Everyone told me I had a really good chance, and I went along to the television recording in Westminster with my carefully prepared speech about this all being so unexpected. There was a lunch and I was put on a table with the other nominees.

But nothing from my parents' middle-class dinner parties had quite prepared me for being seated with a former Tory prime minister. Ted Heath was the bogeyman of my childhood, an almost mythical baddie who my dad used to shout at on the television news. Ted Heath was the man who brought in the Three-Day Week and ordered television programmes to end at half past ten in the evening. Beaten by the miners, beaten by Thatcher, now he was up against the toughest opponent of them all as 'the Grocer' went head to head with John O'Farrell for Political Book of the Year.

Nominees on the other side of the table were chatting away amiably, but I found myself struggling for suitable subject matter for casual chit-chat. *Eat really slowly,* I told myself as I stared down at my plate. *Once you've finished, you'll have no choice but to make conversation.* What the hell was I supposed to say to him? 'Um, so, Ted? Do you think the Spice Girls will get back together?' Or maybe, 'Tell me, Ted, how do you think Keegan's gonna do in the England job?'

I heard a rumour that this award was definitely between me and the former PM. *Pah, but what chance does he have?* I thought. *He hasn't won anything since the 1970 election. And I suppose when I do beat him he'll probably go off and sulk for another twenty-five years!* The decades of undeserved Tory triumphs are over now, Heath! This is the era of Labour victories; from general elections to book awards, you'd better get used to being on the losing side!

The moment came for Jon Snow to read out the winner. With my fingers crossed under the table, I had a few thoughts about who I should thank as I received the award. And then, sure enough, a cameraman knelt down right beside me. *Yes!* I thought. *This is it!*

But instead of pointing the lens at my face, he asked me if I could lean right back so he could 'get a clean shot of Ted Heath'.

Hang on a minute, I thought to myself. *That's a strange thing to say.*

'No – move back a bit more, mate!' said the cameraman. 'But don't block his path to the stage.'

Hmm, I'm picking up clues here, I thought. *I have a feeling for these things.*

Some Vague Utopia

European Parliament Elections – 10 June 1999

I think, at some solipsistic level, I had once believed that if I worked really, really hard for the Labour Party, then they would come to power and all the bad things about our society would immediately be put right. Gradually realizing one's own political impotency is the cruellest part of growing older. I could cope with the loss of hair, the creaky knees the morning after five-a-side football – it's the *insignificance* that is so hard to come to terms with, the creeping realization that the world doesn't change just because you set out to change it.

Labour in Power had once been a fantasy notion, 'some vague utopia' in which fairness and tolerance would flourish and all injustice and exploitation would be forbidden – or at least be confined to the borders of Mordor and Wandsworth Borough Council. But here it was: I was finally living under a government of the party I had campaigned for.

'So . . . did things get better?' asked the first questioner at every book event or library reading. This was such a regular opener you'd have thought I might have come up with some short and witty reply by now, but, perhaps because I was so eaten up

23

with anxiety about it all, I always took far too long to answer, I could almost feel the energy in the crowd slipping away. Oh, no – not nuance! Not complexity! No panellist was ever cheered on *Question Time* for carefully putting both points of view. But this was my life now: bye-bye, certainty, bye-bye, binary politics; I was fair, I saw both points of view; I was the kid in the school whose dad was headmaster.

My friend Pete had always been way to the left of me; he'd briefly been in the Socialist Workers Party before quitting over democratic centralism, feminism and, more significantly, the expectation that he should get up at six in the morning to sell newspapers. Once upon a time, we'd been united in our loathing of Thatcher and Major, but now we argued about the government that followed. He pointed out the failures of the Labour government; I tried to cling on to the positives and not put the word 'New' before 'Labour' quite so often.

'I can't believe New Labour is abolishing trial by jury!'

'Well, that's not exactly right, Pete. I mean, I don't personally agree with that particular reform, but I think Jack Straw is trying to speed up the justice system, and looking at whether a jury trial is appropriate in every single case.'

'They'll probably just lock them all up in the Dome. They'll have to find something to do with it.'

'To be fair, the Dome was first commissioned by the Tories, and though I don't personally agree with the decision to build it, I think you have to put it in context of all the hospitals and schools that are now being built as well.'

'Yeah, with private finance . . . putting private money into the health service – where will it end?'

'Well, I mean I don't personally agree with that particular aspect of the funding . . .'

'Why don't they just tax the rich more and pay for it like that?'

'Well, obviously, I don't personally agree with Labour's pledge not to raise the top rate of tax but, at the other end of the scale, huge benefit payments to the worst off: pensioners' winter-fuel payments, free TV licences for the elderly, Education Maintenance Allowances, Sure Start? The minimum wage has meant a pay rise for two million people.'

'Yeah, a tiny one. It's all just tinkering, trying to put a nicer gloss on capitalism.'

'But credit where it's due – Pinochet arrested!'

'Oh, they'll cop out on that. They always cop out.'

'They didn't with hand guns. Think how many lives that will save. And landmines banned? Peace in Northern Ireland, devolution, six hundred hereditary peers abolished.'

'And ninety-two left in place.'

'Okay. But Labour have cancelled Third World Debt.'

'Yeah, now all the students are going to be in debt instead.'

'Well, I don't personally agree with that particular policy . . .'

That became a sort of catch phrase, an equivocating admission of my guilt by association before we could start discussing whatever Labour were doing. But then Pete had previously been opposed to everything Neil Kinnock had done; he had been against John Smith; it's no good being furious about Tony Blair's changes to the Labour Party, Pete, you've already used up all your go's. He had even opposed independence for the Bank of England, while I had enthusiastically supported it. Obviously, neither of us knew what the hell it actually meant, but it showed where we were both coming from.

But Pete was sincere and consistent, I respected him for that. What I couldn't stand were the privileged liberals who had supported Labour for five minutes and were now wringing their hands in sorrow that it had apparently all gone wrong. One such acquaintance told me with a heavy heart that he was resigning from the Labour Party.

'Really?' I said, a little bemused. In truth, I'd never have guessed this bloke had ever been a member. 'Um – when did you join?'

'In '96.'

Well, that doesn't count, then! I was screaming inside. *If you held off joining the battle until it was obvious it was won, you don't have the right to storm off in a huff at the first scent of difficulty!* Of course, I couldn't actually say that; all members are equal, even if, deep down, I felt that some members were more equal than others.

In the newspapers, I'd regularly read that another famous actor had announced that they'd become disillusioned with Labour, and these fair-weather celebrity supporters annoyed me even more. They'd been happy to associate themselves with Tony Blair when he was the charismatic new star on the scene but so quick to wash their hands when supporting Labour became last year's fashion. We should have launched a support group for these celebs; we could have called it Luvvies Labour's Lost. I was half-listening to the news on the radio one Sunday morning when my ears suddenly pricked up at the novelty item at the end of the bulletin. 'And, finally, the writer of *Things Can Only Get Better* says he no longer supports the Labour government.'

'What?!' I exclaimed out loud. 'I never said that!' And I racked my brains for something I might have said that could have been misinterpreted or distorted. And then I realized who they meant. I had nicked my book title off a songwriter. They weren't talking about me at all. I'd been caught thinking it was all about me, just like so many other people whose politics were more about

26

how it made them look, rather than what was really important.

What the papers were not telling us (perhaps because Downing Street wasn't telling them) was that, after eighteen mean years of the vilification of people on benefits, of increasing poverty and cuts that always hit the poorest, the tide was flowing in the other direction. The income of the poorest tenth of the British population went up around 9 per cent during the first three years of the Labour government and, believe it or not, the very richest saw a small reduction in their wealth. But you had to be a political nerd to pin down these statistics; it was like the Labour government were doing the redistributive bit in secret.

But there were also times when the tone of the Labour government felt so wrong. When Jack Straw talked about crime or immigration, it was like our family had this right-wing grandfather who you didn't want talking to your friends at Christmas. On that dawn after Election Day, Tony Blair had proclaimed, 'We were elected as New Labour – and we will govern as New Labour!' I had cheered along with everyone else in that crowd because, frankly, the mood we were all in, we would have cheered if he'd recited all the lyrics to 'Bohemian Rhapsody'. But what the new Prime Minister was basically saying was, 'You know all that being friendly to business, working with wealth-creators – we weren't just saying all that shit to get elected – we really think that's the way to go!' Stephen Byers, the Trade Secretary, actually said that wealth creation was more important than wealth distribution. This was quite a staggering statement for a Labour minister to make. I tried not to dismiss it out of hand, just to entertain for a second the concept that the best way to help those who get a small slice of the cake is to make the cake bigger. But, in my bones, I knew this could not be right. What's the point of a Labour government if only to be more competent than the Conservatives?

Perhaps they are just being smart? I wondered. *Maybe they are playing the long game, keeping Middle England on-side, avoiding panic in the City and keeping quiet about their steady plan to transform Britain over the long term through winning more than two elections in a row* (something no other Labour government had ever achieved). *Perhaps the more radical stuff is yet to come?* After all, Mrs Thatcher barely got going during her first term – all her really sweeping changes came after she was re-elected. In June 1997, Tony Blair had gone to a council estate in south-east London and pledged to abolish child poverty in twenty years. Maybe, in June 2017, I would be looking back over the endless succession of Labour governments and feeling a sense of enormous pride that this target had been reached. Maybe, by 2017, Tony Blair would be some kind of mythical folk hero, his popularity so much greater than the grudging respect he was granted during his first term?

But, in the meantime, party activists like me had to survive on the meagre allowance of left-wing policies that were grudgingly portioned out by the government. Just as Labour's minimum wage had been criticized for being set at the absolute lowest end of the scale, so was the rate of 'Minimum Socialism' we were granted to sustain us through delivering leaflets and knocking on doors. 'Just a measly review of fox-hunting and the abolition of school-assisted places?' we complained. 'We can't be expected to live on that! We want to feast on the end of grammar schools and Murdoch being banned from owning British newspapers.'

And what made it hardest of all was being fully aware of New Labour's maddening shortcomings, resolving that this was still much better than the Tories, but then being cast as a 'Tory' as a result. Stand-up comics I had known since the 1980s, when we had done benefits together for left-wing causes, were appalled that I could have moved so far to the right by remaining in the same party. I was a panellist on *The News Quiz*, and afterwards, in the pub, the wonderful and much-missed Linda Smith turned to me and said ominously, 'So, you were very funny on the show tonight . . . And you seem like a nice person . . . So how can you possibly be a supporter of the Blair government?' It felt like she was saying, *You seem nice, so I can't understand why you like to torture kittens.*

People accused me of being in 'Blair's pocket', it was ridiculous, I hadn't voted for Tony Blair in the leadership election, I had been critical of him in various newspaper articles, I'd never dream of describing myself as 'New Labour' – how could anyone describe me as being in Blair's pocket? I think it was shortly after this that I got an invitation from the Blairs to dinner at Chequers.

There's a bit at the end of my first political memoir when I recall finally coming face to face with Tony Blair at the Royal Festival Hall on that dawn of 2 May 1997. In my inebriated, emotional state, I had over-emphatically shaken his hand and blurted out, 'We've waited so long! We've waited so long!!' 'He smiled and gave me an affirmative nod,' I wrote, 'which sort of said I know what you mean but I'd better not chat with you 'cos you look a bit pissed.' I learned later that Cherie read this bit out to her husband on holiday and he exclaimed, 'I remember that bloke! And that's exactly what I was thinking!'

A few weeks later, a letter arrived on my doormat with '10 Downing Street' and a fancy crest on the back. Envelopes like that tend to get opened before the circulars from estate agents. Inside was an invitation to join the Prime Minister and his wife for dinner at Chequers. *Ooh-err!* I thought. *Should I buy a bottle of Liebfraumilch to take along? And maybe a box of Ferrero*

Rocher for the lady? I think it was fair to say that Jackie and I were a little nervous in the run-up to this event. We drove up to Buckinghamshire with far too much time to spare, and settled our nerves with a drink in the nearest pub. You get a very warm welcome at the gates of Chequers: armed policemen holding sub-machine guns block the driveway and demand to know if your car has been left unattended 'at any point in the last twenty-four hours'. Obviously, I sleep in my car. 'No,' I lied, but this seemed to satisfy them and we were waved through.

And there in the hallway were Tony and Cherie Blair, immediately putting us at our ease and offering drinks and introducing us to the other guests. Judi Dench was there and John Reid MP, the Minister for Transport, but I grabbed what might be my only opportunity to chat with our host. And every now and then I would catch myself and think, *Blimey, I'm talking to the Prime Minister!* and I would carry on trying to act normal. And, of course, Tony Blair was charming. It made me trust him more. And, later, would make others trust him further than they probably should have done, when his word was all the evidence he was offering.

At the end of a surreal evening, I felt quite positive as we drove away from Chequers in our crappy car with the dent in the side. But then I had a worrying thought. If the Prime Minister and his wife have you to dinner, are you supposed to have them back? Years later, I worried, Cherie would be getting ready for bed with Tony and would say, 'The O'Farrells never had us back, did they?' Anyway, who would we have them back with? See if the Clintons were free on Saturday?

I did at least scribble a quick handwritten note to Cherie to thank her for having us, which I spent ages composing on my computer first to get the casual wording exactly right. All of us are pretending we are something we are not. No one more than one other guest at Chequers, whose presence loomed large that evening, and whose acquaintance I would rather never have made. Sir Jimmy Savile was there that night, just as he had been many times under previous prime ministers. Stoke Mandeville was just down the road and, apparently, Sir Jimmy had to be indulged because he did so much for the hospital, like raising money, attracting publicity and a few other things that wouldn't get into the paper for a while.

The depths of Savile's monstrosity became known only after his death in 2011; back in 1999, he just came across as creepy and unfunny. While I was talking to Tony Blair at pre-dinner drinks we became aware that he was trying to draw attention to something, and we looked across to the wall of this beautiful Elizabethan manor house, where the intricate wood panelling and classical portraits were jarringly interrupted by a glossy picture of a naked woman which Jimmy Savile had stuck up there with some Blu Tack he must have brought along specially. An embarrassed silence fell over the assembled guests. We saw that written across the woman's naked body in thick black marker pen was 'Oh Lord, please send me Sir Jimmy Savile.'

I looked at Judi Dench, who was as speechless as I was. I looked at Tony Blair, who was trying to find the right words. He was like a fish gasping for air: what is the right thing to say when someone is so incredibly inappropriate? Eventually, Blair just shrugged and said apologetically to me, 'Well, he does do an awful lot of work for charity.'

A decade or so later, the news went from 'Sad passing of a great British eccentric' to 'Monster who preyed on the sick and young'. Celebrity is a form of power, and 1970s pop celebrity turns out to have been a form of the absolute power that corrupts absolutely. People complain today about too many background checks and the excessive scrutiny of Scout leaders and priests not permitted to be alone with children. But Jimmy Savile is what you got before political correctness went mad.

There is no doubt that getting to meet top politicians had the effect of making me more forgiving of them, as you learned of all their frustrations and the conflicting pressures they were under. For many, this would be a reason never to engage with them, which to me seems like a rather self-defeating act of contrived ignorance. Hopefully, most of us should have sufficient brain power to be able to think more than one thing about a person. Today, I look at Tony Blair and think, *fundamentally wrong about Iraq with tragic consequences.* But I also think, *key person in securing peace in Northern Ireland.* I think, *wrong to be so close to Murdoch and Berlusconi* but *right to cancel Third World Debt.* And *maybe wrong to want identity cards* but *definitely right on gay rights,* and so on. People are complex, and politicians are human. Once, I hated Maggie Thatcher with every fibre of my body, but now I think that was wrong and actually a little stupid. As someone who hopes we can make the world a better place, who wants the widest possible happiness, peace and fairness for the greatest number possible, I feel I should make it my personal mission to try not to *hate* anyone. However, it has to be said that this would be a lot easier if the Tories didn't keep behaving like such a bunch of total cunts.

Tony Blair seemed like a politician in total command of all he surveyed: a huge parliamentary majority, a pliant Cabinet, a huge lead in the opinion polls and a weak and ineffective opposition. But, in fact, just two years into his first term, Labour managed to lose a nationwide election to the Conservatives. Even though William Hague seemed a vaguely ridiculous figure, his party surprised everyone by coming in a convincing first at the European Elections, ending up with thirty-six seats to Labour's twenty-nine. It was Britain's first national election conducted under Proportional Representation. If it had been truly representative, three quarters of the seats should have stayed empty, because the turnout was a paltry 24 per cent; a record low for any country in the European Union at that point.

It reminded us that support for New Labour may have been wide but it was also shallow. And perhaps the lack of enthusiasm was also because most of us had very little understanding of how our lives were affected by who represented us in Europe. British television news reported every twist and turn of Bill Clinton's affair with Monica Lewinsky, as if we were more interested in sex in the White House than in the complex compromises reached by European ministers. I mean, honestly! Did they really think that we were so superficial that we'd rather hear lots of sordid details about the most powerful man in the world having illicit sex with a young intern than learn about the intricate technicalities of voting procedure in the European Parliament?

A poll conducted during the campaign showed that five out of six voters wanted Britain to remain in Europe. But the only people talking loudly about Europe were the people who hated it. Two Tory MEPs attempted to launch something called the 'Pro-Europe Conservative Party', but they were never seen or heard of ever again. Instead, the United Kingdom Independence Party gained its first MEPs, one of whom was an annoyingly self-assured man called Nigel Farage, who turned out to be the leader of this motley collection of bigots dubbed 'the BNP in blazers'. Like everyone else, I knew that Tony Blair was the most influential politician of his generation. It never would have occurred to me that, one day, he'd have a rival for that title in one of those saloon-bar bores who'd just been elected to a Parliament they didn't think should exist.

Tony Blair's stated mission was to make the new century as dominated by Labour as the previous century had been dominated by the Conservatives. But it didn't get off to the greatest of starts. The Millennium Dome became the go-to stick with which to beat New Labour from left and right. It was expensive, it was ill conceived, and it was naff. And then the opening night was an organizational disaster for all the celebs and hacks who'd managed to wangle a ticket. They should have commissioned Prince to rewrite his hit record about partying like it was 1999: 'Tonight we're gonna queue up for two hours at some ill-conceived multi-faith zone and then shout "Do you know who I am?" at Security.'

Being someone who generally leaves things to the last minute, I finally took my seven-year-old son to the Dome twelve months later, on the very last day of the year. It snowed, and we had a snowball fight before we went in. Then we joined the queue for the Body Zone, we filed through the Play Zone, we watched the show, we toured the exhibits, we looked at the stands.

'What was your favourite thing, son?' I asked him afterwards.

'Having the snowball fight with you.'

Well, that was a billion quid well spent.

Present Imperfect

Lambeth Parents' School Vote – 5 July 2000

It was the pause that killed me. Sitting through that meaningful pause again, trying not to bang my forehead on the empty plastic chair in front of me. Lambeth Council's 'Head of Talking in Empty Platitudes about Education' was giving the same speech I'd heard him give at so many other public meetings, hoping that a passionate display of concern might make up for a chronic shortage of school places.

'I am determined,' he said, sounding determined, 'that we get education right in this borough! Because children . . .' and then came the extended pause; '. . . because children . . . *are the future.*'

Oh, they're the future, are they? I wanted to scream. Right, because up until you did the big reveal, I was racking my brain for what you might be going to tell us. 'Because children . . . are shorter than adults?' No, not very pertinent. 'Because children . . . are what happens when Mummy and Daddy love each other very much?' No, I think most people in the room already know that. 'Because children . . . are *French*? No, that's only some of them and mostly the ones you get in France. But it turns out that children *are the future*! This was obviously a massive revelation to me, because up until that point I had thought badgers were the future. And non-slip shower mats. But no, it would seem not. It's children. They're the future. Who'd have known?

I was sitting in a public meeting I had helped organize which was being held in a local primary school. We would have held it in a local secondary school, but there wasn't one – that was sort of the problem. Despite children being the future, no one had apparently foreseen that, one day, our seven-year-olds would become eleven-year-olds and they would have no school, short of being held back in Year 6 until they were eighteen and studying for their A-levels in the Wendy house by the home corner. Eleven-year-old children were currently travelling great distances across south London to start at schools that no one else wanted to use. What better way to prepare your child for the world of work than a long commute on a packed rush-hour train to somewhere they don't want to be? 2,800 Year 6 kids had left primary school in Lambeth that year, but the borough only had 1,490 places in Year 7. You didn't need the whole numeracy hour to work out that there was a problem.

There is something about the format of public meetings that brings out the worst in people. The manager of your local Sainsbury's store could hold a public consultation meeting about where you'd like them to put the Marmite and, even if he helpfully offered to put the Marmite in every suggested aisle, he'd still be heckled and booed off the platform by Bovril militants. So, when the subject under discussion was our own children and the prospect of them setting off to school in the dark to low-performing schools five or ten miles away, you can imagine that emotions were running a little high.

We were calling for a local, non-selective, co-educational, non-denominational school with a sixth form. Talk about a catchy brand. We took a vote on that model at our first public meeting and support was almost unanimous. There were abstentions from some churchgoers, who thought it should be a faith school; there was a short speech saying we should be campaigning for another single-sex girls' school from the mother of two daughters who hadn't quite bought into the 'school for everyone' message. And I think there were hopes from some of the kids that it might also be open to wizards and have a 'house elf', but we told them, 'One thing at a time.'

I feel it necessary to emphasize that, back at the turn of the century, the notion of campaigning for a new school was a completely different prospect to what became quite commonplace under David Cameron. What we were most definitely *not* doing was demanding our own new school to avoid having to use the 'bog-standard comprehensive' down the road. A bog-standard comprehensive is exactly what we wanted, even though Downing Street press spokesman Alastair Campbell had just told the country it was a thing of the past. A decade later, the political brand of 'parents campaigning for a new school' became tarnished by the Free School model, which generally involved spurning your local state school because you were scared of all those rough kids and getting £18 million off Michael Gove after you chatted to him at the *Daily Telegraph* Christmas party. Maybe these later models were called 'Free Schools' because their snobby founders wanted their kids to do Latin and rowing without paying loads of school fees.

But back in the 1990s, you just didn't get brand-new schools. Lambeth had flogged off a number of educational sites down the years to be used for a variety of purposes, from luxury flats to luxury flats. Then, in September 2000, a brand-new school was opening in the neighbouring borough after a successful campaign by local parents; it was this that inspired us to action. So, our first-ever committee meeting involved the new chair of governors at Dulwich's Charter School sitting in my front room telling half a dozen of us how they had won their campaign. I was quickly disabused of any naïve notion that setting up a new school would be fun and fast, like Judy Garland and Mickey Rooney saying, 'Hey, we could do the show right here!', and you have a quick-cutting musical montage and then it's the first day of term. The Charter campaigners had endured a long and difficult battle, full of frustrations and setbacks, enforced compromises and personal attacks. But they had got a new school. And I thought this was incredible.

Here was a whole new way of doing politics. I could *see* the difference that they had made – kids walked through the gates of the difference they had made. All those years, I had campaigned for a better *everything*, which I'd hoped would come about with a Labour government, with no way of measuring if I ever made any personal difference. But here was something concrete to campaign for. (Oh no, already I'm worrying about graffiti being sprayed on the concrete.) Perhaps it was the fact we now had a Labour government and it was so much more complex and confusing than I'd anticipated that made this new Holy Grail seem so appealing. Maybe I just longed to be one of the good guys again, to be demanding change rather than apologizing for the lack of it – but that evening I felt a certain campaigning zeal returning to my bones. It was like the one I'd felt when I'd under-taken to make Michael Foot Prime Minister or when I resolved to rid the world of nuclear weapons. My work was done there now, it was time for a new challenge.

Upstairs, my seven-year-old was already asleep as we concluded our first committee meeting. Could we really win a campaign and build a new local school quickly enough for him to start there in four years' time? This ideal school was already acquiring mythical status in my imagination, even though it currently had no site, no building, no funding and no staff. How do you even go about asking for any of those things? How long does it take to build a school?

We gave our campaign the slightly clumsy acronym SSCIL (pronounced 'skill', once you'd had it explained to you), which stood for Secondary Schools Campaign In Lambeth. We had thought of Central Lambeth Action for Secondary Schools to make CLASS, but that might have been a rather open invitation for cynics to put 'Middle' in front of it. To be fair, we were more than just a middle-class group of self-appointed busybodies; most of us were governors at our respective primary schools. I'd also been a school governor at a primary school in north Battersea, so I felt I brought a certain amount of experience to the group. Oh, except that they'd shut that school and then demolished it.

Making this campaign up as we went along, we organized a huge petition; we lobbied our MPs; we had meetings with council officers; we got ourselves on the London News and I got my on-screen sound bite down to the suitable fifteen seconds, including punchy full stop. I can't believe I'm still wearing that jumper a decade and a half later.

All this time, we'd had a suitable site in mind, but we'd been waiting for the best moment to lay claim to it. In the 1980s, a local boys' school had been closed down in Clapham, and a further-education college had been built on half of the site. But the rest of it was mostly just a tarmac car park and neglected wasteland with a few cheeky neighbours laying claim to this *Lebensraum* by moving their garden fences back ten yards. With the world's media watching (or rather, me, with my digital camera and a pre-prepared press release), we marched on the site, with cute-looking kids holding banners they had made themselves. One of them had misspelled 'education', but surely that only made our case stronger?

Then the government totally stymied our campaign for a new secondary school for Lambeth with a cunning and completely unexpected tactic: they announced a new secondary school for Lambeth. But their proposal was for something called a 'city academy'; a new type of school that would be run by a 'sponsor' who had to put up £2 million, which would prove that they knew all about education as well as all about selling carpets. Apparently, city academies could select up to 10 per cent of their pupils on the basis of aptitude in their particular specialism. Suitable sponsors might be a private business or charity. 'Selection?' 'Specialism?' 'Business?' Was 'charity' a euphemism for 'private school'? We were smelling rats all over the place. Rumours flew that the sponsor being lined up for Lambeth was the biggest company based in the borough, Shell. It gave us an early chance to practise saying, 'You know, it's all about oil!' Then the talk was of an organization called 'the Church Schools Company'. They sounded perfect, apart from us wanting our school to be unconnected with any church or company. The waters were muddied; we weren't sure if we had won or lost. And now our little committee was threatened with the one thing that has stymied so many progressive campaigns down the ages – division.

That same year saw splits on the left on the national and international stage. Tony Blair clumsily tried to block Ken Livingstone from becoming the Labour candidate for Mayor of London, but was perceived as a control freak for doing so, and when Livingstone ran as an independent and won, Labour's Frank Dobson was pushed into third place. This proved that Tony Blair wouldn't always get his own way and we should fight him on this, said those opposing compromise.

But then, in the United States, Democrat Al Gore lost the presidency by a whisker to the arch-right-winger George W. Bush, partly because the progressive vote was split by the Green candidate Ralph Nader. Gore was about the greenest candidate ever to have a chance of becoming president, but by gaining nearly 3 million votes, Nader inadvertently let in Bush, the former oil man and architect of the Iraq War. It proved that a left that refused to compromise and unite under one banner was a left condemned to impotent opposition.

Both sides in this argument had valid contemporary examples to call upon. We tried to push back against the government's proposals for a few months and managed to secure a meeting with Stephen Timms, the junior education minister, to whom I was perhaps a little too rude about the government's paucity of ambition. And soon after that we received an exasperated letter from Keith Hill, the local Labour MP, who said that there was nothing more he could reasonably do for our campaign. He saw the city academy as a bonus that would be welcomed by most of his constituents, for whom the religious sponsor was not a politically unacceptable deal-breaker. He was basically telling us to stop being such impossible bloody lefties.

I had hoped this campaign would relieve me from feeling tainted. A few months into the Labour government, I somehow felt personally responsible for the various disappointments and sell-outs. And now we were not even through the first year of our school campaign and already I was arguing for compromise, suggesting we had to be prepared to sacrifice some of our original principles. It was the same old argument. What is more progressive? Helping to establish a school that felt politically suspect, or remaining politically pure and protesting so loudly that your community is left with no school at all? Or just following Diane Abbott's example and paying to go private? No, not that one, that was definitely not the most left-wing option.

Eventually, we put the choice to a public vote of parents at another public meeting. They were given an update on our progress, on what was being offered and the dilemma before us. We asked if there were any questions. A slightly incongruous woman stood up and made a very angry speech about the council's residents' parking scheme. One parent wanted everyone to know that her son was gifted and talented, had got top marks in his SAT scores and had read all the Philip Pullman books. But given the choice between a city academy now, or the long shot of an old-fashioned comprehensive at some later point, perhaps under a different sort of Labour government, the room was overwhelmingly in favour of accepting what was on offer now. The mooted specialism for this academy was to be modern foreign languages. We had just decided that the correct tense was 'present imperfect' not 'future perfect'.

I hoped my comrades in the campaign didn't see me as some government stooge, I hoped they didn't think I was totally in cahoots with New Labour. Finally, we went to Downing Street to deliver our petition in person. Apparently, the Blairs were on holiday. 'Don't worry!' shouted one of our campaigners. 'John knows where Tony and Cherie hide the front-door key.'

Look how I am laughing along with everyone! That good-natured smile on my face looks so natural.

Losing My Maidenhead

General Election – 7 June 2001

When I was seventeen, my friend Dave ran the Friday-night youth disco at Maidenhead Leisure Centre, and I would help out: setting out amps, unwinding cables and lugging in boxes of twelve-inch singles. Then lots of fourteen-year-old kids would turn up and dance for a couple of hours – until their fringes were wet and their hearts broken because Tracey from Taplow wouldn't dance with them to 'Disco Inferno'. Our boss at the leisure centre was a short bloke with a moustache and tight jeans who had dubbed the event 'Boogie Nights' in the hope that a little of the glamour of the New York disco scene might rub off on the Magnet Leisure Centre, Maidenhead. And after a couple of weeks he took us aside because he'd had a bit of an inspired idea.

'Yeah, John, Dave . . . what I was thinking was, next week, at the end of the evening, what you could do, right, is say, "Okay this is the last song of the evening. See you next week at Boogie Nights!" And then you could, like, play . . . "Boogie Nights".'

There is something about authority that has always made me want to take the piss out of it.

'Sorry, talk me through that again,' I said. 'It's the end of the evening, and we tell them, "This is the last song . . ."' I said, feigning latent excitement at the creative possibilities he was unveiling before us.

'Yeah,' he said. 'And then you say, "See you next week at Boogie Nights." And then you play . . . "Boogie Nights".'

'That is brilliant!' me and my mate agreed. 'We'll definitely do that next week.' And our boss seemed pretty pleased with himself.

So, the following Friday night, we got to the end of the evening, and the announcement went out: 'That's it for another week. This is the last track of the night, see you next week at . . . BOOGIE NIGHTS!'

And then the opening bars of 'YMCA' burst forth and we tried not to look at him with his confused and disappointed face because, inside, we were both cracking up at this ridiculous little game we had invented for ourselves.

'Great set again, guys,' he said, wanting to start with something positive. 'But, I dunno if you remember . . . I thought you were going to say, "See you next week at Boogie Nights." And then you were going to play "Boogie Nights".'

'Oh shit, yeah. "Boogie Nights". You're right, that would have been better.'

'But you could do that next week, yeah?'

'Definitely. "Boogie Nights". By Heatwave?'

'Yes!'

'That's perfect. It's the same name as this disco.'

'Exactly.'

And the following week, we made the same announcement and then played 'Ring My Bell' by Anita Ward, and the week after that 'Ain't No Stopping Us Now' by McFadden and Whitehead, and me and my mate thought this was the most hilarious joke in the history of the world, that every week the boss would catch us as we were packing away, and remind us that we'd really liked his idea of ending the kids' disco 'Boogie Nights' with the song 'Boogie Nights'.

And then, twenty-two years later, I am back, standing on the same rostrum in the same leisure centre, except this time the authority figure I am winding up is Theresa May, Conservative MP for Maidenhead, and I am the man with the impertinence to stand for Labour in this most middling bit of Middle England; I am rude enough to wear a red rosette in this true-blue town. She is wearing her trademark leopardskin shoes. Those are the shoes I am trying to step into. The returning officer is reading out the number of votes cast, and the number of spoilt ballot papers. And the song 'Boogie Nights' is going round and round in my head and I almost want to ask her if she'd like to dance. Theresa is the local Tory MP secretly aiming for the very top; I am the Labour candidate returning to my home town. It's like the beginning of a really bad rom-com.

The idea of standing for Parliament in an unwinnable seat had been hatching in my head for some time. My book and all the publicity I'd got from it presented the opportunity to fly the flag for the party at a new level. A few people had said to me, 'You should stand for Parliament. You'd be a good MP,' and I'd think, *Yes, I should* and *No, I wouldn't.* But for a politico like me, running for Parliament was one of the great unconquered peaks, a Scout's badge to sew on to the sleeve of my political anorak.

'So, do you want to be an MP, then?' everyone asked.

'Not really,' I would answer confusingly.

'So, why are you standing for Parliament?'

'Because it's a more interesting way of spending the General Election than delivering leaflets round the bloody Clapham Park estate again.'

'But what if you win?'

'I won't win.'

'But what if you do?'

'You don't know Maidenhead like I do. They have £100,000 cabin cruisers called *Just a Whim*. They think racial awareness is playing Motown in the wine bar.' When I was invited to give the annual address at my school's old boys' dinner, they sat me next to a man who told me he wasn't a political person. Except, it transpired, for being a Conservative councillor. That's Maidenhead all over. They're not 'political', they're Conservative.

There are many ways to have a mid-life crisis, and mine was to go back to my home town and be rejected en masse by the people I grew up with. In a perverse way, there was something quite therapeutic about it. I had spent the first eighteen years of my life in this comfy corner of the Home Counties. In the election that brought Mrs Thatcher to power, I had been the Labour candidate in my school's mock-election, scoring 35 votes out of a possible 1,300. I was hoping for at least double that this time. To paraphrase an old gag, you only stand for election in Maidenhead twice. Once on the way up, once on the way down. It was great to be back.

My parents still lived in the constituency, in the once-pretty village of Cookham, where the charming English scenes painted by Stanley Spencer were now obscured by rows of 4x4s. Mum improvised a guest bedroom for me in the loft, where I could sleep, if I didn't mind sharing the duvet with a dead blackbird. My mother was a very resourceful woman. I think she must be the only person in medical history to be given a new hip and ask the doctor if she could have the old bone for the dog. She took her lumbering golden retriever Fudge everywhere. When she saw that the sign on the door of Marks and Spencer's read 'Guide Dogs Only' she put on her tinted swimming goggles and marched straight through to the food section. Fudge immediately took exception to the slippery flooring and lay on her back. As Mum was tugging the dog's lead and lifting one eye-piece, the store manager came across and pointed out the no-dogs rule.

'Oh, I thought guide dogs were allowed?'

'Madam, you're wearing swimming goggles.'

'Well, I'm a bit short-sighted.'

Early in my childhood, I was the one saying, 'Mum, you just *can't* do that!'

As a book dealer and a lifelong Labour man, my father was very proud that his youngest son had written a political bestseller, and he loved to come to my book events, where the wine appeared to be completely free. While I was giving a reading, he would get up to walk across the front to fill up his glass again to ensure all caution had been abandoned by the time it came to the questions.

'So, John, what do you think of this whole *ethnic* thing?'

Inside, alarm bells are going off inside my head. 'Danger! Danger! Elderly parent has steered subject straight on to race!'

'Um, which ethnic thing, specifically?' I stammer, as the rest of this room of bookish lefties shifts uneasily in their seats.

'Well, I mean, I go down to the newsagent's, and I chat with the Pakistani there – absolutely marvellous! And we have a Nigerian postman – absolutely charming – and then of course you have your West Indians and Hindus, and the Arabs, of course . . . so what do you think of this whole *ethnic* thing?'

When I chose this parliamentary constituency to stand in, I

hadn't stopped to consider the fact that my mum and dad would delight in attending every single meeting. I don't mind questions from the audience, but not 'Why didn't you wear a jumper?' At the official selection meeting, I was asked which things the Labour government had done which I disagreed with. This was a tricky question.

'Well . . .' I said thoughtfully.

'Trial by jury,' prompted my dad.

'Er, thanks, Dad . . . I think the jury reforms set a dangerous precedent . . . and um . . .'

'Tuition fees.'

'Yes, thanks, Dad – I don't agree with bringing in tuition fees.'

'The Dome.'

Also, how come Dad was drinking that wine? I brought that bottle for the raffle.

I had had a vaguely heroic image of what it might be like to seek selection for high office, but this was turning out to be nothing like Robert Redford in *The Candidate*. There were only about a dozen or so people sitting around this small room, so it would have been hard for me to pull off that thing American politicians do of pretending to recognize someone in the middle of the crowd, pointing and giving a thumbs-up.

In any case, I was finally selected as Labour's prospective parliamentary candidate for Maidenhead after a tough and closely fought battle in which I always had the slight edge, given that the other bloke didn't turn up. I wrote a press release to send to the *Maidenhead Advertiser* and managed to knock that big story about Bisham's new mini-roundabout off the top of page seventeen.

Maidenhead Labour Party was probably typical of many local

parties across the south of England where members were few but faith was no less firmly kept. The same small heroic team alternated the key party positions – Chair, Secretary and Treasurer – and my agent for this election was to be Bob, a wonderfully friendly and down-to-earth man who shared a nice family home in Cox Green with his lovely wife, their grown-up daughter and seven hundred boxes of Labour Party leaflets. Then there were Stan and Ina, who had been in the party for ever – you imagined they probably knew Clement Attlee and Ernest Bevin. Party Secretary Jenny could be relied to come to every street stall and canvass, so she was usually that 'ordinary voter' I was earnestly engaging in my publicity shots. Shirley, meanwhile, told me that 'Tony Blair's stars were not looking good for May the third.' This might be why the election was moved back a month, even though the media accepted the official line that it was because of the foot-and-mouth outbreak. Mr Kennedy (as I still felt I should call him) had lived at the end of our road when I was growing up. Every winter, before all the local kids went on the big pond beside his house, he would go out into the middle of the ice and jump up and down and make sure it was safe for us. Thirty years on, I apologized for how much we all laughed that year he went right through.

Like me, none of these activists were ideologically New Labour, nor were they automatically hostile to Tony Blair and the direction in which he had led us. They were just getting on with it, diligently attending meetings, delivering leaflets, fighting council elections and, I learned, doing so much else besides. The thing I came to realize over the course of the campaign was that, even in a Tory town like Maidenhead, it was so often the Labour Party activists who were the quiet heroes who sat as school governors, who ran the charities, who volunteered for ChildLine, and, my particular favourite, who looked after Labrador puppies before they became guide dogs. When I first met them all, I had wondered how they found the heart to keep fighting for such a hopeless cause as Labour in Maidenhead, and then I came to realize that this was just a tiny part of what they did; they were making a very real difference to the town in so many other ways.

They were philosophical about their chances of ever winning here. In fact, during a previous General Election, when a candidate had turned up and tried to be inspiring by saying that, if they all worked really hard, Labour could take Maidenhead, I think they'd all found it a little irritating. For myself, after having been so desperate to win all the knife-edge battles I'd fought in London, it was something of a relief to be able to say, 'Remember, every vote *doesn't* count!' 'Comrades, we shall not rest until we have found every Labour vote in Maidenhead! Or maybe we shall, let's just see how the mood takes us . . .'

It felt strange to return to long-forgotten yet familiar streets. The last time I went down Ray Mill Road, my flares got stuck in my bicycle chain. There's that newsagent's where I used to buy cigarettes; 10p for ten Players No. 6; purchased only in order that they could be rebelliously smoked in the alleyway between school and the railway line. There are new houses built over the woods where we used to collect conkers, a private estate on the scrubland where we played football. The smell of the Thames is so evocative, it transports me right back to childhood, the great roar of the weir that I heard every night as I went to sleep. I remembered that I had knocked on every door in Thames Crescent once before; my mum had press-ganged my brother and me into collecting for Oxfam when I was around nine. I can tell I'm not coming across as quite so cute this time. 'I'm not voting for the socialists!' says one angry man. I wasn't quite sure if this was a pledge to vote for New Labour or against. Most voters just say a polite 'Sorry, we're not political,' so I know what that means.

Then I came across a voter's name that I recognized. Oh no, not Hemmett! One of the school hard-nuts, he tried to set fire to me in metalwork. I hadn't seen him since I was fifteen, when he gave me a dead leg for 'being tall'. Nervously, I headed up the overgrown front path of this unloved council house. *What if I can't answer his policy questions?* I worried. *He might give me a Chinese burn.* I rang the doorbell and his grown-up son opened the door to this disastrously scruffy flat, clutching a can of Special Brew. It was ten in the morning. It appeared that the Hemmetts had mastered the art of sleeping rough *indoors*.

'Hello, is Kevin in?' I asked.

'No, he's in Reading.'

'Oh, not to worry. Maybe I'll catch him another time.'

'No, he's in Reading Jail. Six months. I'll tell him you was looking for him, though,' he said, reading my name off the leaflet like I was now in serious trouble.

'Er, no, no – really, best not to worry him. Forget all about it. Please. He can have my dinner money, I won't tell.'

Another council tenant said he would definitely vote for me if I could get him his free NHS glasses. I listened to his complex story of how some bureaucrat had said he wasn't entitled to free spectacles because he was on disability benefit as opposed to income support. All I could say was 'Well, that doesn't sound right. Look, I'll see what I can do,' and, conscious that I was getting his hopes unrealistically high, I emphasized that I didn't have any actual power, I was only a candidate. 'Yeah, but when you get elected you'll be able to do something, won't you?' he said hopefully, and I felt a pang of guilt that I was going to let down this supporter by failing to become his MP.

I gave out leaflets outside the railway station and was told to stop by the station manager, who informed me that I was on private property. 'How can this be private property? It's the train station!' I exclaimed, my mind-set stuck in the pre-Thatcherite days of public space and nationalized industries. I shook hands in the pedestrianized high street, I dug out my old *Spitting Image* Thatcher puppet and put her free pensioners' TV licence in her hands. I wore a suit, I was polite, I found myself calling people 'sir' and 'madam' and saying, 'Thank you, anyway,' if they told me to get stuffed.

With a small team and limited resources, my best chance of raising my profile was via the local newspaper and, in the months running up to the election, I made it my mission to send some sort of press release to the *Maidenhead Advertiser* every single week. I quickly learned that the less overtly political the story, the more likely it was to make it into the paper, so I just sent them endless photos of me giving a talk at a local school or patting the donkey at some summer fête. The best I could hope to convey was a general message of 'That Labour candidate is very busy,' which I hoped might bring with it an inherent subtext of 'So I guess socialism must be the answer.' A digital camera was a fairly new concept back in 2001, but it was the best investment I could have made, because nothing makes the job of an over-worked or lazy journalist easier than providing a story with the picture already attached.

The Liberals had been campaigning for ages to save the old town-hall building, due to its enormous part in our nation's cultural heritage (i.e. playing the hospital in *Carry On Matron*), but although they had worked hard to collect lots of signatures for their petition, I was the one pictured on page two of the *Advertiser* holding the placard. They were furious about that, but that was the trouble with the Liberals in Maidenhead: they were all substance and no spin.

The only other local media seemed to be BBC Radio Berkshire, which featured local traffic news and agony aunts helping distressed callers from Ascot talk through their personal problems, such as 'Our useless Croatian nanny has pranged the Volvo *again*.' I was invited on to take part in a local election phone-in, and confided to my parents that I was a little nervous about all the Tory callers being really hostile. But I dutifully sat on the panel, with the Liberal candidate on one side and Theresa May on the other, and did my best to defend the government's record. And I was slightly astonished to hear a voice coming on the line that I recognized as *my mum*. My mother had phoned up to say that she agreed with John O'Farrell.

'Sorry, caller, we didn't catch your name,' said the host.

'It's Mrs O'F— It's Joy, Joy from Maidenhead.'

'And on which issue do you agree with John O'Farrell?'

'All of them! Every issue,' she confirmed, managing to restrain herself from asking if I wanted chips or mashed potato with my sausages that evening. An hour later, I was standing in my parents' kitchen, saying, 'Mum! I'm thirty-nine, I can manage!'

'But the others were all against you.'

'Mum, they're the other candidates; they're supposed to be against me! When Gordon Brown is doing *Election Call* on the five economic tests for euro convergence, he doesn't have his mum ringing up and saying, "Och, I agree with my Gordon!"'

Back when I was first selected for Maidenhead, I was contacted by the BBC, who said they were making several documentaries following different candidates through their elections and would I like to be the subject of one of them? This was obviously a very difficult decision for someone as shy and retiring as myself.

Hmm, what if it deflects from the seriousness of this important democratic process? said one voice in my head. *But you'll be on telly for a whole half an hour,* said the other one.

But what if it makes the party as a whole seem frivolous and lightweight?

Ah, but hang on – I've just thought of another important new point – you'll be on telly for a whole half an hour.

I decided to call the documentary *Losing My Maidenhead,* and the BBC were happy to go along with that title, long before a single vote was cast. I was now fighting two elections in Maidenhead. The first involved the traditional, unglamorous business of calling on voters, delivering leaflets and making as many contacts as possible. This is a repetitive and sadly not very interesting process and, although it has to be done, there was no way I could film this for a month and hope to produce an interesting documentary. My second election campaign was the one I fought for the benefit of the film crew supposedly just following me around. My political duties were subsumed by all my instincts as a writer; I was thinking, *What's a good visual? What is the candidate's subconscious desire in this scene? What is the narrative arc of leafletting this street?* So, while our organizer was telling me we had a thousand leaflets to deliver in Belmont ward, I was thinking, *Or . . . I could go and call on that kids' TV presenter in Cookham and he could hit me on the head with his inflatable mallet? Yes, that seems like the best use of the candidate's time.*

I ended up going to canvass at massive country houses because it looked so good to walk up an endless tree-lined avenue to a soundtrack of Radiohead playing 'No Surprises', and voiced my fears of ugly crowd violence between the rival fans when I watched a cricket match between Littlewick Green and Chalfont St Giles.

I had an idea for a scene in which I would put on my red rosette and climb into a little boat to pootle up and down the Thames with a megaphone, calling on the millionaires in their riverside mansions to vote Labour, or to pull alongside the towering cabin cruisers in midstream like some Somali pirate – only one who gave out New Labour election leaflets. My producer loved this idea and so boats were arranged and a location chosen.

I arrived at the boatyard, where a boat had been reserved for me. The assistant producer was pretty pleased with it. I looked across and saw this magnificent traditional slipper launch, a real beauty of a boat, all wood and varnish and elegant sleek lines. It was like something that would have whisked Princess Grace across Monte Carlo harbour to a 1950s cocktail party. This was a total disaster.

'We can't use that!' I said, to their astonishment.

'Why not? It looks great.'

'It's not funny, that's why not!'

'But we booked it especially. It was quite expensive.'

'I'm the *Labour* candidate in a *little* boat. That's the gag! They're the rich *Tories* in the *big, expensive* boats! Expensive boat approaches expensive boat – there's no conflict, see?'

At no point in this General Election was I as certain of something as I was about the casting of the comedy boat. Labour's policy on criminal justice? I'd stammer and equivocate and try to see both points of view. Labour's use of private finance to deliver investment in public services? I struggled to articulate why it felt like the wrong route to the right outcome. But the correct comedy boat for my stupid river stunt? I was 100 per cent sure of my opinion and argued with certainty about the rightness of my cause. 'It's not funny unless it's a crappy boat! Posh boat – not funny; crap boat – funny!' The man from the boatyard was listening in and tried to understand the problem with his prized vintage boat.

'What about that one?' I asked him, pointing to an ugly little dinghy with an outboard motor.

'You can borrow that for free,' he said. Thus, the biggest crisis in my election campaign was resolved. And it turned out to be the best bit of the whole documentary. I steered my boat up to some Hooray Henries, who were, obligingly, drinking champagne, and I gave a leaflet to a beautiful young woman in a bikini. She said she was voting for me and you can see me almost fall backwards into the Thames.

I watched that documentary again right after Theresa May became Prime Minister. I couldn't believe how the world seemed to have been so utterly turned upside down since then. She had been just another powerless Tory MP resigned to another term in opposition. I was from the confident Labour Party cruising its way to being re-elected to government. I was just having a laugh fighting the 2001 election: we were clearly heading for another landslide across the country; I could afford to have a bit of fun with this irrelevant sideshow. But watching it all fifteen years later, it didn't seem so funny any more. Labour had gone from being unelectable in Maidenhead to being unelectable across the whole country. There's a moment in the film where I encounter the nutty candidate from UKIP, who, back then, seemed so ludicrous and paranoid it was laughable. But his fringe views on immigration and the Germans would become mainstream, his prejudice and poison against refugees and foreigners would win his side a historic referendum.

When I encountered this bloke, I was out canvassing with my old friend and former boss Alf Dubs. Alf had given me my first break when I was twenty-three, when he took me on as a researcher in the House of Commons, and now he had come to help me in my hopeless attempt to get to Westminster in my own right. That was the only positive thing I could take away from this film; I was reminded that, even in Labour's darkest days in 2016, Alf was still being effective in opposition. He had got the 'Dubs Amendment' passed in the House of Lords and finally accepted by the government; Alf had shamed the Tories into admitting more unaccompanied child refugees into the UK. As a Jewish child escaping the Nazis, Alf was once a refugee himself; he'd come to the UK as one of the 669 Czech children rescued by the 'British Schindler', Nicholas Winton. Winton had lived in Maidenhead and had even stood for Labour here, and lost. And now one of the refugees he had saved was out on the streets of Winton's adopted town, having to listen to all sorts of nonsense about asylum seekers and immigration from some UKIP bigot who has no idea that this particular refugee devoted his entire life to public service.

One of the best things about making this documentary was that I could tell Theresa May found it really annoying. Every time I was at a public event to which the local MP had also been invited, I could see how much her nose was put out of joint by the BBC pointing their cameras at me and not at the front-bench politician. In fact, if ever you stand for election against a high-profile Conservative, I recommend you get a couple of mates to follow you around with a camera and a boom mic – it's worth it just to see the indignant expression on your Tory opponent's face.

When we were doing the candidates' debate, she defended the cuts made by the local Tories, saying, 'The council has had to make some very tough choices.' And then we were on local radio and she said, 'The council has had to make some very tough choices.' So, the third time we were on a panel together, I got in ahead of her and said, 'Theresa May will probably just try to say that the council has had to make some very tough choices.' She looked a bit thrown now that it fell to her to defend the council cuts, and she paused for a nano-second while her brain considered the concept of original thought or creative sentence-construction. Then she said, 'The council has had to make some very tough choices . . .'

I always went into these debates fired up and armed with evidence and supposed killer lines, but she was never up for any real debate. She waited for me to finish my bit, didn't engage with what I'd said at all, and then just trotted out the official Tory line, simply ignoring me if I tried to contradict, provoke or attack her. It was all very disappointing. I thought it was because she had such a safe Tory seat that she wasn't going to even bother with a political scrap. I didn't realize that, in fact, she just didn't know how to have one.

I have to say in all honesty that I never thought for a moment that my unremarkable opponent in Maidenhead might one day become Prime Minister. Theresa May was perfectly competent and polite and diligently turned up to local events and recited her lines without putting her well-shod foot in her mouth. But the new MP for Maidenhead never, ever struck me as a someone so brilliant or inspiring that she would surely end up running the country. I think about some of the really top political brains I've been lucky enough to encounter: Gordon Brown, Barbara Castle, Michael Foot and Tony Blair. I've even met a few brainy Tories, like Michael Portillo and Ken Clarke, and though I disagreed with them, I was impressed with their intellectual hinterland and capacity for big ideas. But Theresa May just seemed like a competent manager; I could picture her as headmistress of a small independent girls' school in Surrey. I watched her all the way from the very beginning, and I never saw her coming. Theresa May rose without trace.

At last, it was Election Day. There was nothing more I could do to win this election; I had already given it 25 per cent. The first thing to do on Election Day is to call on all the doors of the Labour voters who promised to vote for you. That was a busy hour or so. Back in the lonely committee rooms, the polling numbers of electors who'd already voted were methodically read out, only to be endlessly greeted by the word 'against' from the person checking our records. Eventually, the system detected a vote that had been cast by a supporter, and I felt a rare flush of pride. 'Oh, yes,' she said. 'Number 21, the Johnsons; they're very good, they always come out for us.'

'What?' I exclaimed. 'So, you actually know every Labour voter by name, do you?'

My parents were keen to do their bit and came with me in the car as the Labour candidate addressed the voters via the traditional tannoy bolted on top of his brother's beaten-up Ford Sierra. We drove around Bray as the message boomed 'Vote Labour! This is your Labour candidate saying vote for a minimum wage of £4.20!' I'm sure I saw one of the local residents covering up the ears of her cleaner. My mum wanted a go on the tannoy, so I passed the microphone to her.

'Vote for my son!' she said proudly. 'Vote for my son John!' And she only just managed to stop herself telling Maidenhead how well I'd done in my cycling proficiency test. She passed the peculiarly shaped mic to my dad, who seemed momentarily confused by the technology and held the long handset to his ear and said, 'Hello?'

And then the voters were treated to the image of a rusty old

Sierra plastered with Labour stickers driving through Maidenhead booming out the message '*No, darling, it's not a telephone – you speak into it – tell them to vote for John!*' And then an Irish accent came over the tannoy: '*Don't fooking tell me what to do!*' Looking back, it's hard to believe I lost.

I arrived at the count with the loyal band of Maidenhead Labour activists who had worked so hard to keep the red flag flying here in the 'Toxteth of the south'. Ballot boxes were unlocked and papers tipped out on to tables. I still think this is the best way to conduct elections – in fact, under this system, Al Gore would have been President of the United States and the history of the twenty-first century might have been completely different.

The Labour activists could either stand for hours behind the counters in the hall and watch me lose, or we could all go upstairs to the leisure-centre bar and watch Labour win on the telly. It was a surreal way to enjoy a Labour landslide: I was the loser in the room but knowing we were convincing winners in the world outside. 'Labour hold Jarrow,' said the red bar across the bottom of the TV screen. I leapt up and punched the air, and everyone thought I must have had a bit too much to drink. 'Sorry,' I said. 'I always look out for that one.'

When it was time for the declaration, the returning officer gathered the candidates together to allow us all to examine the spoilt ballot papers on which people had voted for all of us, or three of us, or had written in the name of their Labrador retriever. One person had crossed out every name and written at the bottom, 'None of them is left wing enough.'

'Well!' chuckled Theresa May. 'I don't think he can have met John O'Farrell!'

I got a measly 15 per cent of the vote, but I was still flattered that 6,577 people were prepared to put their trust in me. There was a big surge for the Liberals, as a result of tactical voting. During the campaign, I had thought maybe I should stand aside completely to give the Liberals a clear run – if I could arrange to twin with a Liberal somewhere else to stand aside and allow Labour to defeat some incumbent Tory in return. I had actually put this idea to my friend Fiona Mactaggart, who was MP for neighbouring Slough, and though she was supportive of the principle, she thought this wasn't the election to do it. Funny to think that, if I had been able to go through with this radical plan, Theresa May might have lost Maidenhead and wouldn't have become Prime Minister fifteen years later.

When all the votes across the country were counted, the Conservative Party had made a net gain of just one seat. I calculated that, if they repeated this at every General Election, there would not be a Conservative government until the year 2593. Still much too early for my liking. In a way, we were all winners in Maidenhead that night. Actually, no: Theresa May was the winner; I was definitely the loser. But something had happened earlier on Election Day which had prised open my shell of affected indifference. In the last few hours, I'd been knocking on doors in the area where our support was least abysmal and found myself face to face with the disabled voter who'd shown such faith in my ability to help him.

'Oh, it's you.' he said. 'Remember I said I'd only vote for you if you got me my free glasses?'

'Yeah, look, I'm sorry but, like I said, I'm only a candidate, I'm not even on the council or anything, but I sent off a letter about it, I did, really.'

'I know you did, and look – I've got them!' And, triumphantly, he held his free glasses aloft.

'What? You mean, it worked?'

'Yeah. They'd made a mistake and your letter made them check.' And he demonstratively put his new bifocals on to re-read me the correspondence. With a surge of pride, I suddenly understood what it was all about. Being an MP wasn't about shouting over your opponent on the *Today* programme, it wasn't about asking sycophantic questions in the House of Commons or braying like an idiot during Prime Minister's Question Time. It was about winning little victories for ordinary people every day of the week. Battling away on a thousand fronts for unglamorous causes that would never appear in the newspaper or win you a promotion. It was a couple of hours before I would be defeated at the count and, at last, I saw the purpose of being elected.

And ever since losing my Maidenhead, I have had a far greater respect for politicians and all the invisible stuff they do on our behalf, of the ludicrously long hours they work for little or no thanks. I was exhausted after weeks of campaigning, and I hadn't even been trying very hard to win. But, immediately after a gruelling campaign, all the elected politicians would be straight back to the House of Commons, to slog away for endless hours in Westminster before dashing to their constituencies to give up their weekends as well, finding what time they could to squeeze in their families in between. And, for this, they are held in contempt by the general public and mocked by smug media types like me. It's so easy to have a knee-jerk contempt for politicians, to pre-sume they are all vain and venal. It's an easy round of applause on *Question Time*, but it's not true: most of them are motivated by a sense of public service, most of them want to make the world a better place.

I drove away from the Thames Valley with a sense of optimism and a renewed faith in politics and our system of government. That one voter's free glasses had made me see it all so clearly.

Despite all its faults, our democracy really does work; we should respect and treasure it. From now on, I resolved, I would use my *Guardian* column for something more constructive than just taking the piss.

The following week, I was staring at a blank screen. Hmm . . . it's not so easy to get a laugh when you're being fair and constructive. 'But I'll definitely do that, *after* I've written this piece about John Prescott punching that voter.'

Changing Enemies

Tory Leadership Election – 13 September 2001

All through my youth, the Conservatives had seemed like an unstoppable election-winning machine, but now they were coming across more like some ridiculous fringe party. I half-expected to see their die-hard activists next to the Socialist Workers in the Arndale Centre on a Saturday afternoon, trying to sell their newspapers. '*Daily Telegraph!* Get your *Daily Telegraph*! Britain out of Europe! Start the hospital closures!' This world turned upside down had also seen huge demonstrations through central London by right-wing protestors, complaining that they weren't going to be allowed to kill wild animals for fun any more.

'You don't understand the ways of the country!' was the cry of the fox-hunters. It made me want to grab one of the demonstrators, drag them down an alleyway, nick their watch and their wallet, and, when they complained, I could tut, 'Honestly, you countryfolk, you just don't understand the ways of the city, do you?'

The twenty-first-century Tory Party was allying itself with hunting, with vigilantes, with 'Farmers for Action' (apparently *not* a website for rural doggers), with Little Englander symbols like the colour of your passport, and sinking to incendiary talk of Britain becoming 'a foreign land'. Theresa May ruffled a few feathers when she told the Tory Party conference that many people saw them as 'the Nasty Party'. I remembered that, when we had been taking part in the candidates' debate in Maidenhead, a question had come up of a possible referendum on Britain adopting the euro and what might be the correct wording to put to the voters. An elderly Conservative activist had stood up and said that the only acceptable wording could be 'Do you want to surrender your country to the Germans?' *Yeah, that seems pretty neutral,* I thought, *give or take a word.* These were people who were still furious that Britain had adopted the duvet in place of traditional sheets and blankets. 'The continental quilt was introduced without a referendum! The tog rating is completely outside Britain's control!' Their activists were ancient; their values seemed even older.

And under the new system introduced by Hague, these were the people who were charged with choosing the new leader of the Conservative Party. The Tory rank and file had been entrusted to choose a leader only once before, when they had voted for Jeffrey Archer to be the Conservative candidate for Mayor of London. He was promptly charged with perjury and forced to resign his candidacy, before enduring a highly entertaining trial which ran conveniently alongside the 2001 General Election campaign. Now the Conservative Party membership were given the job of choosing the Leader of the Opposition and, in theory, a future Prime Minister. It was their considered judgement that the best person for this job was Iain Duncan Smith. We hear a lot about 'the wisdom of crowds', but this result proved that there is also such a thing as 'the stupidity of crowds'. It was hard to think of someone less likely to win them a General Election. Lord Voldemort would at least have had the recognition factor.

Since most people had never heard of Iain Duncan Smith, his election as leader was his best chance to make a big impression: to grab the headlines and shape the news cycle to his agenda. Unfortunately for him, he was elected to his post on 13 September 2001.

It was the cliché of my parents' generation that everyone remembered where they were when they heard that Kennedy had been shot. The first details of 9/11 were sketchier; the truth was too incredible to arrive fully formed. A small plane had accidentally flown into one of the Twin Towers, then we learned it was a passenger jet; this was a serious, large-scale accident. Then, when the second plane flew into the other tower, a chilling mental leap was simultaneously made by everyone who witnessed it. 'Oh my god – this is *on purpose*.' I think at some level most people immediately understood that the world was fundamentally changed from that moment on.

Some news events are so disorientating you feel compelled to speak to loved ones to try to recover a little equilibrium. I called home, and Jackie said she just wanted to get the kids home from school and have them safely inside our home. Earlier that year, we had visited New York as a family, and the four of us had gone to the top of the World Trade Center and stood outside, just taking in the scale of it all. Our eight-year-old son had been frightened by the immense height and then his scarf had blown away and fallen all the way down to the ground below. That solid concrete floor where my family had all stood had now gone the same way.

There were those on the far left in whom I detected a perverse excitement about what had just happened – a sense that

America had had this coming to them, as if somebody had finally given a bully a black eye. I did not feel required to go back and do a full audit of the rights and wrongs of America's various foreign policies down the years before sticking with my initial gut revulsion at 9/11. For now, Tony Blair spoke for most people in the UK when he said that Britain stood 'shoulder to shoulder' with the United States. In the emotional atmosphere of the moment, I found myself privately feeling a guilty pride that Britain was coming across as America's most loyal friend; that Tony Blair had captured the mood in the UK and had earned the gratitude and respect of the American people more than any other international leader.

9/11 changed everything: the direction of our politics, Britain's relationship with Europe and, in some intangible way, the atmosphere of all Western society. I remembered an evening the year before when I was invited to a charity event at 10 Downing Street. I had been with a comedian friend in a Soho pub beforehand. 'Oh, well, I'll come with you,' said Tony Hawks. 'I've never been to Downing Street.'

'But it's *invitation only*, Tony. You can't just turn up to a posh function at Downing Street and expect them to let you in because you're holding a four-pack of lager.'

But, at the security gate, Hawks confidently told the police his name was 'Lord Hawksworth', and they apologized that they couldn't see his name on the list. He asked them to ring through and check, and they said, 'No, it's all right, sir,' waved us through and said, 'Have a good evening, Your Lordship.' We were still laughing as we helped ourselves to glasses of wine from the tray. God, I miss the days when you could just do stupid shit like that.

What became clear just three months after the General Election was that Labour's second term was going to be very different from the first. We had watched the irrelevant farce of the Tory leadership battle over the previous few weeks, thinking we were preparing for a change of enemies. But the battle lines for the new century weren't going to be Blair versus Duncan Smith; it would be Blair and Bush versus the Taliban, then Blair and Bush versus Saddam Hussein, and then Blair versus Opponents of the Iraq War . . . and, by then, I would have sort of switched sides.

Perhaps in September 2001 we were too hypnotized by the endless tape loop of that second plane flying into the South Tower, by the real-life disaster movie of giant towers collapsing as if in slow motion, the apocalyptic image of dust-covered New Yorkers groping their way towards rescue crews. But in the intensity of that moment it felt like this atrocity completely justified Tony Blair declaring that Britain would be there with America against the people who did this. What it wouldn't do was justify Britain being there with America against the people *who didn't*.

Political Jokes

English Local Council Elections – 2 May 2002

You know the thing that makes me certain that the Conservatives are definitely on the wrong side? They have such a rubbish sense of humour. Their jokes are about as funny as a food bank. You can argue about our different economic policies, and contrasting notions of 'freedom', and the individual versus society and all that – but just picture those party members you see at the Conservative conference or the Republican National Convention and try to imagine being made to laugh by any of them. That's the clinching argument for why we should be in government: we have more of a laugh than they do. Maybe that's why I also struggle with the far left – the humourless, angry new puritans shouting, 'Sell-out!' at you because your joke doesn't first condemn the deforestation by multinational mining companies that put the wide-mouth frog in this situation in the first place.

I read a political commentator once observing that a noticeable difference between the two main parties was that, at the Tory Party conference, they have a cabaret evening where they mock the Labour Party, while at the Labour Party conference, they have a cabaret evening where they mock the Labour Party. I think this speaks volumes about the characters of the two tribes. The biggest laughs I ever got speaking to Labour audiences was when I pointed out some of the madder things about ourselves.

Having spent many years as a local Labour Party organizer desperate to get any speaker that might make our meetings less insufferably dreary, I now found it hard to say no if I was asked to do an after-dinner speech for some far-flung constituency Labour Party. I travelled to constituencies from Devon to Yorkshire, with pretty much the same speech on my prompt cards, usually adding a few local touches to reflect whether I was addressing activists in a Labour stronghold or some no-hope safe Tory seat. I always slightly dreaded it before I set off, and would still be feeling a little self-conscious and awkward as I walked alone into a roomful of strangers in my stiff suit and tie. But once I'd got the speech out of the way, I'd feel an enormous relief, and I could have a drink or two, then later I'd be asked to draw the raffle, and someone would always shout, 'Fix!' and you'd watch the last winner's face change as she saw the only crappy prize that was left on the table. But at the end of the evening the local party might have raised a couple of thousand pounds, which would help pay for their local election campaign in May, and I would be left feeling pleased that I'd come along to be part of this and a little ashamed for ever having thought I'd rather stay at home and watch *The West Wing*.

The local community hall may not have been as glamorous a setting as the White House, but there were just as many inspiring stories to be heard from the people there. I would be seated at dinner beside the woman who'd invited me, and with a little probing I'd learn that she was a Labour councillor and also the local union organizer and she was proud of how they had stopped the main local employer going over to zero-hours contracts; oh, and she was also a volunteer for the Samaritans several nights a week, but it was getting harder because her dad had Alzheimer's and he'd moved in with them, but she was still hoping to finish her Open University degree because she'd had to leave school at sixteen to work in that engineering plant by the canal, until they closed it down in the '80s, but not without a fight, and now they're trying to turn the building into an arts centre and library. I never came away from a constituency fundraiser without thinking, *What an amazing bunch of people. I wish more people could see the difference they make.* The modest, hard-working activists who keep the Labour Party going at the local level – *and this is proven by science* – are the very best human beings on the whole of Planet Earth.

But then, when the local-election results came round, I'd look up the result in that town and I'd be shocked to see that the amazing woman I'd sat next to had lost her council seat because voters were going off Tony Blair. Over three hundred Labour councillors lost their seats that May, including one in my ward in Lambeth. The Tory elected in Clapham Town ward had tried to associate himself with our school campaign by having himself photographed outside the site. It was a perfect visualization of his involvement: he'd got the wrong building.

In the 1980s and '90s, I had been a Labour foot soldier, a canvasser, a local organizer and council candidate, and I had found that pretty demoralizing, given the number of defeats we had endured. Since my previous efforts had been so laughable, it seemed reasonable to head into the problem and make 'comedy' the thing I could offer the Labour movement. It was hard to imagine that all the great political struggles throughout history had had someone doing what I did.

'Comrades, we must storm the Winter Palace and seize power in the name of the workers of all the Soviets!'

'That's all very well, but who's going to write Lenin's gags?'

Long before anyone in the Labour Party had ever heard of me, I'd been writing occasional jokes for a Labour front-bencher, although, back in the dark days of Thatcher's premiership, it was impossible to imagine that a Labour MP could ever become so powerful. I have to concede that the public image of Gordon Brown was not exactly one of light-hearted raconteur of non-stop witticisms, so when people heard that I wrote jokes for him it often left them scratching their heads to remember one. But ever since Gordon Brown had been Shadow Secretary of State for Trade and Industry, I had been at the other end of a phone when he needed a suitable line for an important speech or a media appearance. He would ring up from the airport at the last minute and say, 'Hi, John, I'm just about to speak at the Scottish Trade Union conference – have you got any good Scottish Trade Union jokes?' And I'd think, *Yeah, obviously, Gordon! I have a huge file right here on my desk labelled 'Scottish Trade Union gags – unused'.*

During Labour's years of opposition, this was all part of fighting the good fight; I was helping one of our generals attack the enemy, and my personal motivation was obvious to me. But once Gordon Brown was Chancellor of the Exchequer and the requests continued to come through, I felt less certain about why I was doing it. I tried to tell myself that continuing to help leading Labour players look good was part of the business of keeping the Tories out of power. But I think I was constructing another rationale in my head. Tony Blair had not been left wing enough for me. Gordon was the one making all the redistributive policies. When Gordon was Prime Minister, then we'd see some real change. Gordon is Labour through and through; deep down, we all know Tony's not really one of us. And there I was, back in lefty opposition mode once again – finding it more comfortable to be against something imperfect rather than supporting the inevitable compromise of Labour in power.

Quite often, Gordon would come up with a decent gag himself, and just wanted to bounce it off me to see if I could improve it slightly. Back when Bill Clinton was embroiled in scandal, there was one joke Gordon was particularly proud of and which I agreed was word perfect. His line was 'There will be no U-turns; no right turns, no left turns and, at Downing Street, definitely no interns.' At that time, no one in Britain had heard this new word 'intern', except in the context of Monica Lewinsky. But I told him he couldn't possibly do this gag. I was the former *Spitting Image* writer telling the Cabinet minister he was being inappropriate: 'No, Gordon, you cannot take the piss out of the American President – you're the British Chancellor!' And Gordon would nod, then perform the joke again, enjoying its perfect symmetry and rhythm. It was his political secretary, Sue Nye, who finally had a serious talk with him and banned the intern joke. Tony Blair had just been in Washington, standing by Bill Clinton during his most difficult hour. Maybe that's what appealed to Gordon about taking the piss.

Gordon never criticized Tony Blair to me, but you absorbed the sense of the great rivalry between the two from the people around him. At one drinks function at Downing Street, I couldn't help but laugh when Gordon's maverick press secretary Charlie Whelan blew smoke at the internal door dividing numbers 10 and 11. 'Cherie hates anyone smoking indoors,' he said, with a mischievous grin.

Sometimes the request for jokes came at the worst possible

time, and sometimes it was a good excuse to take myself off to the pub with a blank notepad and tell myself this was all for the cause. Once, on a studio day at *Have I Got News For You*, I had written a series of jokes on a story that had just broken about the Tories, but Angus Deayton hadn't bitten at any of them. Then I happened to get a message from Gordon Brown's office, asking if I had any ideas for gags on the very same story. So I faxed the rejected *HIGNFY* jokes straight over to the Treasury. An hour later, we were in the producer's office, Parliament was broadcasting live from the little TV in the corner and we heard Gordon Brown do a couple of very familiar-sounding jokes from the dispatch box to howls of exaggerated laughter from the benches behind him. A slightly surprised Angus Deayton said to me, 'Um, didn't you just write those jokes for me?'

'Yeah, but you didn't want them, so I gave them to the Chancellor.'

I don't blame Angus Deayton for being a little confused by this, because I felt the same way. I used to satirize the government. Now I was satirizing *for* the government. On one occasion, I had even written jokes for the Prime Minister himself. In the run-up to his conference speech in 1999, his office rang me and told me the sort of thing they were looking for, and I said, sure, I'd give it some thought – it was all very casual. And then, literally about ten seconds later, the phone rang again and a journalist introduced himself.

'John, that's so amazing about you writing jokes for Tony Blair's conference speech!'

'Blimey!' I said. 'That was quick! Who told you?'

'Oh, well, I have my sources.'

'But I only just put down the phone to them. You must be, like, in the same room as them or something?'

A year or two later, I met this hack in person and he told me the truth. Nobody had told him anything; it was a completely speculative call on his part. He'd just thought, *I wonder who they might get to write jokes for Tony Blair's speech this year*, and he'd thought of me at exactly the same time as the people in Tony Blair's office had. After he had gone public with my badly kept secret, I thought, *Oh, well, it's only a little bit of gossip in the* Guardian *diary. Everyone will have forgotten it in a week's time.* But every fortnight after that, *Private Eye* would write the 'Reverend Tony's Parish Newsletter' and include some really cheesy joke, adding, 'Thanks for the really funny joke, John O'Farrell!!' I mean, I know I used to defend the right of satirists to attack whoever they want, but taking the piss out of me – well, that was going *too* far.

I got to do all sorts of radio and TV panel shows and, whenever they were attempting to balance the politics, I would be put opposite a *Telegraph* journalist called Boris Johnson who was still honing his bumbling public-school-boy persona.

'What do I think about Section 28?' he asked me once before we were both about to go on stage for *Any Questions?*

'Well, you're against it,' I told him.

'Am I? Tell me why I'm against it.'

'Because Section 28 makes it illegal to discuss homosexuality in schools in a positive light. So, the only legal choice before teachers is to ignore homosexuality completely or to be negative about it, condemning the very idea of being gay in front of teenagers who may be grappling with coming out themselves.'

'Yes, you're right. I'm against it, aren't I?'

And I felt quite pleased with myself, until I heard him opposing Labour's proposed repeal of Section 28.

Boris Johnson was at the beginning of a journey that would

take him a very long way, because he was the exception to the rule – he was a genuinely funny Tory. When I first met him, we were both writing regular columns for our respective newspapers and then we stood in neighbouring constituencies. He would effortlessly win Henley while, on the other side of the Thames, I would effortlessly lose Maidenhead. During the campaign, the producer of *Campaign Confessions* arranged for us to have a beer on the pub at Henley Bridge, and though Boris was amiable and interesting, it was clear to me that we were polar opposites, both politically and culturally. We could both quote Homer; just not the same one.

I put it to him that becoming an MP ought to mean he gave up all his other jobs. I wish I had been more persuasive. He continued to write his popular articles in the *Daily Telegraph* informing Middle England about the terrible practices in the European Union, and his readers felt vindicated that here at last was hard evidence confirming all their worst fears about Brussels. The only problem was that Boris was making it all up. Perhaps because in his head the line between jokes and facts was so blurred, he could talk about bendy banana bans or eight-year-olds forbidden to blow up balloons – and maybe he thought these cheeky inventions were all just a wizard prank, but across the country a million Conservative supporters were having their prejudices confirmed with myths; the jury was being presented with fabricated evidence.

Boris was catapulted to national celebrity status after he appeared on *Have I Got News For You*; without which, it is my firm belief that he would never have won the selection to be the Conservative candidate for Mayor of London. He was hilarious on the show and so was invited back over and over again. He became a popular politician irrespective of any politics; people weren't really bothered about what he stood for, they voted for him because he was a laugh. Somewhere out in the universe there is an alternative version of modern British history in which Boris Johnson was never invited on to a satirical panel show, never became a celebrity and subsequently Mayor of London, and never wielded any influence in a knife-edge vote on Britain's membership of the European Union.

It galls me that a satire show on which I worked for five years could have played a crucial part in launching the career of such a deeply destructive politician. It's one thing for members of the Bullingdon Club to have a laugh smashing up a restaurant then walking away. It's quite another to do it to the European Union.

But I had already had my suspicions that shows like *Spitting Image* and *Have I Got News For You* helped politicians more than they harmed them. Despite my youthful faith in its political importance, despite my sincere wish that the opposite were true, I came to the disappointing conclusion that *Satire Does Not Work*. All those years when I imagined I was exposing the vicious hypocrisy of Thatcher and Major, all it ever did (if anything) was make people feel a little bit better about everything. You were cross with the government, then you laughed at the government, and there: it had been processed, you'd dealt with it. Which makes satire worse than ineffective; rather than undermining the establishment, I think it actually helps maintain the status quo. George Orwell said that every joke is a tiny revolution, but the effect of all those tiny revolutions is that one big revolution is endlessly postponed. Laughter is the release valve that defuses the tension, it's the enzyme which converts anger into euphoria, a resentful feeling of repression into a sense of mocking superiority.

In any case, I was living proof of the terrifying consequences of daring to mock the powers-that-be in this country. In Iran or

Indonesia, we would be dragged off to a darkened cell. Here, the 'satiratti' were overpaid, invited to media parties and eventually to Downing Street or Chequers to mingle with the establishment we originally set out to challenge. 'Of course I'll write you jokes for nothing, Gordon, and yes, Tony – I'd be delighted to write lines for your conference speech and, yes of course, Home Secretary, I'd love to come and speak at a social event at your constituency.'

Once, I'd had an ambition to become a political satirist. Now, I feared that things had come full circle; the politicians were taking the piss out of me.

Mission Accomplished?

Lambeth Planning Sub-committee Vote –
1 April 2003

There's a dog-poo bin near my house that wouldn't be there if it wasn't for me. You know, they say that politicians never change anything, but I for one can proudly point to this smelly red bin on the edge of Clapham Common and say, 'I got that put there.' I wrote to the council suggesting that the bit of grass between the church and the library was a particularly bad spot for you know what, and the council wrote back and said, 'We've looked at it, we agree with you, we're installing a bin there.' We all change the world in different ways. Nye Bevan created the Health Service, Harold Wilson the Open University. I can point to that bin brimming with bulging little polythene bags and say, 'If thou seekest his monument, gaze ye at all the dog shit in this bin.'

And before the campaign for a new secondary school in Clapham, this was the only quantifiable thing I could point to and say that I had definitely achieved through local activism. After that easy early victory, I was hoping that another single letter might get me a new £24 million school on the other side of the common, but this challenge was proving a little more difficult.

For three years, we had been battling away with letters and public meetings and lobbying trips to the House of Commons, and it felt it was getting closer. The school was agreed in principle, but whether or not it would be in time for our children was another matter – if we were refused planning permission, the whole timescale would be knocked back at least a year. The new academy in Lambeth was being lined up with a sponsor called the 'United Learning Trust', which were three words I felt much better about than their earlier brand of the 'Church Schools Company'. Their background was in Anglican private schools, but I told myself at least that was education, not off-shore hedge funds. Their 'chairman' was Dame Angela Rumbold, a former Tory MP, but she had been an education minister and knew her subject inside out. I worried about having to make small talk with a former Thatcherite Secretary of State but, as it turned out, we could always bond by just slagging off the Liberals. Former Archbishop of Canterbury George Carey was on the board (oh dear, I forgot to tell him that I used to write *Spitting Image* sketches about him), and then there was the real driver behind this organization, Ewan Harper, soon to be 'Sir Ewan', a highly motivated and deeply Christian patrician Tory, evangelical about changing the life chances of children through education. The culture clash with the urban lefties of our campaign was enormous but, in the broadest sense, we all wanted the same thing, even if we were coming from completely different directions. Lord Carey kept banging on about helping 'these poor children in these dreadful inner cities' and I would think, *Hang on, those are my kids and their friends you are talking about . . .*

A cautious circular dance was evolving: we were scrutinizing ULT's every statement, suspicious that they were trying to impose a faith school; and they were listening to our angry supporters shouting at public meetings and thinking, *Are these SSCIL people a total bunch of raging communists or could we possibly work with any of them?* The threat of having no school whatsoever was regularly wheeled out by the council or the government to try to stop us pushing for exactly what we wanted, and at each stage during the campaign we had to make a political judgement about when this was just empty intimidation or a real danger.

It is when you are delicately poised to make some progress during a difficult negotiation that you are guaranteed a loud intervention from *The Person on Your Side You Wish Would Shut Up*. Every campaign group has one of these, every cross-party committee, every political organization that has to arbitrate and listen and be reasonable always has one bull-in-a china-shop campaigner who wants to fight rather than make progress.

Our committee is on the verge of securing a key point of principle from the sponsors that will be written into the funding agreement. 'And so we are agreed that there will be no faith criterion for admissions, and the school will welcome families of all faiths and none,' and I'm thinking, *Yes, this is it, almost there* . . . which is when *The Person on Your Side You Wish Would Shut Up* shouts, '*We don't want your religion stuffed down our kids' throats!*' and *boom*, we've lost them again, the trust is shattered, we're back to square one. Nelson Mandela would probably have been back home after a five-stretch if his parole meetings hadn't always been interrupted by that one ANC bloke from his solicitor's office interjecting, 'You can stick your peaceful transition bullshit up your Afrikaner arse. Nelson is agreeing nothing!'

There was one meeting in Lambeth Town Hall when Sir Ewan Harper was so incensed by the aggressive questioning about his insistence on 'a Christian ethos' that he declared, 'That's it! We are not going to sponsor a school here – if Lambeth doesn't want us, we'll go elsewhere.' I got him into a small side room to try to talk him down off the ledge. In that moment, it felt like I had saved the entire project, though who knows what mood he would have been in when he woke up the next morning. On another occasion, a councillor gatecrashed a meeting at my house and drunkenly insulted each of us in turn because we kept insisting the school must have a sixth form. All this seemed to me to be a pretty random way of deciding education policy; there were so many fragile egos and temper tantrums we had to tiptoe around. I suppose all politics works like this: you start out with political philosophies and moral positions and evidence and research, and you end up with outcomes dependent upon whether or not the people in the room were pissed off with each other.

This was bad enough when it was deciding about one school in south London, but when the debate was whether or not Britain should go to war in the Middle East, you would hope that evidence and legality would be paramount. As my fellow campaigners and I continued to be preoccupied by niggling discussions with council officials and civil servants, an epoch-defining national debate was raging around the case for war against Saddam Hussein.

I came to wonder if there might be a political parallel between city academies and the war in Iraq. Tony Blair had decided early on that what mattered was getting results. He was a man in a hurry, and decided he couldn't wait a decade to improve failing local authorities that might eventually improve local schools. So he would bypass what he saw as the unwieldy and obstructive local council and find another way to do what had to be done. But then, if you delete 'Lambeth Council' and insert 'United

Nations', it is the same basic principle. If cumbersome democratic bodies result in gridlock, we'll just bypass them altogether. You might get away with this when the worst that happens is you annoy the National Union of Teachers, but when it results in chaos in the Middle East, civil war and hundreds of thousands of deaths, the world can be less forgiving. Maybe Blair could have used the academy model in Basra, he could have got the bloke who ran Harris Carpets to be in charge of Kandahar. Maybe the evidence for academies was 'sexed up' by Alastair Campbell; maybe bog-standard comprehensives were going to unleash disappointing GCSE grades within forty-five minutes.

It's really easy to be against the Iraq War now; in fact, it's virtually compulsory. But despite the huge marches, it really was a minority position in early 2003; you were made to feel extreme and naïve. It's one of those issues on which people have upgraded their memories based on the latest version available. Everyone remembers where they were when they heard about the Twin Towers. No one can remember being in favour of the wars that followed.

This is not to say that, back in 2003, I was utterly confident about my opposition to military action. Lots of people I respected put forward convincing arguments that the world had changed since 9/11, that it was immoral to sit back and do nothing about Saddam. Maybe he did possess a dirty bomb that some lone terrorist could detonate in a Western capital – after 9/11, no terrifying sci-fi scenario seemed too outlandish. I understood that the world had changed and why so many Labour MPs voted for the war, and I knew that they didn't do so lightly.

I remember sitting at a Fulham game, arguing with a Labour MP I respected very much. He was obviously deeply conflicted, but I could tell I was failing to persuade him to vote against the war. Tony Blair was, effectively, saying, 'Weapons of Mass Destruction are definitely there, you'll just have to trust me on this one.' And to oppose the war back then was to call Tony Blair a liar before the thing happened that made everyone think Tony Blair was a liar. I think the Prime Minister genuinely believed that WMDs were there, but perhaps because he so needed them to be. He was being very persuasive about something he'd convinced himself was true.

I watched the news with increasing alarm, I argued with friends in and out of the Labour Party, I wrote about it in the *Guardian* every few weeks, but even with this enormous privilege, I felt as powerless and frustrated as the million marchers against the war. I was definitely guilty of giving more consideration to Tony Blair's arguments because he was a Labour leader than I would've done if a Tory PM had put the same case. But I just felt the wrong-ness of it in my bones. Isn't it the eternal lesson of history that, even if a war resolves one problem, it will always create a dozen more that nobody foresaw? I had no answer for what to do about Saddam Hussein. But he wasn't the only appalling dictator in the world, he just happened to be the one Bush had his sights on. The marchers said that Tony Blair was George Bush's poodle. I thought it was a bit more complex than that: Blair was Bush's Labradoodle maybe; his Cockerpoo, at least.

When Robin Cook quit the Cabinet and made his devastating speech against the case for war, it felt like someone at the top of the Labour Party was finally speaking for me. He resigned with great dignity, and his forensically argued speech received an unprecedented standing ovation in the House of Commons. Later, a second minister resigned, but too late and on the wrong issue. Clare Short took the moral high road, tripped over her shoelaces, fell in a cowpat and realized everyone had stopped looking two months ago. Like everything else, it turns out there is a wrong way to do the right thing.

When the statue of Saddam Hussein came crashing to the ground and joyful Iraqis beat it with their shoes (a means of protest which never really caught on over here), opponents of the war were thrown on the defensive. All our doom-mongering had been proved wrong, our disloyal undermining of our brave troops was shown up to be so much hot air. Bush appeared on an aircraft carrier in front of a huge banner that read 'Mission Accomplished', which, in terms of fate-tempting hubris, is up there with the captain of the *Titanic* boasting that he was about to break the transatlantic speed record.

It started to go horribly wrong quite quickly. A failure to plan for the aftermath and some catastrophic decisions by Bush's appointees in Iraq rapidly led to a bloody insurgency that took far more American and British lives than the initial war. Back in Britain, an ugly, macho battle erupted between Alastair Campbell and the BBC over the 'dodgy dossier' that had been cobbled together to justify the invasion. After Downing Street outed the government scientist at the centre of the WMD claims, David Kelly, he was thrust into the media spotlight and ended up taking his own life. And then another car bomb would go off, and another British troop carrier would be blown up, and it was all just so irredeemably awful.

Back in 1996, I had been delighted when Tony Blair declared that his three priorities in government would be 'Education, Education, Education'. But now, we were well into Labour's second term and it felt like it was nothing but 'Iraq, Iraq, Iraq'. Everything was tainted, and ministers doing great work in other areas found that their jobs had suddenly become much harder. I could feel the hostility to New Labour's academies policy growing as the Iraq War and its aftermath triggered a 180-degree turn in most people's opinion of Tony Blair and everything he stood for.

At some naïve stage of my campaigning, I think I had hoped that Lambeth Academy would be a perfect, all-inclusive educational utopia that would put an end to all local class divisions, and gated communities, and 4x4s parking in the bus lane. I was like Tony Blair with New Labour – surely everyone would want to come and join us inside this great big tent. In all the meetings with government ministers or council officials during the previous three years, at least we'd been able to take one basic principle as read: a new school would obviously be A Good Thing. But, late in the day, there emerged a new obstacle we should have foreseen. In the tree-lined avenue where this academy was to be built, residents had become aware of the plan to build a brand-new state secondary school right on the doorstep of their massive Victorian houses. One resident distributed leaflets warning of the triple terror of crime, vandalism and chewing gum. Residents of Elms Road were urged to organize and to do everything they could to ensure that planning permission for this new school was refused.

I optimistically imagined that if I just talked to some of these people I would quickly be able to win them over. I spent forty minutes on the phone with one resident who had worked herself into a state of neurotic hyperpanic about the prospect of local teenagers walking past her house every day. 'I don't want to get mugged every time I go out for lunch,' she said. How did she know we were timetabling double mugging for Monday lunchtimes?

'What about that man who got kicked to death in north London?' she went on. 'Can you guarantee I won't be kicked to death? Can you? Can you?'

I said I could, because I knew a lot of these children and

they didn't strike me as random murderers and, if I was proved wrong, well, she'd hardly be in a position to come back to me. The residents were prepared to spend a lot of money trying to stop the school being built. They hired professionals to produce detailed traffic projections that differed from the council's forecasts. They hired a barrister to make their case.

The planning meeting was held at St Mary's Hall, and it was packed with people both for and against the new school. It was not difficult to tell who was on which side. I sat there nervously picking my nails for hour after hour as each protracted point was debated to death. There were projections on traffic flow and details of planning law. I made a speech, blatantly appealing on a personal level to the seven councillors, saying that, in the frustrating business of politics, this was their chance to make more difference than they would ever know to the lives of hundreds of children they would never meet. Now, finally, it was to be put to the vote. I had no idea which way it would go and my fingers ached from being crossed for so long. Three Liberal councillors, three Labour and one Conservative. Any legal technicality could be used to postpone a definite decision – always the easiest option when faced with expensive lawyers.

'Can I see those in favour of granting planning permission to this proposal?' said the Chair. A half-second pause that felt like a week, then all seven councillors' hands went up. Seven out of seven; unanimously in favour! The parent half of the room burst into spontaneous applause. 'Yes!' I yelled, my fist punching the air. I wanted to cry, but it came out as a sort of ecstatic laugh instead. 'Yes! Yes! Yes!' Parents were hugging one another, it really was going to happen, our own local secondary school would open in September 2004, four years after we had begun our campaign; our kids would walk to school together, grow up together in their local community; whatever class, colour or religion, they would all *know* one another – and knowing one another seemed so clearly the answer to so many of our society's problems.

During that summer, we would cycle across the common to gaze through the fence at the building site in Elms Road; we saw the steels go up, and the kids tried to imagine that inside that space would be classrooms, dining halls and a gymnasium and to picture themselves being at school there. Then we'd cycle back home, and I'd pass the dog-poo bin and think it didn't look quite so impressive by comparison.

The sponsors asked me to be on the project board that would oversee the building of the school, then they asked me to join the panel which would select the headteacher, and lastly, I got a phone call from Dame Angela Rumbold asking me if I would be chair of governors of Lambeth Academy, as the school was to be called. I discussed it with Jackie. I consulted with some of our campaigners, and they said I should go for it. I cared so very deeply about the success of this school, I wanted it so very much to be a success – that would be enough to make it happen, wouldn't it? We were getting a brand-new school, my son would be in the first year and I would be the chair of governors. It was going to be great! 'Come on, everyone!' I said to all the parents of Clapham and Brixton. 'Let's just all hold hands, close our eyes and jump!' And so, in September, we made that leap in the dark. And then we opened our eyes and looked around.

Oh, not everyone had jumped.

Oh, Happy Day!

Election of Chair of Governors,
Lambeth Academy – 1 September 2004

One of the secrets of the right is that they are so comfortable with power; being in control comes to Tories as naturally as inconsiderate parking or talking too loudly in restaurants. But from the moment Labour came to power, it became clear to me that there is a significant section of the left who will always be more comfortable remaining untainted by the compromises of office, who would rather snipe from the sidelines than do the difficult bit of effecting change. Now, I was being presented with my own microcosm of this unglamorous transition from protest to power as I made the difficult metamorphosis from impatient school campaigner to responsible chair of governors.

I studied the greatest left-wing icons, trying to find a clue to how they kept their integrity and reputation beyond their early successes, and the path ahead for me became clear. My best move now would be to die. Or rather, be gunned down by the fascist Bolivian army or assassinated by a white supremacist; anything less tragic and heroic, like getting on with the mundane business

of governing, would just end up with me being a big disappointment to everyone. If Tony Blair had died in 1997, he'd be our very
own JFK.

For years, I had been encouraging a culture of exasperation
and outrage among local parents, but then I neglected to write
that memo informing them that, from 1 September 2004, all
criticism could cease, and henceforth we required only unbridled
enthusiasm and lavish praise for the efforts of the school leadership team.

'It's a beautiful building, John, you must be very proud.'

'It is, isn't it? I think we should all be proud.'

'That bamboo looks a bit dry, I think they might need to
water it.'

And I think, *God you don't have to get so personal, I can't
believe you're having a go at me about the bamboo.*

I wasn't so much proud as relieved. For four years, I had been
weighed down by this huge cloud of vague worry: worry that
we would never get the school, worry that the school wouldn't
be finished in time, worry that no one would come to it. Now,
Jackie and I were waving off our eleven-year-old son on his first
day at his new school. Not just new to him and to us, but a new
build, a new type of secondary school, one of the very first in
the country. His blazer is slightly too big, his face is full of
trepidation as he tolerates me taking a photo of him at our front
gate.

A hundred and seventy-nine other local children were arriving at the school gates as the last bit of rubble was swept up by
the builders and the kitchen staff were still struggling to work
the ovens. As chair of governors, I was the only parent lucky
enough to see all the new kids arriving, so I followed my son
at a respectable distance and did my best to let him experience

this day without catching his father in his eye-line, grinning and giving him the thumbs-up every five minutes.

I felt excitement and optimism as I looked down on the children gathering for the academy's first day. Yes, there was some disappointment that many middle-class parents had felt unable to make the leap with us. We all want our children to be tolerant and comfortable around minority groups, but I'd always presumed that the minorities would be other people. Despite the small number of families like mine who pay extra in Waitrose for the Special Gullible Range, there was just enough of a social mix for us to claim we had attracted a broad cross-section of the local community. Our first intake had twenty-four different first languages, in particular Portuguese, Yoruba, Somali and I think they were probably joking about Klingon.

The students filed into the building where they would grow into young adults, a building they had not been able to visit before because it was only finished at eight o'clock the previous evening. The first thing they saw was a magnificent circular atrium, like the reception of some expensive New York hotel. There were two halls, one of which could be converted into a theatre with retractable seating, a large gym and two canteens with a free salad bar. Every classroom had state-of-the-art interactive whiteboards, there were language labs with screens and audio facilities for every pupil, there were workshops, a reprographics room, art studios, a fully equipped digital recording studio . . . at one of the public meetings, one parent was a little indignant we weren't providing a heated swimming pool.

At that moment, seeing the building through the students' amazed eyes, I didn't feel much like arguing about academies versus comprehensives, or New versus Old Labour; all I could see was the front-line reality of a Labour government in power, spending money on the right things. This was progressive politics being effective. I felt vindicated, righteous, proud. And eventually I went home, closed my office door and still brimming with emotion, I turned my stereo up to full volume and played 'Oh Happy Day!' by the Edwin Hawkins Singers.

The plan was to grow Lambeth Academy year by year. This little group of eleven-year-olds would have this huge building all to themselves until next September, when another 180 Year 7 pupils would arrive. But then I got a call from a Labour councillor I knew. 'John, you know we have this terrible problem of an overspill of excluded troubled teenagers from our Pupil Referral Unit? Well, I've just had this brilliant idea! Lambeth Academy's just opened, with all these empty classrooms. It's perfect!'

When I had picked myself up off the floor, I politely explained that, as much as I appreciated her problem, my idealistic spirit of social inclusion only went so far. We were not going to market our new school as 'the perfect place for your precious eleven-year-old. Plus, a whole load of big scary hoodies – in fact, all the most difficult and disturbed adolescents of the borough, who'll be in the same building!' I didn't tell Sir Ewan or anyone else in any authority that I'd unilaterally rejected this enquiry. They might have wanted to give it due consideration.

My son knew that his dad was the 'chair of governors', but he was only eleven and a half, he couldn't be expected to know what that meant. The problem was that I was forty-three and a half and I didn't know either. Traditionally, the governing body is there to ensure that a school is running as it should be: to set targets and scrutinize academic progress, to monitor behaviour, to deal with admissions, appointments and generally observe the big picture from the outside. And the chair of governors will work closely with the headteacher to make sure the school never sinks to the level of the Bash Street Kids, where the same ten pupils have been held back for sixty-three years in a row. The principle of independent scrutiny is based on generations of experience which have taught us the enormous importance of holding those in power to account.

Tony Blair had to explain himself to his Cabinet and to Parliament, a chief executive must answer to their shareholders. Whenever an individual becomes all-powerful and is able to wave away all advice and criticism, it nearly always goes horribly wrong. So, in your local schools, the headteachers are rightly in charge and make all the day-to-day decisions. However, every term they should be answering questions from the governors about their progress and their plans and explaining why there is always one student with a massive tie-knot and chewing gum in his hair.

Back in the 1980s, I had been put on a school governing body as an appointee of the local Labour Party. Then political party governors were banned by Thatcher, so the clerk to the governors said to me, 'What do you do for a living?'

'I'm a comedy scriptwriter.'

'Perfect. we're re-appointing you "Local Business Governor".'

So now I approached a sympathetic local entrepreneur I knew; I got the best of the councillors for that ward; I got the leader of the council, who was on his way to the House of Commons. I asked Mike Richardson, who'd been Chair of Lambeth Governors' Forum and was very knowledgeable about education; then there was the project manager who had overseen the building of the school. The ULT had, annoyingly, stipulated there must be a church appointee, and I was offered a slightly eccentric local minister, but since he ran that Saturday school for the local Afro-Caribbean community I thought he'd be a good fit. Before governors' meetings, he would lay out a purple cloth on the side table then arrange on it a selection of Christian books we might like to purchase afterwards. I could have said, *Can you* not *do that, it's not really appropriate*, but my embarrassed response was just to smile and pretend to browse, as if I was briefly considering buying *Stand Up for Jesus!* before continuing on my way. 'Um, I've got a few other Christian bookshops I want to look in, but I may come back . . .'

Governance had been one of the key battlegrounds during the campaign for the school, so I was pleased I was free to adopt the community model I'd seen work well in the past, even if I did think it was a bit weird that I'd just been left to pick whoever I wanted. We had our first meeting, and Mike said, 'Well chaired,' afterwards, which meant a lot. I had requested that governors be provided with tea and biscuits; it's not much to ask for volunteers regularly giving up a couple of hours of their time, although my tea often went cold because I was concentrating so much on the meeting. Being the chair reminded me of the one time I was a referee. I found it harder work than playing in the game – you can't drift off for a second. Drifting off is what I'd always done best in meetings. But now I didn't doodle a single spider's web in the corner of the agenda. To wake up the other attendees at the end of this particular meeting, I had one small announcement under 'Item 8– School Opening Ceremony' in which I casually mentioned our special guest for that day.

Sir Ewan had failed to hide his excitement when he told me that Lambeth Academy's official opening would be done by the queen. For a split second, I had an image of the late Freddie Mercury singing 'We Will Rock You' in the main hall as the kids stamped and clapped in unison. Then I understood what he meant. 'Oh, *the* queen! Right. Queen Elizabeth the Second. Wow!'

I was going to meet the queen! *I wonder if she'll recognize me from that time we waved at each other during her boat trip through Maidenhead in 1975?* This didn't seem like the moment to confess that I felt a little conflicted about our school being opened by the United Kingdom's head of state. I had never been a monarchist, though it was never really an issue that bothered me a great deal. But set against this default lefty position was the obvious kudos that would be gained for our school by being opened by the world's number-one ribbon-cutter. Until Great Britain comes up with something better than a hereditary monarchy, I'd much rather she opened our school than the one down the road.

With the benefit of hindsight, however, I would say that, if you ever think of asking Her Maj to open your kitchen extension or new vaping shop or whatever, just be aware of how much you're taking on, because the self-important flunkeys at Buck House who make all the arrangements for her are not the sort of unassuming visitors who say, 'Look, we'll fit in with you. We really don't want to be any trouble . . .' Planning the queen's visit became like a full-scale military operation. On top of all the other challenges of opening a new school, there were endless pompous edicts and annoying diktats. Along the way, I learned that Her Majesty didn't want a steel band (she'd heard enough steel bands) and that you have to provide one special toilet designated for the sole use of Her Majesty and no one else. I suppose that's fair enough, really. You can't have one of the kids outside banging on the door shouting, 'Come on, Liz, how long are you going to be in there?' And then the queen coming out and saying, 'I'd give it a while if I were you.'

On the day in question, we lined up in the atrium, waiting to be introduced to her, and then stood there for twenty minutes because she was running late. Maybe she'd stopped off at

Ladbrokes to place a bet? A boy I knew from my son's old footy team was in charge of holding the door open for Her Majesty. He gave me a mischievous grin and whispered to me that when the queen came through he was going to trip her up. *He is joking, isn't he?* I thought.

At last, she arrived, and Lord Carey walked her along the line. I can't pretend she looked anything other than quite bored to meet me. She didn't say, 'Oh, it's you! I loved *Spitting Image*. How did you know what Philip and I say to each other in bed?' She shook my hand, and I feel I did well not to say 'Blimey, you're much shorter than you look on the stamps.' In the main hall, all the parents had gathered, and the queen was presented with a big plate and a couple of Lambeth Academy mugs. There were performances from the students, many of whom I'd known since nursery; the kids were so up for it and I felt ridiculously proud of them. I did a speech saying that the campaign for a great new school wasn't over, it was only just starting; a sort of 'this is the end of the beginning' kind of thing, but with less gravitas than Churchill. I decided against offering Her Majesty a high-five on the way out but, when she was gone, we all breathed a huge sigh of relief and thought, *Well, now we can get on with making this school work.*

There was so much optimism and confidence, it reminded me of Labour's victory in 1997, a real sense of a new beginning and the feeling that so much was possible. I showed TV crews round, and Fleet Street journalists, who reported that this school was massively oversubscribed (which was true) and attracting a great social mix (which I hoped would come true if we kept saying it often enough). Because I had been the one taking the principal around the primary schools or writing the articles in local magazines, I was getting a disproportionate amount of the credit for this apparent success story. One local grandmother came round to my house with the present of a bottle of wine to thank me for the school. I tried to explain that it took hundreds of people to make this school happen, but then I thought, *Well, one bottle wouldn't really go far between all of us,* so I said, 'Thanks very much.' Years afterwards, she still said 'Thank you for the school' every time she passed me in the street. But, a word of warning about taking too much credit for something that is a result of the efforts of many, many people. You might regret it when it all starts to go horribly wrong . . .

It would take a whole separate and rather boring book to document the many and complex ways in which things turned sour in the first couple of years at Lambeth Academy. Suffice to say that, during the short period I tried to work with our first headteacher, I aged about fifty years and the bags under my eyes got so big Ryanair would have charged me extra for them. No one individual has ever caused me so many sleepless nights, so much anxiety and, ultimately, so much anger. My solution had always been for everyone just to be nice to one another; I would have been useless in the Spanish Civil War.

To begin with, our first headteacher talked a good talk, and she seemed caring and sincere about the power of education to change lives. But that book I read on screenwriting had a name for a character like her; this archetype is the 'shape-shifter'. In this particular fairy story, I was embarking upon a scary journey with the most precious thing in the whole world – my own child. But it was okay, because I had this wonderful fairy godmother who would protect us all along the way. So I convinced the first-born of all the other families in the village: 'It's all safe; let your children come with me, we're following the fairy godmother . . .' And then we travelled deep into the forest and headed into the caves, and then we reached the innermost cave and that was when the shape-shifter pulled off her mask and revealed that she wasn't the fairy godmother at all, she was in fact the complete opposite.

Both parents and teachers were contacting me with complaints and concerns. Families started to move their children to other schools. I tried for too long to focus on the positives, perhaps because it was easier to repeat the excuses of the leadership team than to challenge them. One of my best friends was also a parent at the academy and tried to have a conversation with me about his concerns. He confessed later that he came away from it thinking, *Okay, I can't talk to John about this any more.* But the evidence was piling up; teachers were angry, parents were angry. Then one mum got in contact with me about the unwatered bamboo by the entrance to the school, which was now all dried up and dying. *You think that's the worst of our problems?!* I wanted to shriek at her. *You have no idea of the shit going down behind the scenes, and you're worried about watering the stupid bloody plants?*

I was in so deep. I had totally committed to this project on every front. I'd even just published a novel about state education versus private which was being adapted for the telly. I couldn't keep telling everyone how great this new school was and sack the headteacher in the second term. And it wasn't even in my personal power to do so. The academy's sponsors were still learning how to do this, I was learning how to do this and, at the same time, discipline was breaking down and staff morale was in free-fall. Then came one particular day when everything seemed to go wrong all at once. I had my worst argument yet with our headteacher, who I felt had been very rude to some generous volunteers. I discovered that the school office was even more chaotic and malfunctioning than I'd feared. I learned that yet another family was pulling their child out, and there was a particularly ugly incident in the playground involving a boy I'd known since he was little.

I could not help but think, *What the hell have I done?* The kids are out of control, the headteacher is out of control, and in the middle of it all is my own child and the children of all the families whom I had reassured that this new school would be a huge success. Was I like Rudyard Kipling, whose burning patriotism made him determined to see his boy volunteer for the Western Front, despite the poor eyesight of his doomed son? Was my own political zealotry putting my kids on the modern-day inner-city front line?

I stood alone in my kitchen, thinking, *I just don't know what to do.* Within just a few months, this great success story felt like it had turned into a disaster and I could see no way out. Stuck on the fridge, I saw a picture of my kids when they were much younger, smiling out at me in their primary-school uniforms, and I felt overwhelmed by an enormous guilt and burden of responsibility and I broke down in tears. It was that trust in my kids' smiling faces, it just killed me. 'God, I just don't know what to do?' I said out loud, and our dog came over, sat and looked at me. *I just don't know what to do . . .*

Are You Thinking What We're Thinking?

General Election – 5 May 2005

I was watching the Champions League semi-final when suddenly the home phone rang. *Who the hell is this, ringing me up in the middle of the football?* I wondered. 'Hello!' said a recorded message. 'This is John O'Farrell!' continued my own voice. Oh, it was *me*! It was that appeal to Labour Party members I'd recorded earlier in the day. I hadn't realized I was doing one of those really annoying cold-calling things, I'd thought I was recording an answerphone message for volunteers *when they rang in*. I hate those bloody automated calls, especially when they ring back again ten minutes later, like this one did.

'Hello! This is John O'Farrell!' said the annoying voice again.

'Look, piss off, John O'Farrell! I'm trying to watch the footy!' I shouted at myself down the line.

This was going to be a very difficult General Election. The polls were closer than they'd been for over a decade and, under their new leader, the opposition were widely expected to make significant gains. Eighteen months earlier, the Tories had got rid of the charisma black hole that was Iain Duncan Smith, demonstrating once again a level of ruthlessness and political expediency that Labour has never quite been able to match. Tory MPs had felt they had no choice but to act, following some damaging revelations about IDS which had been mysteriously leaked to *Newsnight* from a top-secret source. Well, okay, it was the same Tory MPs. Despite the fact that Michael Howard had finished fifth out of five last time he'd stood for the leadership, he became Leader of the Opposition without a contest. Other likely contenders came out for Howard or declined to stand, so he was elected unopposed and it was all over quicker than you could say 'something of the night about him'. That description would follow Howard to the grave, or 'bed', as Michael called it.

So the big worry at this election wasn't so much from some appealing new Conservative Party leader, the danger came from an increasing sense of disillusionment with the Labour government and politicians in general. My idealistic hope was that their supporters would be even more uninspired than our supporters.

It had been so easy to be Labour when we were in opposition and all we had to do was attack the discredited Tory government. And it had been so easy to be Labour back in 2001, when memories of the Tories in power were still fresh and Tony Blair was still trusted slightly more than an email from a deposed Nigerian monarch. But now there were so many apologies to get out of the way first, every slogan felt like it needed an extended self-justification before you got to the point where you tried to enthuse the voter. There had been a time when I had been a tiny bit proud to have received a Christmas card from the Blairs with their smiling faces on the front. That year, I had just added 'and John O'F' under their signatures and sent it on to a friend in the SWP.

Under Britain's electoral system, all of your vote goes to one candidate, whether you are wholeheartedly behind them or whether they only just shade it over the others. In this binary choice, I had always been happy to be a rock-solid 1 for Labour and 0 for the Conservatives. But the truth was that, currently, I only felt 0.6 for Labour, with 0.2 of me sympathetic to Charles Kennedy's opposition to the Iraq War and perhaps 0.2 for the Greens and maybe a tiny bit of support for the Independent Working Class Party, just so I could go to one of their meetings and ask for a cup of lapsang souchong.

Of course, I understand that no political party in power can ever be expected to fulfil all the hopes and dreams of all its supporters but, as political wrong turns go, they don't get much bigger than invading Iraq under false pretences, which led to a massive death toll and greater instability in the region – not to mention betraying the trust of a whole generation of British voters. The situation in Iraq had continued to worsen as the insurgency mutated into a nightmarish civil war while the occupying powers lost any last shred of moral authority as images of torture by the US Military were shared around the world.

I suppose it begs the question, 'So what exactly would Labour have to do before you stopped supporting them?' After a lifetime of grappling with this, the honest answer has always been 'Cease to be the best chance by which we can get progressive government in this country.' I understood and respected those who felt that a huge moral line had been crossed, but there were still thousands of other issues which would continue to need decisions, whether it was saving the local library or cancelling global debt – and I still believed we needed our guys in there making those choices rather than the other lot. There are so many contradictions and illogicalities, it's almost too much to hold in your head all at once, but in the end you have to make a call for the least imperfect option and embrace the compromise. I wish there was a purer, more idealistic choice on offer, and there probably is if you want to waste your vote, but what if that helps the very worst of them, isn't that an immoral act in itself?

A few years earlier, my French niece had cried all the way to the polling station when her first election saw her forced to vote for the Conservative Jacques Chirac, whom she had to support to block the fascist Jean-Marie Le Pen. She'd been hoping to vote for the socialist in the final run-off for President, but he had finished third, just 0.6 per cent behind the National Front. In the first round, there had been no shortage of other left-wing candidates who had helped make this happen: Workers' Struggle, the Citizens' Movement, the Greens, the Radical Party of the Left, the Revolutionary Communist League, the French Communist Party; every one of these got way more than the 0.6 per cent that kept the socialists off that final ballot. But each of them made their own politically pure choices, which left French voters with the final choice of Tory or fascist.

My politics keep coming back to, what is the left's best chance? Which imperfect party do we unite behind, not just for this General Election, but in the long term? Which movement do we organize around to try to make us as progressive and effective as we can be? So this was why I had recorded a telephone message for Labour voters telling them which marginal seats needed extra volunteers and where their efforts would be most appreciated. Someone told me that I had rung them up at three o'clock in the morning. Another Labour voter lost. I still hadn't lost my touch.

Slightly more successful were my attempts at fundraising for the party. Someone from Labour Head Office got in touch to ask if I would write some emails to party members asking for donations to our election chest. Once he'd explained to me that I wouldn't have to write to each member individually, I was able to agree. I felt bad about some of the old friends I hadn't contacted for a while. They said they saw my name in their inbox and thought, *Ooh, look, I've got an email from John. I was worried we might be losing touch . . . Oh, hang on, it's a begging letter from the Labour Party.*

I decided that the key to these missives was to make people feel good about being in the Labour Party by being as rude as possible about the Labour Party. My first email requesting money for the election listed all the ways in which donations would be completely wasted – on badly targeted direct mail (to 'Mr Michael Howard' of Westminster) or printing thousands of leaflets that would never be delivered. I included the word 'socialism', saying that every time I wrote that word the Head Office computer automatically crossed it out. And the response from Labour Party members was phenomenal. The bloke I was dealing with at Labour Head Office kept ringing me up in astonishment; money was pouring in. And I love Labour Party members for this! That they were more likely to give their money to an appeal saying that Labour would waste it than to an earnest and urgent demand to help secure Tony Blair's third term. The request for members to fill out their name and addresses got a much better response when I told them we would immediately sell on their personal details to a telephone marketing company. We didn't have to say, 'Not really, only joking!' – they got that, and the fact we'd made them smile made them more inclined to get on board. It made me feel that Labour Party members were smart and sophisticated. The wider message was, of course: we have a sense of humour about ourselves, we are not uptight, we are human. I think in the end, a few jokes just made people feel a little better about still being in the Labour Party.

Halfway through the campaign, I was asked if I'd come to speak at a rally focusing on world poverty. 'Who are the other speakers?' I asked casually. One was the Prime Minister, one was the Chancellor, and the name Bill Clinton definitely rang a bell. *Best not argue about the running order*, I thought. I practised my speech in my bedroom to an audience of one, and my nine-year-old daughter gave my jokes the thumbs-up. I wonder if Chelsea Clinton did the same for her dad. When I arrived in the Green Room, Alastair Campbell was on the phone to his boss, helping him reach a key decision before he arrived. 'But Gordon *always* wears a tie,' he pointed out, before glancing at me. 'John O'Farrell's not wearing a tie.' The make-up lady dabbed a bit of powder on my face. 'Hmm, you're a bit of both,' she said. I asked her what she meant and she pointed to the two shades of face powder she kept with her at all times. 'That one's Tony; that one's Gordon. You're a bit of both.' It felt like some sort of metaphor for New Labour: 'I'll just dab a little bit of Tony Blair on your forehead, and a little bit of Gordon Brown on your cheeks, and there! Now you look all radically moderate!'

Then, in the spirit of World Poverty Day, I went out on stage and did a load of jokes slagging off Michael Howard. I made a point about it being easy to be on the left in opposition, 'But supporting Labour in power, that's much harder – that's like being a Beatles fan when the Frog Chorus is in the charts.' Next up was Bill Clinton live on the screen from America. Thankfully, our speeches didn't overlap – in fact, he didn't have any Ann Widdecombe gags at all. He did back-reference my Beatles line, though, which made me so chuffed I think I would have agreed to be his intern.

But all these speeches, emails and phone calls were only talking to our own supporters; the point of elections is to reach out beyond your base and venture into more challenging territory. And in the 2005 General Election, I was going deeper into Middle England than any socialist had gone before. I was heading into the belly of the beast – I would be the Labour pundit on the pastel sofas in the BBC *Breakfast* studio.

In my youth, I had thrown myself to the ground across the entrance of a nuclear weapons base, I had fled a police baton charge outside South Africa House, but nothing had prepared me for making polite chit-chat with political opponents in the cosy setting of *Breakfast* TV. Opposite me in this weekly panel were Frederick Forsyth for the Conservatives and Rosie Boycott for the Liberals. Inside, I was outraged at Forsyth's support for Michael Howard and his position on just about everything, but the BBC *Breakfast* sofa does not lend itself to angry confrontation. So, while one part of me wanted to scream, *How can you possibly be a Tory!* a bigger part of me was seduced by the chummy atmosphere of daytime TV, and I was all gentle smiles and 'Hmmm, that's really interesting, Freddie – and I love that cardigan you're wearing, by the way – but I worry that Tory policies might actually *increase* poverty . . . but then, life would be boring if we all agreed, wouldn't it?' And we all shared a good-natured chuckle as our host said, 'Well, lots to think about there from our political pundits. Now over to Lianne with the breakfast weather . . .'

Tony Blair had said that this would be the last election he would fight, and though he claimed he would serve a full third term, no one really believed him. And, of course, waiting in the wings was Gordon Brown. No, 'waiting' is perhaps too polite a term for it; he was wrestling with the stage manager after trying to open the trapdoor under Tony's performance, he was pulling down the curtain and setting off the fire alarm in the wings. The defining image of the 2005 General Election was Tony buying an ice-cream cone for Gordon, which seems faintly ludicrous now but at the time felt significant and oddly reassuring. It suggested a truce at the heart of Labour, the passing over of the symbolic 99 of power (with extra sprinkles). Because of everything we had read up to this point about their toxic relationship, I watched this news footage with a certain amount of tension that Gordon Brown might shove the ice cream in Tony Blair's face, making sure that the stale Flake went in his right eye for good measure.

When I was in my twenties, I would feel deeply guilty if I ever missed a single night's canvassing, but now there always seemed to be some excuse not to go out knocking on doors, Tuesday night was my five-a-side football game, on Wednesday I was seeing my parents, Thursday – oh, that's Election Day, I'm leaving this quite late. But whenever you worry that your motivation to campaign for Labour might be slipping, along come the Tories with some offensive poster campaign or election broadcast to get you fired up all over again. In 2005, Michael Howard looked at the many issues that impact upon people's everyday lives, such as housing, health, education and transport and thought, *No, I think what I need to do is go on and on about asylum seekers and Gypsies.* These issues immediately shot up the list of voters' concerns and, unsurprisingly, there were increased reports of racist incidents across the country. The Conservative posters had the straight-talking byline 'Are you thinking what we're thinking?' To which the answer was 'Not unless you're also thinking that the Tories are running the most shameful, racist campaign I can remember by a major party, designed primarily to whip up fear and divide communities.' Michael Howard kept telling us it wasn't racist to discuss immigration but, by talking about little else, he was just saying in polite code what the Tories had said in 1964 when they'd won a seat on the slogan 'If you want a nigger for a neighbour, vote Labour.'

Thanks Michael, I wasn't going to go canvassing tonight, but you give me no choice. My own constituency of Vauxhall was a safe Labour seat, so I did my doorstep campaigning half a mile away in highly marginal Battersea. Every time I went back there, I knew fewer and fewer faces; the new organizer would say to me, 'So, Queenstown Road is at the end of Lavender Hill, just turn left,' and I had to stop myself saying, *Yeah, I know, I've knocked on every one of those doors a hundred times* . . . There's nothing more annoying than trying to run a campaign and having volunteers turn up to be foot soldiers but giving off the air of senior officers. Just nod, take your canvass pack and get on with it; they've got enough to think about without you patronizing them about how things used to be done round here. (But then, obviously, I couldn't help thinking, *Oh, they're putting those streets together, are they? Hmm, I would have put Emu Road in with Stanley Grove and Prairie Street.*) I was one of 163 outsiders who had signed Battersea Labour's visitors' book. Weirdly, Labour ended up holding the seat by 163 votes.

On Election Day, our kitchen was transformed once again into the operational HQ for our local ward. The doorbell rang so many times that, in the end, the dog gave up barking and went and sulked somewhere upstairs. The polling station was only at the end of the road, so my nine-year-old daughter wanted to do her bit for the movement by taking cups of tea to the Labour number-takers sitting outside the library. Some of the tea was still in the mug when she got there.

I had gone and voted as soon as I was dressed. I always think I'll wait until I'm going out anyway, but then I realize I just can't relax until I've done the great deed and pressed that pencil very hard in two clear strokes to declare my emphatic endorsement beside the name of the Labour Party candidate. Double-check? Yes, that is the right box . . . look across . . . yes, 'Labour', that box there . . . there's my big X. It's really not that complicated. I don't know why I always worry and stare at it for so long after I've done it.

On the way out, I give my number to the Labour Party teller sitting outside the polling station and we share a joke about how I might possibly have voted. We have both been local activists for over a decade – or two decades, if you count the silent pauses in ward meetings when they asked for a volunteer to be membership secretary. I also recognized the man collecting polling numbers for the Tories. At that point, Stuart Wheeler was a major Tory donor, reckoned to be worth in excess of 80 million quid. Even though he was wearing the blue rosette of the enemy, it sort of restored my faith in democracy that a man that rich and power-ful was still prepared to put himself out there and keep doing the boring stuff.

General Election Day is a very special festival in our national culture, and we should treasure the rituals and customs of this shared British experience. Strangers nod and smile as they head down the street clutching their polling cards; there is a great dignity to it, a silent sense of trust and collective consent as we each of us play a very small part in something very big. It's sort of miraculous that it all works, that we continue to put our faith in the notion of democracy, when it seems so constantly under attack. Whenever talk resurfaces of having a British National Day, centred around the anniversary of Trafalgar or something equally irrelevant, I always think we should make it about democracy, about the Mother of Parliaments and the best system of government anyone has yet to devise.

The BBC has always been my automatic choice for Election Night, despite the fact that they were still using that bombastic Rick Wakeman theme tune. It was so overblown and portentous, you imagined Rick playing it on five different keyboards in the Albert Hall, the long fringes swinging from the sleeves of his white leather jacket. At the slightly more reassuring sound of Big Ben striking ten o'clock, we were mollified with a projected Labour majority of sixty-six. Exit polls had been unreliable in the past and would prove so again in the future, but this one turned out to be spot on.

It was a new experience to spend an Election Night watching Labour lose seats yet look like it was still heading for victory. It's like your football team is 3–0 up from the first leg and you go along and see them lose 0–2 and at the final whistle feel a bit weird about celebrating winning on aggregate. I was sad but not surprised to see Stephen Twigg lose in Enfield Southgate, and I was annoyed to see the Wandsworth Tories regain Putney. I was appalled to see George Galloway oust Oona King in Bethnal Green and Bow. I've met many politicians of all shades over the years, and only one of them left me thinking, *Wow, if this bloke ever came to power, there would be bodies floating down the river.*

In the circumstances, Labour's majority of sixty-six looked pretty healthy, and it was amazing that Labour would carry on breaking records for its longest period of government. You wait ages for one Labour victory and then three come along in a row. But behind the result were some alarming statistics. Labour had won the smallest share of the vote for any majority government in British history. Tony Blair got fewer votes winning this election than Neil Kinnock had losing either of his. The Tories were not far behind Labour in terms of number of total votes cast; in fact, in England, more people voted for Michael Howard than for Tony Blair. The seeds were being sown for a series of disasters that none of us could possibly have foreseen. I had thought that the re-election of Tony Blair would bring us closer to Europe. I had thought victory confirmed us as the natural governing party of the new century. But as I watched the General Election results being declared and felt that now-familiar relief of seeing 'Labour Victory' flash up on the screen, a moment in history might have passed by that I may have just missed.

Looking back years later, I felt this deep sense of dread that 5 May 2005 might have been the last time I would see a Labour victory in my lifetime. I saw no clues back then to suggest that, over the following decade, the Labour Party would go into a catastrophic tailspin and end up nearly destroying itself as a potential election-winning force. Was it really possible that Labour's longest-ever period in office was also to be our very last?

Power Surge

Conservative Leadership Election –
5 December 2005

David Cameron became leader of the Conservative Party at the age of thirty-nine. That was the day I officially became old. When even the leader of the Tory Party is younger than you, you're formally inducted into the association of over-the-hill, decrepit old blokes. Stop listening to 6 Music, it's Classic FM for you now; you'll find the details in your *Radio Times*, which you must keep in its own special binder on the coffee table by the National Trust coasters.

Michael Howard had announced his resignation the day after the General Election, although he wanted to remain in post until the autumn, as this had a pleasing 'un-dead' feeling about it. David Davis was the front runner to lead the Tories, and it looked like his clever tactical move back in 2003 might be about to pay off. At that time, Davis had surprised everyone by throwing his support behind Michael Howard when he might easily have won the leadership himself. *Ah*, I had thought, *he's calculating that whoever leads the Tories into the 2005 election is doomed to fail and will have to resign afterwards. Whereas if he makes himself look generous to Howard now, he'll be well placed to inherit the leadership next time round, when a Tory Prime Minister might become a possibility.* Except, as with so many cunning plans, the rest of the world doesn't always co-operate. Davis led the first ballot of MPs but gave a lacklustre speech at the Tory Party conference and posed with a couple of large-breasted women wearing T-shirts with the slogan 'It's DD for me!' Classy. 'Vote for me because my initials are like a big bra size!'

All this was in stark contrast to the fresh approach of the relative newcomer who emerged to join Davis on the final ballot. Young David Cameron did something radical and exciting, never witnessed before at a Conservative Party conference. He gave a speech while wandering around the stage with no notes! But what did he say? Well, no one remembers, but he wasn't reading it from a lectern, and that's the point. The Conservative faithful were wowed by his thrilling new message of whatever-it-was-he-memorized-rather-than-read, and David Cameron overwhelmingly won the final ballot of party members.

Look how modern and metropolitan he is – he's cycling to Westminster! Okay, so his chauffeur is driving behind him with all his papers, but you can't have everything. Cameron had first been spotted at the scene of a crime back when, as a twenty-five-year-old, he worked as a special assistant to the Chancellor Norman Lamont. On so-called Black Wednesday in 1992, Britain crashed out of the European Exchange Rate Mechanism in the most disastrous manner possible, despite the Chancellor blowing billions that day trying to prop up the pound. At the end of his 'extraordinary day', Lamont appeared in Downing Street to face the TV cameras. And standing there behind him was the puppy-faced David Cameron, trying to look sombre and grown-up as his boss failed to apologize for the way Britain had just been humiliated in Europe. *I could do better than that*, young Cameron was probably thinking. Yes, David, one day you will do much more than take us out of a European currency arrangement. One day, it will be you facing the cameras in Downing Street, after you have accidentally sent us crashing out of the European Union altogether.

In 2001, the Tory leadership election had been completely upstaged by the terrorist attacks in the United States. Four years later, the terms of Britain's political debate once again became focussed on the fear-induced agenda of surveillance and security, with a generous sprinkling of anti-Islamic rhetoric and increased racial prejudice. London had woken in a good mood on the morning of 7 July; the previous day, the city had unexpectedly won the right to stage the 2012 Olympic Games. Then came news of a 'power surge' in the London Underground, but that didn't seem to chime with the sense of urgency being conveyed and the fact that the entire Underground was being evacuated for the first time in its history. Then it was euphemistically described as a 'network emergency', but with memories of the Madrid train bombings the previous year, many of us had already guessed the grim truth. Only when we saw the pictures of the exploded London bus in Tavistock Square were our worst fears confirmed.

I watched the dust clear on this awful news as I was sitting at my desk at home, supposed to be writing a funny column for the *Guardian*. I had agreed my story with the comment editor Seumas Milne; I was writing a piece mocking Jacques Chirac for being so arrogantly certain that Paris would win the Olympics, and for being so rude about the cookery of Finland that they then switched their votes to us. This would be one of my last regular comment pieces. I'd told the paper that I wanted to stop doing a weekly column after the election, but they had asked me to stay on until July. The news in July turned out to be not very funny.

Should I carry on with this? I thought. *It doesn't feel appropriate to be writing stupid jokes for a newspaper when something really awful is clearly unfolding.* I rang the *Guardian* comment desk.

'You're not going to want a comedy column in tomorrow's paper, are you? Shall I just stop now, so you can put something more serious in my slot?'

'No, no, John, keep going. Nobody quite knows what's happened, the Olympics is a big story.'

So, all morning, I ploughed on with jokes about English cooking or great British sporting failures, and I would flick back to the BBC News website and there were pictures of bombing victims, bloody and bandaged, and I didn't really care if I was professionally obliged to deliver a satirical column that week, I didn't want them to run it and I was glad when they didn't.

It was London's worst terrorist attack, killing fifty-two and injuring seven hundred. Four young British men (two of them still in their teens) had travelled to the capital to kill themselves and as many other people as they possibly could, believing, I suppose, that this would make them some sort of hero. Perhaps they sought a special sort of posthumous fame, perhaps on some level these young men wanted to prove how hard and committed they were, but they certainly demonstrated once again that *absolute certainty* is the most dangerous mind-set in politics. They were so very wrong and yet must have been so very sure they were right. What a precious political virtue is doubt. How civilized doubt is.

Some were quick to blame Tony Blair for getting Britain involved in the Iraq War, but France kept out of Iraq and would suffer worse atrocities than this. My ageing father was perplexed by it all. 'What do these people *want*?' he kept saying. 'When the IRA were bombing London, at least we understood why. They wanted Britain out of Ireland, and the British government said, "Not unless Ulster agrees," and, well, you knew where you stood. But with these new terrorists, I just don't understand what they want us to *do*?' My father's nostalgic lament was, basically, 'The old terrorists were much better than these new ones.'

As with the IRA attacks of my childhood, terrorism was not just an external assault on our society, it also led to enormous strains on our liberal democracy from within. There was a racist backlash against the people in whose name the terror acts were supposedly executed, the government pressed for further curtailments of civil liberties, and, just as the police had abused their powers after the Guildford and Birmingham pub bombings, now a group of armed policemen made themselves judge, jury and executioner of one suspect, who turned out to be a completely innocent Brazilian electrician.

The Stockwell shooting was a mile from where I lived, in a station where I regularly changed train; I could easily have been walking through that station at the time. And yet, looking the way I do, I would have been completely safe from the hyped-up, jittery armed policemen. I would have had this protective force field around me that said 'Middle-class white man – what harm have they ever done to the world?' (Answer: 'Most of it.')

But all of us in London just got on with our everyday lives, not because we were brave or defiant or because we would not be cowed, but simply because we had no choice. You can't stop going to work, or stop going to buy food or stop seeing friends. People glanced around more nervously on the Tube and I became aware that the number of fellow cyclists waiting at the traffic lights had doubled overnight. But barely anyone left the capital because of terrorism. The people I knew who left London always went for the same reason – schools.

People would move to temporary addresses for schools, they would involve their children in lies for schools, they would abandon all their declared principles for schools. People would not be driven out of London by terrorism, but the fear of mediocre GCSE results was another matter. I had already witnessed an exodus of families escaping to the countryside just as their children approached secondary-school age, and I'd always thought that was the wrong way round; that the teenage years would be just when the kids would want to live somewhere exciting.

And yet here I was, late at night, looking on the internet at houses in Sussex, studying maps of places I didn't want to move to, thinking that maybe we'd have to leave London, maybe we should leave the country altogether, maybe we should move abroad and start a completely new life elsewhere? I wasn't thinking straight, my mind was all over the place, the crisis in Lambeth Academy was driving me slightly mad, I would regularly wake at three in the morning and then be unable to get back to sleep. Deep down, I knew I had to stay and see this through. I had no choice.

Back when the school had just opened, I had always reached for the Lambeth Academy mug when I made tea. Now I chose the plain white one; the school logo was nudged further and further to the back of the cupboard. I didn't want all that anxiety at the front of my mind; just because the problems were always there didn't mean I had to face up to them. Piles of school admin grew higher, letters were still awaiting replies. Before the election, Jackie and I had been at an event with the Labour Party top brass, and Tony Blair had cheerily asked, 'How's the school going?' Jackie didn't hold back on how the school was going. I think Security probably pulled her off the Prime Minister about ten minutes later.

Of course, all parents worry about their children's schools, but when you are chair of governors you are more aware of all the various problems and it gives you so much more to worry about. I felt powerless to prevent the middle-class flight from Lambeth Academy, but we felt we had to stick with it and keep the faith.

So I was particularly perplexed to see a bizarre attack on me in the *Daily Mail* under the headline 'How the Smug Left Give Their Kids a Leg-Up'. The essence of the article was that instead of paying for a privileged education, people like me gave their kids a 'faux private education' by being actively involved in their kids' schools. The journalist suggested that I used my position on the governing body to make sure that my kids had the best teachers and received favourable treatment. My son was incredulous when he read this. 'Are they kidding me?!'

'Yes, well, it's not *that bad*, mate, I mean, marvellous inner-city melting pot, children from all backgrounds and all of that, eh?'

'And it's a nightmare having your dad as chair of governors as well . . .'

I'd thought I was familiar with every pressure group or think tank in the complex world of left politics, from *Labour Left* to *Left Futures*, but I have to say the *Smug Left* was a new one on me. I was pretty pleased with myself to be its founding member. Not just pleased, but self-satisfied, superior, self-righteous and sanctimonious. I suppose the Smug Left is the *Mail*'s fall-back position from the Hypocritical Left. The Right are always so desperate to hear that, although you go on about state education, you actually send your own kids to Eton. And then when you say,

'No, I don't, I send my kids to their local state school,' they can say, 'Well, that is so typical of the Smug Left. *To do what they say they should do.*'

We had limped through the first academic year, clinging desperately to the occasional positives when brilliant young teachers brought the best out of the students, but then we would be knocked back into despair again when discipline broke down, when promises were broken or another family pulled their child out of the school.

'I'm my own worst critic!' the headteacher was very fond of saying. And, inside, I always thought, *Oh no, no, no – you really aren't your own worst critic. Believe me, there are dozens of parents, teachers and governors who are much worse critics of you than you are.* At the end of this first academic year, two of the three Directors of Learning resigned, and now I was convinced that the headteacher simply had to go; no amount of extra training days or supportive action plans were going to turn things around. In an empty home on a hot summer's day, I opened up my computer to write to the leadership of the ULT and started calmly setting down the reasons against the continued employment of the headteacher of Lambeth Academy. And soon it was just all pouring out of me. I was writing like a demon, typing faster than I thought I was capable of; this was so liberating, there was so much to say.

Before the end of her fourth term, and after intense scrutiny from the ULT, Sir Ewan Harper rang me up to tell me that the first headteacher of Lambeth Academy would be 'retiring'. Jackie said later, 'Who'd have thought the Tory Christians would be the good guys?' Staff would be informed on their first day back in January. It was the hardest secret I ever had to sit on. When the day came, I sat beside the headteacher in the staff room as she announced this surprising news after only four terms. My face was sombre and inscrutable. I had decided it might be inappropriate to take out a party-popper and pull the string at the moment she said she was going.

It seems to be a generally accepted cliché in modern politics that we should not get side-tracked into discussing personalities; it is policies and principles that matter. But this just isn't true: character matters a great deal in delivering change, and the personality of a leader can make the difference between war and peace. The first leader of Lambeth Academy actually had very sound politics; we'd initially bonded over our views on comprehensive education and Iraq and what a pain-in-the-arse one particular mum was, and I think, at some simplistic level, I believed these values were the most important thing. But the beliefs you espouse are not enough to make you the right headteacher, or the leader of the Tory Party or the next Prime Minister. Great leadership requires so much more. The Labour Party and the entire country was about to learn that the hard way.

Waiting for Gordon

Labour Leadership Election – 24 June 2007

'So, next on the show we have a very funny guy from England. This dude is gonna be hysterical. Believe me, we are gonna have a lotta laughs right now ...' Already I can sense that this American radio host is going to be disappointed. I was promoting a book in the United States; I'd had an interesting chat for a New York podcast and a thorough interview with a Californian presenter. But then I made the mistake of appearing on a radio show from the big bit of America in the middle. It was probably called something like 'Redneck FM'.

'So, get ready for some HIL-AR-IOUS topical humour as we ask our guest – you're live on air – John O'Farrell, what would be your favourite way to execute Saddam Hussein?'

There was a slightly stunned pause on my end of the line before I recovered myself. 'Er, well, um, I'm a pretty liberal sort of chap. Er, I think that we should perhaps try to understand the anger within him . . .'

'Oh, come on, John! Does he swing or does he fry?!' Before I had time to respond, the zany host had gone over to the phonelines, where listeners were ringing in with their own creative suggestions for the best way to execute Saddam Hussein. On line one, Brett from Phoenix suggested, 'We should peg him out in the desert till dem buzzards peck his eyeballs out.' The DJ laughed heartily at this one. 'John what do you think – you like that one?'

'How lovely,' was all I could say. 'What a charming thought.' And I looked at my watch and saw that I was one whole minute into my half-hour booking on this show.

The following month, I got the chance to do a broadcast interview with Tony Blair, and I thought, *Maybe 'Arizona shock jock' could be the way to go.* 'So, tell us, Tony, what would be your favourite way to execute Saddam Hussein?'

During the Prime Minister's last few months in office, someone at the Labour Party decided that the launch of Labour's YouTube channel should feature an extended question-and-answer session with the party leader. Because nothing provokes a string of intelligent and thoughtful responses like an internet comments section.

'But who on earth can we get to cross-examine the Prime Minister on his entire time in office?' they asked themselves. 'Paxman, maybe? John Humphries?'

'Too easy – we need someone who will really put him through the mill, who'll bang the table and shout and demand straight answers.'

'Oh, no, not *him* . . . Not John O'Farrell? That's too tough on Tony!'

I filmed an appeal for questions and, the next day, I got the bus up to a little studio in Victoria, where they told me I would be the first person in history to conduct a live on-line interview with a British prime minister (a fairly empty claim, since it was never that likely to happen with Gladstone or Disraeli). I have to concede that this interrogation did not turn out like Frost–Nixon or Oprah Winfrey skewering Lance Armstrong. In fact, I wish I'd thought a little harder about a few ways to liven it up a bit. I could have got hold of Rod Hull's Emu puppet and wrestled the Prime Minister to the floor.

I'd start with what I thought was a really tough question, sent in by a member of the public, and then come in with a challenging supplementary of my own. Then Tony Blair would start explaining his reasons for the choices he'd made and then I found myself just listening and nodding and thinking, *Well, that sounds fair enough, good answer, I'm sorry I even asked.* I think I'm always far too worried about remaining polite ever to make a tough political interviewer. I came away with a strong suspicion that he might have done a few more of those than I had.

But I did offer him the chance to announce his resignation there and then, live on the internet. I suggested to him that it would be a very modern way to go. He declined my kind offer, as if I was only joking. And then he shuddered slightly when I proposed that, for his next job, he could become Gordon Brown's Chancellor, as a chance to get his own back.

Tony Blair's final few months were intended to be a triumphalist swansong, though none of the leaked memos planning his farewell tour included the landmark of becoming the first Prime Minister to be questioned by the police. Blair was interviewed as a 'witness' about the Cash for Honours scandal, which followed allegations that the Labour Party had accepted anonymous loans from rich donors who subsequently received knighthoods or peerages – or a signed copy of Cherie's book, if they only gave a fiver.

The Cash for Honours scandal was exactly the sort of sleazy

mess that used *to prove* to me that the Tories were unfit to govern. When it happened in the '80s and '90s, it was emblematic of everything the Thatcher and Major governments stood for: rich businessmen buying themselves titles by giving millions to the party that helped them keep their ill-earned millions. Now I had to square that old certainty with the fact that my own side had been engaging in the same slimy business. I filed this new disaster under 'Uncharacteristic blunder forced upon Labour by unworkable system'. That file was bulging by now.

Even during his brief third term, Tony Blair still managed some amazing achievements. Alongside Gordon Brown, he persuaded other world leaders at the G8 summit at Gleneagles to write off $40 billion of debt owed by the world's poorest countries. In his final year, Blair worked tirelessly to rescue the Northern Ireland peace process, just as it looked like it was about to fall apart again. Tony Blair did great things, and he did terrible things, but by now the public and the Labour Party had lost patience with him. Some of his more cutting critics had noticed that 'Tony' rhymed with 'phony' and also that you could invert the two vowels in his surname to suggest a certain level of mendacity. Well, he was never going to survive that.

Gordon Brown had nearly forced the Prime Minister out the previous year, when Brown's supporters had signed a letter urging Blair to step down. When they faxed this to Downing Street, they were slightly surprised to get no response whatsoever, but it turned out that this was because they had faxed it to the wrong number. One of the key conspirators, Tom Watson, then resigned from the government. His involvement in the plot became pretty obvious when he was spotted entering Brown's house in Scotland, even though he claimed he was just visiting Brown's new baby and that 'they had watched *Postman Pat*'. Apparently, the subject of the Labour leadership had never come up, so gripping was the complex love triangle between Pat, his cat and Mrs Goggins at the post office. Although the coup attempt failed in its immediate aim, it had forced Blair to announce that he would be leaving the following summer.

There was only ever one serious contender to be Labour leader after Tony Blair. No other Labour minister had put in quite so much thought and planning towards getting the top job as Gordon Brown (i.e. twenty-four hours a day for the past fifty-six years). But then, at the last minute, the Campaign Group of MPs attempted to put up John McDonnell as a candidate. Gordon Brown was incandescent about this attempted challenge from the extreme left of the party, while my armchair observation was that this was a ridiculous over-reaction on the Chancellor's part. *Relax, Gordon*, I thought. *So what if the far left put up a candidate? They're never going to win.* On this occasion, there was definitely not going to be any 'widening of the debate', as intense lobbying from Brown's camp kept MPs from indulging McDonnell, who fell well short of the number of nominations required. *That's the last we'll ever hear from him*, I thought. (Actually, I didn't, but I have my irony targets to meet.)

Gordon would become leader and Prime Minister without having to go through the scrutiny of an election process. At Lambeth Academy, we had organized focus groups of twelve-year-olds to interview prospective candidates for our headteacher, and I had found their feedback to be incisive and devastatingly honest. Maybe the Labour Party should have tried that when choosing the person for the top job. I can imagine what the kids would have said: 'Gordon's clearly very highly motivated and experienced – but I worry that he will not be able to micromanage

every single government department in the way that he has dominated the Treasury.' (Sally – Year 8)

'Yes, and is he even-tempered enough to take the relentless
criticism that goes with being constantly in the public eye? I worry
that a bunker mentality might develop, driving a wedge between
Number Ten and the Parliamentary Party. (Nadim – Year 7)

The students had helped me and the ULT pick an excellent
new headteacher for Lambeth Academy. Stephen Potter had been
a deputy head at the Charter School, which had inspired our
original campaign, and so had first-hand experience of building a new school year by year. Our original headteacher had
stayed on until the end of the school year in order that scientists
could follow me into the school and record the iciest relationship
since records began. But the good news was that Stephen Potter
had been able to start straight away, doing succession planning,
managing new appointments and generally cheering me up.

He occupied an empty classroom on the top floor of the school
that looked over the enclosed courtyard. Down in the pond
below, he pointed out some tiny ducklings that had just hatched
and were now being cared for by their mother, who had chosen
to lay her eggs in the heart of Lambeth Academy. *What a perfect,
optimistic image*, I thought. *Baby ducklings being nurtured
within the protective haven of our inner-city school.* Next time
I was there, I asked Stephen how our symbolic ducklings were
getting on. 'Oh, yeah,' he said. 'Well, a great big crow swooped
in and ate them all.' Okay, let's scrap plans to put the story of the
little ducklings in the next parents' newsletter.

Before the school had opened, our first headteacher had
unilaterally selected a colour for the uniform that could be best
described as 'shit brown'. (Obviously, that wasn't the name of
the shade in the brochure; the marketing people always invent

something more pretentious, its actual name was probably 'Diarrhoea Sunset' or something.) It made our students look like they were from a borstal in a bad TV drama; now, I lobbied Stephen Potter to lose the brown prison sweatshirt, saying that a decent new uniform would be an important symbol of change. As with so much else, I was pushing at an open door. Stephen was full of ideas, solutions and optimism.

And, maybe, a few miles across London, Gordon Brown was planning all the big changes for when he took over? Was there an FAQ document he was compiling to give to all those Labour MPs who were as anxious about the future as we were? I was excited at the prospect of a Brown premiership because I anticipated that the left-wing instincts he'd shown as Chancellor would now be applied across the whole government. I hoped we'd be back to good old down-to-Earth 'Labour' again, none of this 'New' nonsense, which still made me wince (and got us elected three times in a row). I hoped that the real Gordon was more radical than the New Labour he'd helped to create, but you could never really be sure.

What would be Brown's Big Idea that he would unfurl to define his long-awaited premiership? we all wondered. We looked forward to it with great anticipation; he'd been waiting for a decade to inherit the top job, so he'd had plenty of time to come up with it. A friend of mine thought he might immediately pull all British forces out of Iraq, to draw a line under that political disaster and signal a different kind of relationship with the United States. I was secretly hoping he might do something really radical on council housing – a massive public house-building initiative to reverse years of rising rents and crippling house prices. Others mentioned the re-nationalization of the railways, the cutting of Trident, or Proportional Representation, which would keep the

Tories out of power for ever and allow the Labour Party to stop compromising on what we really stood for.

As a young drama student, I studied Samuel Beckett's *Waiting for Godot* and had been a little baffled that Godot never turned up. Thirty years on, I was a bit player in another national drama, *Waiting for Gordon*, in which we all discussed our hopes and dreams of what would happen once socialist Gordon finally got here. And then we waited, and we waited, and we waited . . .

Death Throes

London Mayoral Election – 1 May 2008

I was standing in a swimming pool, half-heartedly chucking a Little Mermaid ball about with some mates, when I became aware that Paul was not taking part but pacing around the pool, talking anxiously on his mobile phone. It was my football team's annual trip to Italy – every October, we played a couple of village teams in Umbria then ate and drank too much and discussed how we could have won our games if only our shots had gone in and theirs had not. One or two of our players had the temerity *not* to work in the media – but obviously I had never asked Paul exactly what he did; as a bunch of blokes in a football team together, we had more important things to talk about, like what would have happened if Hitler had been French or whether I could get this ball into that little rubber ring from here.

'What's up with Paul?'

'Oh, I think it's something to do with the financial crash, or some shit. Here, catch!'

'Oooh, missed! Oi, Paul! Paul! Kick the ball back in the pool, will you?'

Still hunched over his phone, a worried-looking Paul gave a little wave of his hand and obligingly kicked the ball back to the pool so we could continue with our game.

'What does Paul do, anyway?'

'Oh, he works for an Icelandic bank. Except it just collapsed.'

'Oooh, bad luck! Here – on yer head! David, did you know Paul works for an Icelandic Bank? Or rather, he doesn't – ha ha ha! Sorry – Paul! Can you get the ball for us again, mate?'

During this period, saying 'Icelandic bank' was like saying 'Chernobyl nature warden' – Iceland was emblematic of the global financial meltdown no one had seen coming but which, in retrospect, had so clearly been hurtling right towards us. So perhaps the rest of that weekend really ought to have been spent reflecting upon the massive political economic implications of a global financial crisis. Instead, we just took the piss out of Paul for managing to get a job with an Icelandic bank. 'Paul, have you thought about a job at the Iraqi Tourist Office? Or selling life insurance at Dignitas, maybe?' 'Or just work at Woolworths? Oh, no, hang on, they've gone bust as well . . .' And Paul did his best to force a good-natured smile, hoping that perhaps the bankers would get a more sympathetic treatment back at home.

The origins and causes of the crash of 2007–8 are incredibly complex and intricate, and I just about understood it all while I was reading those books on the subject, and for several days afterwards. But basically, it boils down to this: lots of greedy people (who had already made an awful lot of money, anyway) didn't think that they should be held back by a few restrictions and safeguards that were put in place after the last great crash in the 1930s, precisely to stop this sort of thing ever happening again. This liberalization of the banking laws was carried out by right-wing governments, under pressure from even more right-wing ideologues who claimed that free-market principles were being undermined by a regulation that said perhaps you shouldn't be allowed to lend a million dollars to an unemployed alcoholic who lived in a broken-down Nissan Micra.

And here's the punchline – Labour got the blame! Yes, the global meltdown of 2007–2008 was all the fault of the British government of the day, apparently, because who can forget those mass rallies of Conservatives demanding *more* financial restrictions, the endless pressure from the *Mail* and the *Telegraph* calling on Labour to reverse the banking liberalization enacted by Reagan and Thatcher? It's so obvious when you think about it – the banking crash was all the fault of us lefties! The banks around the world collapsed because the British Labour government spent so much money on schools and hospitals. I'll be organizing a collection later for bankers who were forced to sell the weekend cottage in Suffolk – I feel so responsible.

But as tempting and easy as it is to blame 'the bankers' for the financial crash, few of us would not have welcomed the massive salary if we'd found ourselves in that position, we would have convinced ourselves we deserved it because we were so clever. That's why the market cannot be completely free – because everyone has to battle against their 'inner banker'. That's why we need governments to intervene in all sorts of areas of society where it's too important just to hope that individuals will make responsible and altruistic choices.

So that's all 'socialism' means to me – we put 'social' considerations ahead of financial ones. If the free market prices the poorest out of a roof over their head, we have to intervene and provide social housing. If the free market leaves people queuing at food banks, then the government has to step in and legislate to ensure they have enough money to buy their children food. I have always struggled with what that loaded word 'socialism' really means. I think it could have made for a very interesting episode of *Call My Bluff,* with special guests Hugo Chavez, Karl Marx and Tony Blair. My version of socialism doesn't still think that the solution to all the ills of capitalism is to nationalize everything. Believe me, no Labour government would want to be responsible for that late-night kebab shop in the high street. But whenever the Labour Party is struggling to express what it stands for, we should assert that we are simply led by what is best for society as a whole. The 'social' in 'socialism' is about putting people ahead of the 'capital' in 'capitalism'. The level of freedom enjoyed by the market should be determined by the maximum freedom that this affords the people (including freedom from poverty, exploitation and having to watch Kelvin MacKenzie on *Question Time*).

The economic crash of 2007–8 should have been the wake-up call that putting profit above all else has terrible social consequences. It should have put unbridled capitalism on the defensive. It should have had British Conservatives and American Republicans hanging their head in shame for all the safeguards they tore up over the years. Instead, we had to listen to David bloody Cameron, with his tiresome home-improvement metaphor: 'Labour didn't mend the roof when the sun was shining!' (or 'They didn't get the little man from the village who mends the roof,' if you heard his first draft).

It's hard to blame Gordon Brown for failing to get the right spin on the situation. It's not like he wasn't busy doing other things. Finally the new Prime Minister had found his purpose and, while other Western leaders froze like rabbits in the headlights, Gordon Brown was decisive and dynamic, pumping billions into the failing banks and urging others to do so. Soon, fellow G8 leaders were following his example. It may be that Gordon Brown saved the world from total economic collapse, I really have no idea, but the rules of the game decided that he wasn't going to get any credit for anything any more.

Gordon Brown had enjoyed positive ratings for his first few months as Prime Minister, so much so that he considered holding a snap General Election to secure his mandate and gain an extra couple of years in office. Unfortunately, this notion was so openly touted it looked certain to happen, and when the polls narrowed and it seemed too much of a risk, the non-election was perceived as an embarrassing climb-down and Brown's un-spun straight-man image evaporated overnight.

Brown had managed to spend ten years at the very top of government without ever gaining a particularly high profile. He never did the chat shows, and rarely commented on news stories or sought the limelight, like so many celebrity politicians. You felt that this afforded Gordon a little more dignity than Edwina Currie on *I'm a Celebrity . . . Get Me Out of Here!* But it is not possible to keep out of the media spotlight once you are Prime Minister; it comes with the job to respond to every crisis, to have an opinion on everything and to perform for the cameras whenever they demand it. And Gordon Brown just wasn't as good at this stuff as the actor-politician who had preceded him. And while it had just about been possible to micromanage the Treasury, he couldn't do that with a dozen other departments as well. Brown was unable to delegate but also slow to make decisions; he worried about negative press coverage but never offered any positive narrative of his premiership as an alternative. But it wasn't just about perception. The abolition of the ten-pence tax rate was hitting the poorest in their pockets. This was a disastrous policy that Brown had inherited from whoever was Chancellor before he became PM. Labour MPs were shocked that he refused to see how much damage it was doing to their constituents.

I struggled to accept the growing consensus that Gordon Brown might not be a good Prime Minister. I felt like I was part of Team Gordon, I had presumed for so long that he would be better than Tony Blair, that we would see far more radical changes once Gordon was no longer held back by the man next door. I tried to tell myself that others were just falling for the Tory media's onslaught on him. But there had been no major shift in policy, he seemed like he was reacting to events rather than driving them.

People went off Gordon Brown very rapidly. In just eight weeks, Labour went from being ten points ahead in the polls to ten points behind. Vince Cable got a big laugh in the House of Commons by saying that Brown had gone from being Stalin to Mr Bean. I thought the hysterical laughter was actually more than this half-joke deserved, it seemed to me that the audience enjoyed the choice of target rather than the choice of words.

This was the atmosphere in which Labour approached the local elections in May 2008. Labour councillors were offered pictures of Gordon Brown for their campaign literature, but there seemed to be a recurring software problem. 'Oh dear, I can't seem to open the JPEG. It must be my computer, don't worry, I'll just have to manage without it.'

In London, Gordon Brown put aside a lifelong animosity to Ken Livingstone to offer him all the support the party could muster, but it was looking like an uphill battle. Ken had always been something of a political maverick, but whereas, before, he used to offend people on the right, by now he'd become far more balanced and was offending everyone.

'So, Ken, can we ask you about your plans for London Transport?'

'Well, of course, Tory privatization left the trains in a terrible state, worse than the trains that Hitler used to take Jews to the concentration camps.'

'Erm – right. Could we just record one bit of the interview without you mentioning Hitler or saying "Jews"?'

'That's what Hitler wanted, you know, not to have to think about Jews. Particularly the really Jew-y Jews, he hated those Jews more than the less Jew-y Jews. And today's Tories and New Labour – they're basically the same as the Nazis. Did you know Peter Mandelson is a Jew?'

Boris Johnson had won the selection to be the Conservative Party's candidate for Mayor, beating off such political visionaries as DJ Mike Read and the boxer Winston McKenzie. The Tories didn't need any second-rate celebrities to become politicians; they had a second-rate politician who was already a top TV personality. The young estate agents and City boys who were starting to populate the pubs of Clapham boasted about hating politics but were voting for BoJo 'for the LOLs, 'cos he gives no shits, he's a #MassiveLegend'. This wasn't an election, this was a light-entertainment casting choice.

In the middle of the campaign I remember cycling home from central London and realizing that this was the first time I could remember seeing more Conservative posters than Labour ones. After fifteen years of being too embarrassed to show themselves, Tory voters were coming out of the woodwork and declaring their allegiance again. In the back of taxis, in the new-build luxury flats – even the Park Plaza County Hall had a Boris poster in the window, which particularly offended me. The hotel was only there because Thatcher had closed County Hall, evicted Ken Livingstone and abolished London-wide local government. *Right, that's it*, I told myself. *If I ever need to stay overnight three miles from my house at the cost of £200 a night, I am defi-nitely never using the Park Plaza County Hall Hotel.*

I told Jackie when I got home. 'Boris Johnson is going to win,' I said. She was shocked to hear me being so pessimistic; it was so unlike me. But it was no great act of political prophecy that, eleven years to the day after Tony Blair's landslide, Labour were going to be comprehensively stuffed at the polls. But it turned out to be far worse than any of us had imagined. Labour finished third across the country, a full twenty points behind the Conservatives, for the first time in its history. Labour's supremacy was in its death throes.

Boris Johnson won easily in London, gaining over a million votes, at that time the largest personal mandate ever gained in a British election. He reassured us of his commitment to the new job by announcing that he would not be giving up his £250,000 column in the *Daily Telegraph*. Johnson did, however, resign as the MP for Henley, so Labour faced a by-election near where I had grown up and where my parents still lived. Since I was in the area anyway, I went along to support the Labour candidate and tried not to look too ridiculous as I talked up Labour's chances on the lunchtime news when they interviewed me in the posh bit of Henley (i.e. in Henley).

I was surprised when the Labour candidate told me that he only joined the Labour Party because of me. Apparently, when I was standing in Maidenhead, I had given him a leaflet outside the train station, a moment that was captured in my documentary. I made some rubbish joke about his furry hat and Russian socialism. He read the leaflet, then my memoir about helping the Labour Party lose elections at every level, and that had inspired him to get involved and now he was a parliamentary candidate himself. Labour finished fifth in Henley and lost its deposit. Wow – that guy really took my style to heart.

My dad turned eighty-nine on the day that Labour won its lowest share of the vote in his lifetime. To be honest, he was now looking in an even worse state than the party he'd always supported. Growing thinner every month, he seemed to exist mainly on a diet of red wine, chocolate and the news. His lifelong interest in current affairs had become an obsessive dependency; if Mum drove him up to our house, he would get through the front door and, almost before he had seen his grandkids, ask if I could put on the television news.

'You just had the news on in the car, dear,' my mum would tut.

'I know, but John has all those news channels, I want to see what they are saying.'

And I'd push the armchair right up to the television and fix him up with a saline drip of news, monitor his regular news intake, give him additional news supplements. It was a great blessing that his mind remained so sharp, even though, eventually, his body became too weak to travel and so our time together was confined to his new bedroom downstairs in my parents' cottage, between the dusty houseplants and rows of his old leather-bound books. Dad and I could still talk about anything, except on the hour and at half-past, when he became desperate for a new dose of exactly the same headlines. But in August something happened that pulled me up short. We chatted for twenty minutes or so, about 'George' Brown's problems ('It's *Gordon* Brown,' Dad) and the history book I was writing. I even learned something new about his war years: that he'd had to turn around at Dunkirk and head back towards the German guns in the deserted streets to destroy reams of secret British papers.

'Weren't you scared?'

'Not really. There was all this wine in a shop window, and

if we hadn't drunk it, the Germans would have done, so, you know . . .'

I laughed and then, for the first time ever, he said that he was too tired to talk any more. And I said, 'Okay, Dad,' and I just sat there with him.

He died the following Sunday.

But the weird thing was that it was okay. Dad was old, he was tired, the last time he had seen his grandchildren he told them he'd had a great life, as if he had known he wouldn't see them again. I could cope with his death because it seemed sort of fair. Jackie's father had died at sixty-two, just when he was beginning a retirement he had looked forward to for so long. That had been so unjust; the narrative had been all wrong. Maybe it's the writer in me, but I felt that my dad's death had come at the correct point in the story.

It was my mum I was worried about. They'd been together sixty years; that's a long time interrupting each other's anecdotes. Her purpose over the past few years had been caring for her husband. She'd been beside him, helping with everything. When he'd had his eye test, she was there, prompting him with the names of the letters he couldn't see.

Mum wasn't alone when I got there. Two policemen were sitting in the dining room having a cup of tea. They informed me that this is normal if someone dies at home; clearly, it was a quiet day for crime in Cookham, the mystery of the dropped crisp-packet would have to wait. So trained were the policemen to look sad and sympathetic that everything Mum said was greeted with a tragic nod.

'John's been on *Have I Got News For You*, haven't you, John?'

'Er, not now, Mum.'

I went through to the next room to behold the first dead body

I'd ever seen and gave my dad a kiss on his forehead. How weird life can be, I thought, sitting there beside him. I had expected to spend the day with my daughter at a music festival on Clapham Common watching Iggy Pop. And instead, here I was, sitting beside my dead father. Somehow, I always thought Iggy would go first.

A few days later, my brother, Mum and I sat around in the undertaker's, and the immaculately dressed assistant sombrely talked us through the options. There were a variety of coffin choices, he explained. They had beautifully crafted scale models so you could see what the wood looked like, each the size of a shoebox, but properly varnished and embellished, with handles and everything.

'This is the oak,' he said, and he placed the model oak coffin gently on the table. 'This is the pine. As I say, that's less expensive.' And we stared silently at that one, too.

'And, finally, this is the mahogany . . .'

Still slightly stunned from the bereavement, my mum, my brother and I stared at the selection of little ten-inch coffins arranged before us.

'The thing is, though,' I said, 'all of these are much, much too small.'

Mum laughed so long and so hard I thought she might have a heart attack there and then and we'd have to ask if they did a two-for-one deal. The poor undertaker was professionally obliged to remain utterly dignified and serious the whole time. But the sad thing is, Dad would have really loved that moment, we would have laughed about it in the pub, but they'd called last orders, they had rung the bell, and here we were now, standing around his grave, his ashes being interred in the churchyard overlooked by their cottage.

In a failure to arrange things the way Dad would have done, the gravestone was placed the right way up and we didn't get the dates wrong. We had asked the vicar if we could have Dad's stone engraved with 'I'd rather be in the Bel and Dragon.' But the reply came back that the bishop had deemed this not sufficiently reverent – and as a humorous P.S. the vicar had added that, splendid though my dad's favourite pub was, he was sure that heaven, where he was now, was even better. Hmmm, not when we sat round that table by the fire, drinking pints of Brakspear's and laughing and joking all evening, it wasn't. That had been heaven right there on earth, back when Dad had his whole family in the pub together and we had all just laughed and laughed and laughed.

Yes We Can

American Presidential Election –
4 November 2008

There was a time when we thought that George W. Bush was the dumbest, crassest American President we could possibly imagine. 'This guy has got to be the worst it ever gets, hasn't he?'

'No, believe me, by 2017, you will feel a burning nostalgia for this kind of mainstream intellectual.' After 9/11, when Bush was interviewed on the golf course, he called upon all nations to do everything they could to stop these terrorist killers, adding, 'Now, watch this drive.'

'Oh, for such sensitivity and self-awareness today!' we'd say fifteen years later. 'If only we had someone moderate and rational with normal hair like George W. Bush.'

Dubya had, of course, come to power at the turn of the millennium in extraordinary circumstances. The election was a virtual tie, with the decisive result coming down to who had won Florida. The Democratic candidate, Vice President Al Gore, had won more votes across the whole country (and, it was later argued, more votes in Florida) but, with the situation looking deadlocked, the Republicans went into aggressive media and legal overdrive, claiming victory on their news channels and in their newspapers, and creating an atmosphere where it would appear deeply partisan for the Supreme Court to rule any other way. The Republicans got the Presidency by being the meanest bastards in the game, which is some sort of lesson for the left, considering the enormous consequences of that victory for America, Iraq and the whole wheezing planet.

Bill Clinton had been the only Democrat in living memory to be re-elected to the White House; just as, in the United Kingdom, the progressive party is always pushing uphill. The Democrats had endured similar existential debates about whether to lean to the left or to the centre, and about what sort of candidate might best appeal to the wider electorate. But in the run-up to the 2008 Presidential Election, this debate took on a new dimension when the Democrats chose Barack Obama as their candidate. It was exciting and scary at the same time. Would the lid be lifted on the deeply ingrained racism of Middle America, sending the Democrats to a crashing defeat? Or was it possible that we could enter a new era of tolerance and racial harmony? 'Yes we can!' repeated Barack Obama, in his powerful and inspiring speeches. With his famous *Ich bin ein Berliner* speech, President Kennedy had updated the classical Roman philosopher Cicero. With 'Yes we can!' Obama seemed to be channelling Bob the Builder.

Since I had to go to America for a few weeks, I decided to make my trip coincide with this historic Presidential Election. The polls were looking worryingly close and I'd decided that what the Democrats needed was my years of experience campaigning for the British Labour Party in the 1980s. I have to say I was amazed how little the Democrats seemed to have studied the electoral strategies of Michael Foot. Did Barack even own a donkey jacket?

I was staying with a fellow writer in Los Angeles, as I had an exciting Hollywood commission; together, we would be co-writing the screenplay for *The Film That Won't Get Made*. This particular film project had defeated thousands of writers and producers down the years, but I felt pretty optimistic that we would definitely crack it and it would go straight into production. 'What are you going to wear to the premiere of *The Film That Won't Get Made?*' I asked my collaborator as we started work on our sure-fire Oscar winner. 'Not sure. I was just wondering who would be good to play the lead in *The Film That Won't Get Made.*'

My hosts, Karey and Nada, were both registered Democrats and, on the wall in his office, was a picture of Karey shaking hands with Barack Obama. 'Most expensive chicken dinner I ever had,' mused Karey, on the Hollywood fundraiser that probably earned more than Labour's annual income. They lived in one of the more prosperous areas of Los Angeles, and there were quite a few Republican signs stuck in the manicured lawns of their neighbourhood, in between the ones saying '24-hour Surveillance – Armed Response'. I think the general message was 'If you attempt to deliver a Democrat leaflet here, we will shoot you.'

The Republican candidate for President was John McCain, who had to endure suggestions that he was too old for the top job. So it was a bit weird that some of his supporters were so slow to take down their Halloween decorations. If you are going to put a John McCain placard on your front lawn, you might think twice about that cobweb-covered skeleton dangling right above his name.

Karey made some telephone enquiries on my behalf about where a volunteer from the British Labour Party might be of most use, and if any of the Democrat organizers immediately hung up he was kind enough not to tell me. Soon, I was being dropped off at a huge film studio which had been temporarily converted into a campaign headquarters and phone bank. I gulped and walked towards the door. Karey had given me an official Obama T-shirt, which I had put on, but at the last minute I buttoned my shirt to cover it up. I felt like an imposter, like I had no right to present myself as a bona fide Democratic activist.

But true to form, the Americans were welcoming and friendly. They seemed extra pleased that someone from England had turned up to help; the receptionist explained to her boss that I had done work for the British Labour Party, though I could tell she was leaving out the letter U when she said it.

I was put into a short training session on telephone canvassing, and it was explained that, because California was a 'slam dunk' for the Democrats, we would be calling swing states, where the election would be decided. Our group would be speaking to voters in Wisconsin. 'So no jokes about cheese,' she said, and everyone else laughed. I felt nervous calling a state when I didn't even know its comedy attributes. Finally, I was led to my table. There was a little plastic Stars and Stripes by every phone. In tiny writing on the handle it said 'Made in China'.

Most of my years contacting voters in Britain has been via the old-fashioned method of knocking on doors. You waste an hour discovering that thirty people are not home. Telephone canvassing is far more efficient; in the same time, you can find sixty people who don't answer.

The script was quite strict. At no point was I allowed to scream, 'What do you mean you are voting Republican!? Are you insane?' No, I had to read exactly what was printed on the sheet in front of me. 'Hello, THEIR NAME, this is YOUR NAME . . .' Oh no, let me try that again. If they were voting Democrat, I told them where their polling station was and reminded them that the election was tomorrow. Amazingly, one voter called by a man on my table had actually been unaware of this. Each party had spent about a billion dollars on this campaign and, still, one bloke in Minnesota thought the election was the following week. I had wondered if my British accent might not be well received, but not a single voter raised it. They probably thought the Democrats were subcontracting their canvassing to call centres in the Third World, from places like Bangalore and England.

There was a generously stocked food table, and I volunteered to run that for a couple of hours. It gave me a chance to chat to local activists and tut at the size of their portions. Other activists toured the tables with baskets of candy to help you put on weight and empathize with the voters of Middle America.

Although there was an infectious optimism in the air, all of them still shared the same worry that the opinion polls might be lying, that, when it came to it, millions of white Americans might not be able to bring themselves to vote for a black man. Was that why that iconic campaign poster showed him in blue and red? Barack hadn't made it easy for them; Clinton's middle name was Jefferson; Reagan's was Wilson – both American presidents. Barack Hussein Obama also shared his middle name with a president, except that his was the president of Iraq. Followed by a surname that sounded like 'Osama'.

There were probably a couple of hundred volunteers there, of all ages and ethnicities, unlike the elderly white demographic I'd seen manning the Republican stall at the farmers' market the day before. It was really encouraging to see just how many young people had turned up to be patronized by us telling them how encouraging it was to see so many young people. 'Fingers crossed for tomorrow,' I said, but that didn't really do it. Everyone there was aching for an Obama victory; this was more than just another battle between Republicans and Democrats, it was the old America versus the possibility of something new and tolerant and inclusive. 'Hope,' read the poster by the door. 'Change,' read the banner on the other side.

I woke early the next morning because there is something exciting about the day when the campaigning stops and a nation finally decides, and this election above all others might be a truly historic day in American history. Oh, and also because I was still jet-lagged and it felt like it was two o'clock in the afternoon. Because I am such a political anorak, I wanted to go with Karey when he voted. His local polling station opened at seven o'clock. We got there at five past and he said he'd never seen queues like this before. The lady behind us told us she was going to spend the rest of the day visiting other parts of Los Angeles, taking coffee and doughnuts to people who were having to queue for hours to cast their votes. 'My family are back in Mississippi,' she told us. 'I'm ringing Domino's later and sending pizzas to the queues at the local polling stations out there.'

I have never queued to vote in the UK, where we generally have a higher turnout. Queues at polling stations usually feature on the news as part of a positive story reporting voter enthusiasm, but I can't help feeling it just shows the local council being a bit rubbish. To be fair, this election was a little more complex than ours – there were votes to cast for the House of Representatives and for California's state assembly and the state senate, not to mention a dozen propositions on matters from housing for veterans to renewable energy. Karey explained how this generally worked. 'Everyone votes for more spending on everything, and then for lower taxes. That's why California is trillions of dollars in debt.'

'We don't really have referendums in the UK,' I said to Karey, perhaps emitting a little premature pride at the British way of doing things. 'We just elect our politicians and leave it to them to get on with putting us massively in debt.'

It seemed to me that, on both sides of the Atlantic, we were losing sight of the value of electing representatives to work full time on the business of government on our behalf. People are busy, they have work and kids, and it's okay to be more interested in your allotment than in international trade agreements – that's why we delegate and give our consent to elected representatives to govern on our behalf. The *parler* from which 'Parliament' comes is a really important part of it all; politicians spend time debating the options, listening to evidence and identifying priorities. You can't have everyone voting on every topic from their sofas, however democratic it might sound to have the great issues of state decided by popular vote on *Ant and Dec's Saturday-Night Foreign Policy*: 'So, should we nuke Iraq? Call the numbers on your screen now to decide whether Baghdad goes bang! Calls-will-be-charged-at-your-network-rate; viewers-in-Baghdad-may-still-be-charged-even-if-they-are-obliterated-in-a-nuclear-holocaust.'

While Karey went and voted, I got into a conversation with a woman who was there to lobby on one particular controversial ballot proposal. I'd never heard anything about it until then, although it would later become world famous. 'Prop 8' would eliminate the right of same-sex couples to marry. This was in a state that had already recognized gay marriage, so if this measure was passed, it would effectively unmarry California's gay couples. The campaigner said that traditional views about marriage were being pushed hard by the black churches in California. Obama had inspired black voters to come to the polls in greater numbers than ever before, but she worried that, while this represented a great leap forward on race, it looked set to help bring about a backward step in the politics of sexuality. I tied myself into linguistic knots trying to discuss this with the gay campaigner – she was forceful and certain about homophobia in the black community, while I winced to hear a white person generalizing about black people in this way. If you ever want to make a liberal's head explode, describe victims of prejudice displaying prejudice themselves. We're just not programmed to cope with it.

Proposition 8 was passed that day, but the campaign against it went all the way to the US Supreme Court and it was finally over-turned five years later. The politics of identity – of race, gender and sexuality – is one area where progressive campaigners have won significant victories over the past few decades. It is said that the left won on social freedom, while the right won on economic freedom. Except there is no 'economic freedom' if you've just had your trailer home repossessed and your family is dependent on food stamps.

Election Day has a different narrative in the United States than in the UK; it was still only mid-afternoon in California when actual results started to come through from the other side of the country. McCain won Kentucky, Obama won in Vermont. A few more 'fly-over' states declared and McCain took an early lead, but there were no upsets as yet. The map on the television had the good guys in blue and the baddies in red; I had to keep catching myself. American coverage is much more studio based and graphics led than Election Night in the UK. I missed the cutaways to the provincial leisure centres in the Midlands, the nervous council officer mispronouncing candidates' middle names and famous politicians having to share a platform beside a loony candidate with a bucket on his head.

Florida was declared too close to call and, for a nervous hour or so, it looked like we might be in for a repeat of the stalemate of 2000. 'Can't we just give Florida back to the Spanish?' suggested Karey. Nada had wiped down that surface in the kitchen a dozen times; she was too anxious to come in and just sit down and watch the TV.

At 8 p.m., we expected to hear them call California but, instead, from nowhere, the screen filled with a newsflash announcing that Barack Obama had been elected President! The whole West Coast had declared for the Democrats, and that was more than enough to put the first black man into the White House. The screen cut to huge crowds of Democratic activists cheering and hugging, and you could feel their joy and the relief. The cameraman picked out one black woman who had sunk to her knees and was sobbing, her head in her hands, and I could only imagine how overwhelmed she must be feeling right now, how huge this moment was in her life. Karey's HD telly was so big and loud I felt like I was right there with them in Times Square, or at Spelman College, Atlanta or in Grant Park, Chicago. The smiles were wider than anything I'd ever seen back in England, plus, they all had much better teeth.

Karey opened a bottle of vintage champagne which he had been saving for a special occasion and I suggested that this would be a good night to let his kids have their first-ever taste. One day, they would be able to tell their grandchildren, 'I first drank champagne on the night Obama was elected President!' Obviously, the kids recoiled in disgust at the taste, but the symbolism still stands.

Finally, in front of thousands of supporters, the President Elect walked out on stage with his beautiful family, Michelle, Sasha and Malia, but I said nothing to my hosts because I couldn't trust my voice not to crack. His first policy announcement was that he was going to get his kids a puppy. This was my kind of politician. I never did find out if the Republicans in Congress blocked that policy as well. Soon we got to see Obama the great orator. He told us about one particular voter down in Mississippi who had cast her vote that day – 106-year-old Ann Nixon Cooper. Born just one generation after slavery, as a young woman she was prohibited from voting on two counts, because she was black and because she was a woman. He spoke of all the great obstacles that had been overcome in this one voter's lifetime: winning women's suffrage, overcoming the Great Depression, fighting a war against tyranny, challenging racial discrimination. 'Yes we can!' he said at the end of each challenge. 'Yes we can!' shouted back the crowd.

Barack Obama being elected that night felt like a huge step forward for the whole world. Surely there could be no going back now. Surely progressive politics were on an unstoppable upward trajectory. Racism and misogyny would become things of the past, and the financial crash had shown that our fate could never again be left to the whims of the markets. Governments had to intervene, and we would elect principled, inspiring leaders like Barack Obama to make this happen. I was going to bring all this optimism back to England, and just hope I didn't have it confiscated at the airport.

The night after the election, I came out of a bar in a busy part of town, Americans were weaving their way home at the end of the second night of celebrations. But one elderly black man wasn't going anywhere, he was just standing in the middle of the square, shouting, 'President Obama! *PRESIDENT* Obama!' He clearly hadn't believed he would ever see it in his lifetime. He caught my eye and I heard myself say, 'Yes we can!'

'Yes, we did,' he said back, stopping me to shake my hand and look me right in the eye. 'Yes, we did!'

Say Your Prayers

European Parliament Election – 4 June 2009

'Are you a teacher, sir?'

'No way, man, he's the Governator!' explained her friend. 'He's Don John – he could, like, sack all the teachers!'

'Er, no, I could not just sack all the teachers,' I interjected.

'Aw, will you sack Miss Essaye, sir, please? Will you sack Mr Aylward?'

'You're on telly, aren't you, sir? Do you know Russell Brand, sir? Do you know La Toya Jackson?'

They were a bit disappointed that I didn't know Michael Jackson's sister from *Celebrity Big Brother*. I did know other, slightly less famous people, like Jenni Murray from Radio 4's *Woman's Hour*, but I worried they might not be as impressed with that.

Being around Lambeth Academy during the school day was the best part of being chair of governors. The students had got used to seeing me around and sensed that I had some sort of authority, though they weren't quite sure what it was. Many of them had seen me on *Grumpy Old Men*, and seemed to presume that this was somehow related to what I did there. As if every school had one: Chestnut Grove would have Arthur Smith and Dunraven Des Lynham, and governors' meetings consisted of us all sitting around going, 'And why do train buffets give you little sachets of bloody creamer that say, "Tastes just like fresh milk"? I'll tell you what else tastes just like fresh milk . . .'

Under the rigour and stability of our new regime, I had felt calm returning to the corridors. 'These children are begging for boundaries,' one of the teachers had said to me. It was so true; they just needed fair rules, consistently applied, and everyone would be much happier, especially them. When I walked my dog in the mornings, I used to see our students leisurely strolling across the common twenty minutes after they were supposed to be in school. Now if I saw someone late for school, they were running.

I loved seeing hundreds of students heading to Lambeth Academy. They trudged towards Elms Road, lugging oversize backpacks filled with books and PE kit. I worried that if one of them fell on their back they might never be able to get back up again. But then, walking across the common in the opposite direction were all the children with their mums heading to the private schools, dressed in bright green and red blazers with stripy caps and straw boaters, like they were in a BBC costume drama set in the 1920s. Perhaps the private schools had such colourful uniforms to make up for the lack of colour in their intake. We went past a local girls' private school once as the kids were coming out, and my twelve-year-old daughter said, 'God, I never knew there were so many blonde children in London!'

Every political person has one particular issue they cannot help getting way out of proportion. Jackie has an intense loathing of the Liberal Democrats, which I've always found bizarre and slightly endearing. The young Neil Kinnock used to get into a fury about South African oranges. My personal bugbear has always been private education. It's the arrogance of so many privately educated men that I find so maddening: the sense of entitlement; the presumption of superiority that sees them waltzing into so many of the top jobs or standing right in front of the screen, oblivious to the fact that everyone else in the pub is watching the football, too. 'No, you stay right there. I'd much rather stare at that Pringle sweater draped casually across your shoulders . . .'

Of course as a middle-class white man, I experience the opposite of discrimination on a daily basis, so perhaps posh boys patronizing me is the only chance this privileged lefty gets to feel a tiny bit oppressed. My kids were aware of my chippy attitude towards private schools and sometimes would call me out for being so intolerant. On one occasion, my family was at a Labour event attended by Andrew Adonis, and the man behind the academy programme turned to my son and said, 'How are you liking your school?' And, just to wind me up, my son said to him, 'I'd rather have gone private!' The little bastard. I struck him out of my will after that; his sister is getting everything.

As some sort of karmic punishment for my prejudice, the great gods of politics deemed that, if I was to get deeply involved with the front line of state education, I would have to do it working with a load of private-school providers. The sponsors of Lambeth Academy ran two dozen independent schools around the country, and believed it was their Christian duty to apply their experience and expertise to the problem of Britain's inner cities. They were completely sincere about this, and their spirit of philanthropy is to be applauded. It's just that, when I sat there in their board meetings and heard a comment comparing the results from our academy in Moss Side to those of their private girls' school in Surbiton, I wanted to smack my forehead against the large oak table in front of me.

The ULT held their board meetings at the Athenaeum, one of the most exclusive private clubs in London where the staff could probably make one of the Habsburgs feel socially inferior. There should have been a sign saying 'Please leave your smile at the door'. One of my first memories of infant school was of feeling embarrassed during prayers, of not closing my eyes and then worrying that the teacher might open her eyes, too, and see me. And here I was in my forties, feeling exactly the same way as the former Archbishop of Canterbury riffed an extended prayer at the beginning of our schools meeting. 'Amen!' chanted everyone else. I didn't want to appear too defiant or disrespectful, so I sort of mumbled, 'Mmnn,' which is liberal-atheist speak for 'I don't believe any of that stuff but I appreciate it means a lot to you guys, so let's just move on.' I think they regarded me as something of a novelty left-wing mascot. If there was a presumption about 'problems with the unions', I would cut in and suggest the problem might also be with the employers, and they were like, 'Oooh, yes, good point, John! He always brings a different perspective, doesn't he? Well done. Well said. Anyway, these problems with the unions . . .'

I did my best to get to grips with all the jargon, although sometimes I gave myself away if they said things like 'All students should have an ILP.'

'What, Independent Labour Party?'

'No, *individual learning plan* . . . But we mustn't lose sight of the CP issues . . .'

'What, the Communist Party?'

'No, *child protection* – oh, John, you do betray your heritage somewhat!'

The United Learning Trust was soon running more academies than any other sponsor in the country, and here I was, sitting on their board when I wasn't even convinced that we should be in charge rather than the local council. But if I was to make a difference, this was the place I had to be. I was the Minister for Lambeth Academy, and the ULT board was our regular Cabinet meeting.

Dame Angela Rumbold died the following year, and I went to the funeral of a former Conservative minister, bowed my head for the prayers and sang along with the hymns. Who would have predicted that when I was twenty-one, despising the Tories with every fibre of my body. But, decades on, we had worked together for something good, and I had come to like and respect her. An old friend said to me, 'I thought you hate the Tories?'

'Hated,' I corrected. 'Past tense. Now I just disagree with them very firmly, but very politely.' What use is hate in politics? No one ever built a new school with hate.

I had come to appreciate that, most of the time, politicians of all political hues were just trying to help people, solve problems or speak up for their constituencies. It's not surprising that none of this mundane stuff ever makes the evening news, but the general attitude of our national media was like that of a cynical sixth-former: 'Oh, they're all in it for themselves. Look how lazy and venal they all are, it's all a big stitch-up.' We woke up to John Humphries interrupting them and went to sleep to Jeremy Paxman sneering at them, and in between we protected ourselves from appearing naïve by displaying a world-weary cynicism about what they were obviously up to. And so, when a politician really did screw up, there was no reserve of goodwill left to make people think, *Okay, this doesn't look good. Let's try and understand how you got yourselves into this terrible mess.*

The 2009 expenses scandal was a perfect storm of greedy MPs, failed cover-ups and botched apologies, outrageous, petty and bizarre claims – high-profile resignations, ruined careers, jailed politicians, all spiced up with a daily window into the curious and embarrassing lifestyles of our elected politicians. There was a £380 claim for horse manure, an eighty-nine-pence claim for a bathplug from B&Q, and a £43.56 claim for *three* garlic crushers, because it's so annoying getting all the little bits out; you might as well just get yourself another free one. One Tory MP famously made a claim for the cleaning of his moat. I don't know about you, but I always clean my own moat, I've never expected anyone else to pay my moat bills. The biggest recurring scandal was around the 'flipping' of houses, a ruse whereby taxpayers paid the mortgages on homes in which MPs weren't really living. We were basically buying lots of them a whole house; you'd have thought they might have let us off the eighty-nine pence for the bathplug. The embarrassing claims ranged from new toilet seats and fancy-dress wigs to 'cutting the hedge around the helipad' and, most famously of all, a £1,645 claim for an ornamental duck house. We never established whether it was the ducks' main house; maybe the ducks flipped houses and claimed on the more expensive one?

When initial rumblings of the scandal were heard, my fool-hardy first instinct had been to attempt to defend the politicians. I felt that there was more than a little hypocrisy to the feigned outrage of journalists who lived by fiddling their expenses. Plus, I was one of those rare activists on the left who actually thought that Members of Parliament should be paid more. This opinion was even less fashionable than my zip-off hiking trousers, but I saw how much we were paying the headteachers to run our academies, and it didn't seem unreasonable to me that the people we were asking to run our country should be paid roughly the same. As the old saying goes, 'If you pay peanuts, you get Lembit Öpik.'

But, pretty quickly, this seemed like an untenable position. It turned out that the politicians had in fact been paid a lot more, but via a grubby, secretive system in which the most unscrupulous claimed the most, with nobody in the fees office ever stopping any of them to ask, 'Are you really sure that you want to put down your husband's porn film as a legitimate business expense?' I still wanted to believe that politics was a noble calling, but I felt like some pathetic establishment apologist as more and more evidence piled up against this naïve position. 'You know it's only a small minority who have made unreasonable claims? What? Oh, it's not a small minority, apparently, it's the majority. But then everyone puts down a few bits of extra stationery into their business expenses . . . What? They've claimed entire houses?'

The whole thing was a dog's breakfast – in fact, one of them claimed for that, too – and the crisis climaxed with the ousting of the humiliated Speaker of the House of Commons, for the first time since 1695. Trust in our politicians was massively damaged as a result of the expenses scandal, and I couldn't see how this could be put down as anything other than an utter disaster for all of us – unless you're someone who wants Westminster razed to the ground to see what happens when our liberal democracy is completely done away with.

There was a national test of the political climate in the weeks immediately after the scandal first broke. The Euro elections are never the surest test of the deep-seated political beliefs held most dear by the British electorate but, as this election approached, I feared that this might really be no more politics as usual.

The openly racist British National Party had been making

steady ground over the previous few years, gaining council seats and even getting a member elected to the London Assembly the year before. Now, the polls showed them likely to make a significant breakthrough in the European Parliament. The European Union was created out of the ashes of the Second World War, after Britain had sacrificed so much to defeat fascism, and now it looked set to have some British fascists sitting in its Parliament. At home, I railed against the apathy of the non-voters who could let this happen; my children learned whole new combinations of swearwords every time Nick Griffin appeared on television.

Then, a couple of days before the election, I came out of Clapham Common Tube station to see a home-made poster taped to a lamp-post. 'USE YOUR VOTE! STOP THE BNP!' read the big black letters smudged across the A4 sheet of paper. I felt cheered that somebody out there cared enough to put up their own poster in my corner of London. So what if it looked a bit amateur? And then I saw another one; 'STOP THE RACIST BNP! USE YOUR VOTE!' *Good for them!* I thought. *They've really gone for it. Oh, look, there's one Sellotaped to the window of that derelict shop, and there's another on the railings by the paddling pool.* There were home-made flyers everywhere. One person seemed to have gone completely overboard in telling my local community to exercise their democratic right and stop the neo-fascists spreading their hate and poison. On my road, an ordinary residential street, there were even more posters, if anything, and then I was nearly at my front gate and now on a lamp-post I spotted a little pink, heart-shaped Post-it note reading 'STOP THE BNP!' and I thought, *Oh my god, I recognize those!* My dear daughter sticks those pink Post-it notes on everything. I walked through my front door to see her standing over my noisy printer with two classmates as another batch of A4 flyers churned out of it, then the three of them headed out to plaster the streets of Clapham again with their pro-democracy message of hope and tolerance.

Just how proud is it possible for a father to be? Here was my thirteen-year-old girl with her friends from Lambeth Academy, black and white, all of them really offended by the idea of a racist political party making headway, so they had taken it upon themselves to take direct action to try to stop this happening. Without me ever really noticing, my daughter had become politicized. She had never seemed that interested before. I mean, she'd thought Mussolini was a type of pasta. But now she was really fired up and had found a way to express her point of view. I might tell her about writing to her MP or letters to the newspaper, but there was plenty of time for that later and, anyway, she'd used up all my bloody ink cartridges.

The results of the Euro elections were terrible. UKIP finished in second place, ahead of Labour, while the BNP won two seats which would earn Nick Griffin an appearance on *Question Time* later in the year. Labour was imploding, with a ministerial resignation as polls closed and talk of a coup to topple Gordon Brown. Our period in office was very clearly coming to an ugly, ignoble end.

But my kids and the loyal students of Lambeth Academy had given me a sense of optimism that defied the national mood, and that was the saving grace for me as British politics started to go badly wrong. Because somebody very wise once said that children are the future. *God, that's so true, children, they're like, the future* . . . I thought as I purchased more ink cartridges and dreamed of a more tolerant politics based on hope, honesty and trust.

Ink cartridges, I said to myself. *Well, that's a business expense. I must keep the receipt and claim that back.*

'I Agree With Nick'

General Election – 6 May 2010

Britain's new Prime Minister, David Cameron, was standing on the steps of 10 Downing Street side by side with his Deputy, Nick Clegg. After waving to the cameras, the two of them turned to walk through the famous front door. Cameron placed his hand on the small of Clegg's back but Clegg countered by putting his hand on Cameron's back. So Cameron's hand did an extra little pat that said, 'No, this is me asserting my domain. *I'm* doing the patronizing back-patting, not *you*,' but Clegg's hand was having none of it and did an extra assertive little pat of its own. Once the door closed, they were probably wrestling, grappling and rolling around on the floor, trying to have the very last back-pat that said, 'I'm your boss' or, 'No, I am your equal.'

But the big black door had closed, and Labour was most definitely on the outside. The Labour Party had lost power after thirteen years; it was all over. We had known this day was approaching for years now; the timing may have been uncertain but the upshot had been pretty clear. It was like the Grim Reaper getting out his diary and saying, 'So, when's good for you?'

Just a few months earlier, I had been invited to a function at 10 Downing Street and, as I left, I had passed my phone to a friend and asked him to take my picture on the steps outside. *This will probably be the last time I come here for a long time,* I was thinking. *Maybe I'll never see our lot in Downing Street again.* Maybe that was it: 1997 to 2010, the only time in my adult life when my party would be in power.

It had been painful to watch the last months of the government, the savagery of the chasing press pack, the desperation of this limping wildebeest of a government that was clearly never going to get away. In one particularly low blow, the *Sun* savaged Gordon Brown for the manner in which he wrote personal notes to bereaved families of British soldiers. This was the level of political debate in his final months in office: 'Brown shows contempt for war dead with messy handwriting'; 'Brown fails to dip head sufficiently at Cenotaph'; and, probably, 'Brown personally to blame for unpronounceable Icelandic volcano causing giant ash cloud'.

But Labour was always going to be vulnerable without that holy trinity of key election-winning factors: unity, competence and good leadership. Lacking one of them makes winning almost impossible; without all three, we were heading for a total wipe-out. Labour MPs had been faced with a harsh choice of going for a change at the top or resolving to unite behind the leader they had. Instead, they reached a compromise: 'I know! Let's stick with the leader we've got, while making it crystal clear we'd much rather have someone else!' No wonder Gordon Brown's smile looked so awkward.

The Tories actually used a big photo of Gordon Brown smiling all over their election posters, which is never a good sign. Beside it were captions such as 'I doubled the national debt, let me do it again.' Other posters featured an air-brushed photo of a baby-faced David Cameron with the slogan 'We can't go on like this.' One wag sprayed on an Elvis quiff and added, 'with suspicious minds'. The Tories had twice as much money to spend as Labour, just to add to the imbalance of having all the newspapers against Labour. Even the *Guardian* urged people to vote Liberal Democrat, which wasn't at all embarrassing when Clegg went and propped up the Tories.

Despite all this, the polls narrowed a little in the last few months and it seemed that David Cameron might fail to win an outright majority, which, given everything that had gone before, would be an abject failure on his part. The Liberals were polling quite well off the back of their policy of not being Gordon Brown or David Cameron. All three political parties had acquired new leaders since the General Election, most recently the Liberal Democrats, who had elected Nick Clegg by the tiniest of margins over Chris Huhne, a former Labour student activist. In fact, more party members voted for Huhne, but 1,500 ballots were held up in the Christmas post and missed the deadline, so it was only by accident that the Liberals got a leader more sympathetic to the Conservatives.

In the run-up to the campaign, there were lots of articles declaring that this would be the first social-media election, the first campaign that would be decided on the internet. In fact, the transformative medium in 2010 was television. With little to lose by remaining aloof, Gordon Brown agreed to hold televised debates with the other leaders in the hope that David Cameron might make some disastrous gaffe, like punching one of the Dimblebys or turning up in the buff.

I went to watch this little bit of history in a local bar that was screening the debate. A Lambeth councillor had hired the place out for all us Labour activists as a sort of mid-campaign party, an extra precaution in case we didn't have reason to have a big victory party after polling day. *This is great*, I thought. *The room is packed out, but only with people who agree with me. I wonder if we might develop a way of replicating this on social media?*

I was aching for Gordon Brown to do well. Everyone in that room was aching for Gordon Brown to do well. By the end of the debate, we all agreed he had done really well. I got home and my son told me, 'Everyone's saying Nick Clegg did really well.' Well that's ridiculous – they obviously weren't watching it in that bar with me and my Labour Party friends. Brown had tried to look non-tribal and reasonable by saying, 'I agree with Nick,' several times. After the recording, he asked his aides how that went down.

'They responded well to that, Gordon, they definitely listened to you when you said, "I agree with Nick."'

'So they all agree with me now?'

'No, they all agree with Nick.'

The last joke I ever wrote for Gordon Brown was for Britain's first televised leaders' debate. I say, 'joke'; it was more of a line really, and, frankly, it lacked the wit and satirical edge to bring waves of laughter from the studio audience, then cheers, then a standing ovation and finally a stage invasion by the crowd to lift Gordon up on to their shoulders and carry him all the way to Downing Street. Maybe he didn't deliver it right. He sent me a short handwritten note to thank me for all the stuff I'd written for him over the campaign. *Blimey*, I thought. *His handwriting really is terrible.*

But for all the preparation, and planning and posters and photo opportunities, you can never know exactly what will be the defining moment of an election. In this campaign, it came from an elderly lady in Rochdale who was placed in front of the Prime Minister in order for him to demonstrate his powers of diplomacy. Brown then got back in his car and described her as 'a sort of bigoted woman'. What he did not realize was that he was still wearing a live microphone that had been fitted by Sky TV. 'All these Eastern Europeans, where are they flocking from?' she had asked him. One explanation was that Gordon Brown thought she'd said, 'Where are they fucking from?' which might have explained his slight over-reaction. Jeremy Vine played the recording back for the Prime Minister, while he covered his eyes with his hand. 'Yes, that camera is live as well, Gordon! Like that microphone you'd been wearing – this stuff was all on day one at Politicians' School!'

Election Day started early in our household. With our home serving as the Labour Party committee rooms, the first volunteer arrived straight from the 6 a.m. leaflet drop. I hadn't actually been able to do any of the dawn delivering on the local estates, because my diary had revealed an unfortunate clash in which I was forced to be tucked up in bed, snoring.

Throughout the day, volunteers came to my front door and were quickly given a bundle of leaflets and a map. I was slightly worried that one of them only came to read the electricity meter. Many were strangers from outside the constituency, so I just had to take their word for it that they were Labour volunteers as they marched through the door. Basically if you fancy burgling my house at the next election, just put a Labour sticker on your jumper, and I'll let you in, no questions asked.

Throughout the day, they returned from knocking on doors to report that most voters had not actually taken the day off work so they could wait in to be reminded that it was Election Day. But gradually the tempo of urgency increased as afternoon turned

into evening. Messengers ran back and forth from the polling station with lists of those who had voted, and these polling numbers
were crossed off our records. I waited all day to vote, thinking
my fourteen-year-old daughter might want to come with me and
watch me do it. When she got home from school, her reaction
was 'Yeah, yeah, you've showed us how to vote in, like, every
single election since we were born. We get it! You put a cross on
a piece of paper!' I wondered if Emily Pankhurst had had teenage kids. To be fair to my kids, they had both been enthused by
this election, doing far more delivering than myself; my daughter
even did a week's volunteering in the offices of Martin Linton,
soon to be the ex-MP for Battersea. I had started my own political
career losing Battersea to the Tories, so if it was good enough for
me . . .

My son was doing A-level politics, and he and his friends
had become exasperated with the barrage of clichés saying that
young people were just not interested. At one point, we had four
of them helping in the committee rooms and, in the bellwether
marginal of Lambeth Academy, the school's mock-election produced a landslide for Labour, with 70 per cent of the vote and the
Tories limping in fourth.

As 10 p.m. approached, the rush to get out those last few
votes had volunteers coming in panting and exhausted, and
eagerly accepting a glass of beer as Big Ben finally called time.
Packed into our front room were about twenty eager viewers:
family, volunteers and councillors, plus a sprinkling of non-party
members who nevertheless had to pass the test of 'Tribal Labour
Supporters Only'. If Labour lost Jarrow, you wouldn't appreciate
some half-interested neutral cheerily saying, 'Oh, well, it's probably good to let the other lot have a go.'

This time round, there was genuine competition over which

TV channel to watch. We've always voted BBC, but a late surge for David Mitchell and Channel 4 threatened to split the anti-ITV vote. How could this be settled? By a first-past-the-post vote of viewers present? Should the under-eighteens have a vote? Should we opt for the Alternative TV system, switching between channels, depending on the proportion of votes cast? I've always been for democracy and all that but, on the other hand, I had hold of the remote control. In any case, what Channel 4 had failed to realize with its alternative line-up is that the BBC's coverage is already a self-parody. Jeremy Vine leaping about the election battle-ground as 3-D ministers explode and computer-generated MPs sprint over finishing lines – it's already a comedy show.

The BBC election studio looked like it cost more than the national deficit, but no swingometer has yet been designed to cope with voters making different decisions in every single constituency. This time, the graphics had Jeremy Vine striding through the gates of Downing Street towards the door of Number Ten – although they skipped that ten minutes it takes to get through the police security cabin. The first result was expected to come in from Sunderland South, and we cut to the council workers up there racing into the leisure centre with their big boxes of votes. It's a whole recognized sport up there. If you see joggers on Wearside, they're always carrying a huge ballot box; and on the athletics track you can watch relay teams practise passing a ballot box on to the next runner.

The exit poll had predicted a hung Parliament, with the Conservatives as the largest party; it turned out to be very accurate in terms of the seats won. As the night wore on, gloom descended over my front room as huge Tory swings seemed to suggest Cameron might win outright. But then a huge cheer went up for a local result as Sadiq Khan held on in Tooting. The only pattern was that there was no pattern. Watching the results with friends and activists somehow always throws up the same cast of Election Night stereotypes. There is the unrelenting pessimist: 'Look, the Tories have just won Surrey South-west – oh no, there'll never be a Labour government again.' And there is the ludicrous optimist: 'But on this result Brown could form an anti-Tory coalition with Sinn Fein, the Greens, and Esther Rantzen, if she wins in Luton.' Then there is the psephological bore (this part is usually played by myself): 'No, it may look like a big swing, but that's based on the 2007 by-election result, and the seat's had minor boundary changes, though it did go Labour in 1929.' And, most maddening of all, is the person who seems to have no understanding of what is happening whatsoever. Imagine Phoebe from *Friends*, only with less grasp of current affairs.

'Has that man won or lost?'

'No, that's Nick Robinson . . .'

'Is he a Tory?'

'No, he's the BBC's political . . . well, actually, yes he is . . .'

Eventually, it became clear that this drama would not be resolved by daybreak, and our guests staggered off to sleep in their beds or our front garden. There was some relief that Labour had not come third, and a little satisfaction that 'Cleggmania' had been exposed as just media hot air, with the Liberals actually losing seats. The Greens gained their first parliamentary seat, and I added Caroline Lucas to the 'J. K. Rowling List' of interesting people I was at Exeter University with but never managed to meet. And there was also a certain amount of relief that the feared BNP breakout had failed to materialize. Despite the levels of public disgust with the main political parties, despite the political class being perceived as self-serving and corrupt, the British people had still held back from switching to the extremists.

Hundreds of BNP deposits were lost, as the electorate turned away from the ugly face of politics (owner: Mr N. Griffin). The BNP had peaked as a political force; their overt hatred seemed to be a step too far for the British people. Racism would have to be stealthier; the phial of poison was passed unnoticed from the repellent thugs looking for a fight in the pub car park to the well-spoken chaps in the saloon bar, still as yet limited to moaning in code about the euro and the accents of mini-cab drivers.

Nigel Farage was lucky to be alive that day. He had spent Election Day riding around in a light aircraft towing an annoying UKIP banner around his constituency. As an unsubtle metaphor for what his party would do for the United Kingdom, his plane plummeted out of the air and crashed into a field. A stunned Farage was pulled from the tangled wreckage, and led towards the ambulance, his head bleeding and his clothes ripped. It would have been in very poor taste for some creative computer whizz to paste the image of the staggering, blood-soaked figure of the UKIP leader into some horror-movie shot of the zombie apocalypse. I mean, even to think of such a thing on seeing that image of a stunned and ragged Nigel Farage, his mouth hanging open, blood on his face, his arms groping forwards, even to associate that with a zombie horror flick, there's no point in googling it for a cheap laugh at what was in fact a very serious accident, because I'm sure no one on the internet would ever be so insensitive.

A far more mundane thought went through my head when I heard about that plane crash. Even though Farage was the enemy, the election organizer in me couldn't help thinking, *What the hell was the candidate doing riding around in a plane on Election Day? He should have been down in the high street, talking to voters, knocking on doors, getting out last-minute waverers, not skiving off by cadging a free ride in a plane so he can enjoy the pretty view and literally look down on everybody.*

Farage later said that, as the aircraft was about to crash, he felt sure he was about to die. It's strange, the element of chance in politics. Had Farage been killed that day, perhaps the Euro referendum would never have happened, perhaps Jo Cox would not have been murdered, perhaps British history might have gone in a different direction six years later.

Five days after the election, David Cameron became Prime Minister, with Nick Clegg as his deputy. A fair share-out of government responsibilities had been agreed between Cameron and Clegg.

'We Conservatives will do all the bastard things we wanted to do all along, but you Liberals can have the bit about getting all the blame for everything.'

'Mmm, that sounds fair!' said Nick Clegg. 'Also, don't give me a government department with any actual power, like the Treasury or the Home Office. I'll just have a general role of walking around and checking everyone's got enough paper clips.'

The days in between had passed in a weird political limbo, it was as if our divorced parents were settling the custody arrangements while we waited outside the solicitors' office with no say in whether we would live with Mum or Dad. The electoral arithmetic had always made it unlikely that Labour could stitch together a coalition, and the Liberals were not prepared to do any deal that involved Gordon Brown staying on as Prime Minister. More to the point, Labour's share of the vote had been so low we would have lacked any moral authority to govern. We had won a smaller share than the Conservatives in 1997, and lost more seats than in any election in our history.

On the Monday evening, Gordon Brown resigned the leadership

of the Labour Party, which briefly made us hope that some sort of alternative deal might be in the offing, but as a constructive gesture it had come too late in the day, and Dave and Nicky were already picking out their wedding rings. On the Tuesday, Gordon Brown quit Downing Street with a strong and humble speech at that lonely lectern in the middle of the road. Then, with Sarah and their two little boys, he walked away from Downing Street.

I watched this with my family, all of us feeling the sadness of the personal moment mixed up with the bitterness of political defeat. It was sort of weird that I knew Gordon Brown quite well, but I didn't really know him at all. It was two decades since I'd first sat down with him on the terrace of the House of Commons, and yet I don't think I'd ever seen him really relaxed, off duty, not being a politician. You got the sense that he was probably thinking about politics twenty-four hours a day. And now he was walking off with his wife and children to begin a whole new life away from it all.

Gordon Brown gave everything to his decade in 11 Downing Street, and then there was nothing to give when he moved next door. But the country still owed him an enormous amount, and the world's economy perhaps even more. But, disloyal though it now feels to someone I used to know and like, I can't pretend that Gordon Brown ultimately possessed the qualities necessary to go down as a great leader of the Labour Party. The tragedy was that his shortcomings for the very top job allowed in a very different sort of prime minister, who understood little about the plight of the poor and seemed to care even less, just at a time when they desperately needed someone on their side. The following month, the new Conservative Chancellor announced a rise in VAT to 20 per cent and a 25 per cent cut in public spending, before cutting the top rate of tax for the rich. 'We're all in this together,' he said.

Yeah, right. The transition from Blair and Brown to Cameron and Osborne was the starkest demonstration in my lifetime of the central philosophical difference between us and them. Left-wing politicians try to make the world a better place; right-wing politicians try to make *their* world a better place.

The Brothers

Labour Leadership Election – 24 September 2010

I was in a huge, packed-out hall in Canary Wharf listening to David Miliband outline his vision of what Labour needed to do next in order to re-engage with voters and I found myself unfolding my arms and thinking, *Yes, that's a good point, I agree with that, but then I agreed with what Andy Burnham just said as well. I agree with all of them. This really is a very interesting discussion, I'm so glad I came.*

And then a voice came in my earpiece: 'That's it, John! Time up!' and I was jolted back to the fact that I was on stage and supposed to be moderating this debate; I had to stop being so interested and start focussing on keeping the candidates to their allotted times and making sure they answered the questions. But then after I had told Ed Miliband he had two minutes for his statement, I would become so focussed on his argument I would zone out again, and forget that it really doesn't do for the Chair to keep nodding emphatically at what one of the panellists is saying, looking around, as if to say to the others, *He is good, isn't he?*

The Labour movement was founded on the idea that brothers

should stand together. And so, in the 2010 leadership election, the Miliband brothers did stand together. The campaign had begun almost immediately after Brown's resignation, with David Miliband the first to declare himself a candidate and looking like the most likely person to win. David was clearly very smart and articulate and he seemed like the logical next leader. But two days after David entered the race, his brother Ed announced his candidacy as well, and suddenly I felt really conflicted.

One day, there will probably be a worthy historical film about this tragic tale of brotherly love and rivalry at the top of British politics called *Miliband versus Miliband*, and Michael Sheen will play both parts. Opening in the mid-1970s in the north London home of Ralph and Marion Miliband, the transistor radio will be playing 'This Town Ain't Big Enough For The Both Of Us' as little David and Ed sit on the floor with their maps of South Vietnam, crossing out 'Saigon' and writing in 'Ho Chi Min City'.

'Dad! Ed's taken my red crayon! And I need it to colour in the Mekong Delta!'

'Will you boys ever stop taking each other's things! Remember what Marx says about the value-relation of products of labour and the fetishization of commodities? Now, run along and have your tea.'

The Miliband brothers had followed similar paths into politics, both studying PPE at Oxford, both becoming special advisers and eventually MPs and ministers; the first siblings to sit together in Cabinet since the historical period known as 'The Olden Days'. But while David had previously worked for Tony Blair, Ed had been next door working for Gordon Brown; it was as if the poisonous rivalry between the two founders of New Labour was so toxic it had infected the next generation to turn brother against brother. David became perceived as the heir of Blair, whereas Ed was seen as to the left of his brother and, perhaps crucially, he had not voted for the Iraq War (since he'd not become an MP until 2005). I had known both the brothers since they worked in Downing Street, and I felt a little embarrassed to have to choose between them.

There had been a moment a few years earlier when I first realized that Ed was ambitious. I was speaking at a Labour gala dinner and I ran a half-joke past him that I was planning to do from the stage. He didn't mind having the mickey taken out of him, it was just that the wording of my joke placed him in some crappy make of car and he wanted me to know that he actually drove a Prius. *Oh, okay*, I remember thinking. *Of course, Ed the Environment Minister is a different person to the back-room policy wonk I used to know. I should have realized he might care what people think.*

I think, even then, he was probably harbouring private ambitions for the very top job, though he must have grappled with the possibility of an enormous family rift. Apparently, David was incandescent on 14 May 2010 when his little brother stood against him and risked blocking his expected succession. But my feeling at the time was that neither of them had a God-given right to inherit the leadership, so surely the younger brother was perfectly entitled to stand. Except the other thought that came into my head as I heard the news was a worry that Ed might not be as appealing to the electorate as his older brother.

There is a subconscious test that the British public do with their leading politicians – let's call it the 'Number Ten Wave Test' – in which voters make a very rapid and brutal assessment of whether or not they could picture a party leader waving on the steps of Downing Street as their new Prime Minister. Thatcher had passed that test, except that, rather than a wave, we pictured her flicking us all a V-sign. Tony Blair had passed it; David

Cameron had instantly passed it, dammit. It's hard to pin down exactly what constitutes prime ministerial material: a sense of natural authority, of being comfortable in your own skin, someone who exudes a sense of gravitas and direction. It was the same with the leaders at Lambeth Academy. You have to remain dignified and unruffled, however appalling the behaviour of the Year 7s or the British tabloids.

So it should be plastered in giant letters across every party office that *Thou Must Never Pick a Leader Who Fails the Number Ten Wave Test*. When the Tories chose Iain Duncan Smith, it was obvious to the rest of us that this was an act of certain electoral suicide. But, down the decades, I worried that it was more often Labour who made this self-indulgent mistake, choosing leaders who appealed to ourselves, rather than the people who didn't come to our meetings.

By my own strict criterion, David should be the one who got my vote.

I had a vague plan to go along to one of the hustings and hear the candidates speak, which was firmed up when the Labour Party rang me up and asked me to chair one of them. What better way of picking the next leader of the Labour Party than watching the back of their heads as they spoke? The event was to be held in the ultra-modern setting of Canary Wharf – once a hotbed of socialist dockers' unions and working-class terraced housing, now all international high finance and expensive wine bars. It felt like somebody was trying to make a point.

The hall was huge and was full to capacity. Jackie and our teenage kids were in the audience, my son had joined the Labour Party that very week and had brought a friend from school. The prospect of cocking this job up in front of my children was the thing that made me most nervous.

Three other candidates had managed to get enough nominations for the leadership: Ed Balls, Andy Burnham and, at the last
minute, Diane Abbott. Having just four white men lined up for
the Labour leadership hustings had not been a good look for the
party of equality, so Diane Abbott was nominated by a number
of people who had no intention of ever voting for her, including
the favourite to win. Thus the precedent was set for nominating a candidate you were completely opposed to, as it made you
look politically generous and advanced the seemingly harmless
notion of 'widening the debate'. You patted one of the far-left
candidates on the head and told them, 'Of course you come and
have a go, nobody will vote for you, but good for you, dear, for
giving it a go!' Jeremy Corbyn was one of the few who nominated
Diane Abbott sincerely, knowing that this would never be anything more than a symbolic gesture.

One of the questions I'd selected from those handed in by the
audience was one about who the candidates would vote for if
they were not standing themselves. I put this question to David
Miliband, who without hesitation said he would vote for his
brother Ed.

'But you were one of the people who nominated Diane Abbott!'
I reminded him. 'Are you not duty-bound to vote for her?'

There was a glint in his eye as he looked back at me. It said,
'Er, I don't think so, John!' 'No, blood is thicker than water,' he
insisted, and Ed gave the same fraternal answer back.

I invited the candidates to step up to the microphone to do their
final summing-up, since the rules prevented me from settling the
whole thing there and then by inviting Ed Balls to lead a *Strictly-*
style dance-off. I was still privately unsure who I'd be voting for
myself but, although I was seated behind them, I had the best
possible view of the effect the candidates were having on this

huge audience. David was very good, but perhaps a little sensible and perfunctory. And then Ed spoke, and he was all about progressive optimism and the potential of politics to do great things, and I felt inspired and excited by what he said. And afterwards, I spoke with my family, and they had felt the same hope-filled exhilaration, and we agreed that Ed had succeeded in winning us over, and so I ended up voting for the poetry, not the prose.

There would be many other hustings after this one, including four televised debates, and the final announcement was not to be until Labour's conference in late September. The older brother had been ahead at each stage of the votes, but it all came down to the final tally of second preferences and the complex arithmetic of the three electorates who each constituted one third of the total: Labour MPs and MEPs, ordinary party members, and members of affiliated organizations such as trade unions and socialist societies. The atmosphere in the hall was split between tension over the result and exasperation at having to explain the voting system yet again.

The five candidates were seated in the front row of the conference hall as the results were announced. I struggled to decipher the figures being read out; I only knew who'd won from the way the others suddenly turned and applauded Ed Miliband. I was surprised, pleased and disappointed for David all at the same time. David was first to his feet, applauding his brother and then embracing him – there was no visible sign of bitterness or anger; it seemed like a genuinely emotional gesture.

Given the choice between hard news and character drama, the news organizations will always feed our appetite for the latter, and so the story was immediately presented to us as some sort of Shakespearean family tragedy – a story of betrayal, ambition and self-destruction. For Labour's fresh start, it was not a particularly satisfactory way for Ed to launch his leadership. He had come second with ordinary party members and second with Labour MPs; it was only with the support of union affiliates that Ed had just squeaked it. It meant putting up with some very bad cartoons in the Tory papers of 'union dinosaurs' coming back to life. 'Hmmm . . . better write "union dinosaur" on the side of that dinosaur to make it absolutely clear.'

In 2010, I felt that Ed Miliband had demonstrated that he'd been justified in challenging for the leadership, because he had won the contest. But then maybe he was wrong to challenge for the leadership, because he ended up losing the election that really mattered five years later? Would David have fared any better in 2015? I was suspicious of the certainty of those who swore he would. Whenever we construct an alternative version of history, we never include all the other crappy little things that might have gone wrong. But there are plenty of people I respect who are convinced that the younger brother should have recognized which of them had the wider appeal. It is one of the eternal dilemmas of politics: how do you separate your ambitions for your party from your personal ambitions within it? You need a healthy ego to be a politician, but at some point you also need the self-awareness to know where your hopes of advancing your values and your hopes of advancing yourself have met a fork in the road.

I voted for Ed Miliband and then wondered why I felt nervous that he'd won. And then a Labour councillor friend of mine berated me, as if I must have some sort of political deathwish, while on Facebook another friend was screaming, 'What have we done! We've just lost the next election!' and on the radio, a satire show was getting big laughs from mocking the choice Labour had just made and I was left standing there uncertainly, like the man who cast Mickey Rooney as the comic Asian neighbour in

Breakfast at Tiffany's. Everyone was shouting, 'Who chose that guy?! He just ruined the entire movie!' and I was looking around self-consciously, saying, 'It's not *that* bad, is it? I mean, I think he's making some interesting choices.'

Later that autumn, a memorial service was held for Michael Foot, who had died that year. A great political mind, a wonderful man, but the leader who'd seen Labour suffer its worst-ever defeat. Back in 1983, I'd learned the hard way that the politicians I liked were not the same ones that appealed to the great British public. Or I thought I'd learned it; some lessons, you just keep learning over and over again . . .

Up the Junction

Alternative Vote Referendum – 5 May 2011

Of all the reasons for the way politics started to go badly wrong in the second decade of the new century, I think perhaps the most overlooked is pure and simple poverty. Not just the poverty of the voiceless underclass and the unemployed which Thatcher had presided over, but now the poverty of people in work, sometimes holding down more than one job, working longer days than their parents had done, both husband and wife working all the hours they could get – and still finding themselves reduced to going to the food bank to feed their kids. Not because of any economic downturn but because the right had broken union power and continued to remove employees' rights so employers and shareholders could make greater and greater profits at the majority's expense.

Somewhere along the line, a contract was broken between the government and the people. The unspoken understanding had been that, if you worked hard and obeyed the law, then things would work out okay: you'd have enough money to live on, and you could clothe and feed your children and still have enough at the end of the week to buy a lottery ticket in the hope you might just become a multimillionaire, lose all your friends and split up the family.

But when this contract was broken, people, understandably, became angry. Angry at MPs on the make, angry at politicians who said one thing and did another, angry at bankers who still got massive bonuses while we paid for their mistakes, angry perhaps at the foreigners who their newspapers told them were the cause of all their problems, angry at anyone in perceived authority or privilege who had no idea what they were going through.

In the middle of all this came a chance for people to express themselves. A national vote on adopting a complex and not very satisfactory reform of the voting system, as demanded by the now deeply unpopular Deputy Prime Minister, best known for solemnly pledging one thing and then voting for the opposite. And so this is how the 2011 AV referendum was perceived by millions of voters:

☐   *Nick Clegg can fuck off*
☐   *Nick Clegg does not need to fuck off*

No wonder the result was so decisive.

2011 was the year when the Tory led-coalition started to implement its brutal austerity programme; it was the year of riots across England and the tabloid phone-hacking scandal and the Occupy movement and the Arab Spring. And in these tumultuous times, I was right there in the middle of it all, campaigning in favour of a Yes vote in the AV referendum. Bliss was it in that dawn to be alive. No wonder buildings were burning in cities right across the country, as masked youths smashed windows and looted shops.

'We're angry because the Alternative Vote system was not even the best PR option on which to be balloted!' screamed one youth, over the cacophony of sirens and alarms.

'Yeah!' shouted another masked rioter through the smoke. 'Why weren't AV Plus or STV also offered as more genuinely proportional options?'

The AV referendum is another one of those pivotal historical moments that gave us a chance to change direction before it was too late. A fairer voting system would have prevented David Cameron winning an outright majority in 2015 on less than 37 per cent of the vote; there would have been no EU referendum, no Brexit and no lifting of the rocks to release the dark insect life that was always lurking underneath.

And yet I look at who else was in favour of this modest proposition and I see what a tiny minority bubble I inhabit. Pretty well every borough in the country voted against electoral reform: working-class Labour areas, prosperous Conservative areas, rural constituencies, market towns and suburbs. The tiny handful of boroughs that did vote in favour of AV were places where there is an extremely high concentration of educated liberals: Oxford and Cambridge, Islington and Camden, Ivory Tower North, Dinner-party Central. That doesn't make it wrong; it just means that we were wasting our time. It is the perennial lesson of liberal left politics that we keep having to relearn; make our causes chime with working-class voters or watch the other side win.

I had been a bit ambivalent about the whole thing to start with. I said to my son, 'This isn't even the electoral reform we wanted.' And he replied, 'No, but this is what's on offer, and if it is rejected, electoral reform will be off the agenda for a generation, so we have to get behind it.'

Oh, okay! I thought. *This is a new thing. Having my political opinions shaped by one of my children.* He had just turned eight-een. Today, when he and his friends recall the first election in which they voted, his always gets the biggest laugh.

But he was right, and so when someone I knew rang me up and asked if I would get more involved I was a firm 'Yes', with a single transferable 'Maybe' listed under the second preference system. I spoke at the campaign launch alongside some proper famous people. I gave a quote for a leaflet. I put my name to one of those round-robin letters to the *Guardian* which are signed by lots of people who all then worry that they might not be famous enough to make the print edition. Every time you see a list of celebrities who have signed a letter about some outrage, pity the D-listers at their breakfast tables as they desperately seek their own name until they reach those chilling words at the end: 'Full list of signatories available online.'

My abiding memory of that campaign is being in the Green Room at the launch with a lot of very interesting and creative people and then Paddy Ashdown coming in and shouting, 'With the talent in this room, I could govern the country!!' and all of us looking around slightly irritated and then just continuing with our conversations. *Oh gawd,* I thought. *If AV means Paddy Ashdown governing the country, is it too late to join the other side?*

But even though a Yes vote had started out ahead in the polls, the referendum was lost because the No side were much more aggressive and ruthless in their tactics and the Yes campaign were all well-meaning and wishy-washy and just much too polite. I wish politics were not such a dirty business, I really do. But if the other side are coming at you with an agricultural muck-spreader, it's no good saying, 'I'm not going to play dirty' – you're already covered head to toe in shit. I knew we were sunk when I saw a big poster of a newborn baby in an intensive care unit with the caption 'She needs a new cardiac facility, not an alternative voting system.' Fancy a referendum campaign using the NHS as an emotive decoy to the real issue!

If ever you are running a political campaign against the right, take a moment to try to imagine the biggest lie, the most outrageous distortion, the nastiest slur they could possible throw at you. Because it will be coming your way on day one.

It's hard to think of two extremes of protest further apart than a group of media luvvies seeking a refinement of the voting system and the horrendous riots which gripped London that summer. I'm not claiming for one second that setting fire to Debenhams or looting Curry's is a legitimate form of political protest but, clearly, the origins of all riots are political; they say something about our society. The spark for the 2011 riots was the police killing of a twenty-nine-year-old man in Tottenham. But it's never about what it's about. The specific anger in that part of north London mutated into random violence across the capital and beyond, including down the road in Clapham Junction, which saw some of the worst looting and arson in the country. 'How could someone set fire to the Party Shop?' said my dismayed sixteen-year-old daughter, looking at the burnt-out remains of her favourite store, where we'd hired fancy-dress costumes and bought so many silly novelty presents down the years. 'What harm did they ever do anyone?'

She was trying to impose logic on to collective madness. I don't think the rioters who trashed our local shopping centre were expressing anger about the murder of Michael Duggan. I think that, for the only time in their lives, they were gripped by some euphoric sense of raw power and invulnerability; from years of powerlessness at the bottom of the pile to just one thrilling night when they felt like they ruled. In a speech in his Witney constituency, David Cameron attributed the riots to many factors: 'Irresponsibility. Selfishness. Children without fathers. Schools without discipline. Reward without effort. Crime without punishment. Rights without responsibilities. Communities without control.' It was worse than we thought – they'd nicked all the fucking verbs as well.

It would need a whole book to get inside the psychology of riots and their socioeconomic context, but there is one simple historical fact that rings louder than the burglar alarm at JD Sports. The countries with the narrowest gaps between rich and poor are the least likely to have riots. Greater inequality is worse for everyone; more equal societies almost always do much better. If you can't grasp that, David Cameron, then you're no smarter than those rioters taking pictures of themselves holding up what they just looted to post on social media. Actually, no, everybody is smarter than that, you have to worry about our education system when the police were able to make hundreds of arrests simply by scrolling through all the selfies on Twitter.

Being the chair of governors of one of the local secondary schools meant that another frightening thought went through my head as the broken glass was still being swept away.

'We didn't have any of our kids down at Clapham Junction, did we?' I asked Stephen Potter.

'Did you not see the photos?' he said, and my heart sank. *Oh no*, I thought, *this could be a disaster; they'll throw the book at any kid stupid enough to get caught up in this; their lives could be ruined, and our school and all its pupils will be tarnished by association.*

'Yeah, some of our students were straight down there the next morning with their brooms for the big volunteer sweep-up.

The staff were sharing some lovely pictures on Facebook.'

There were, however, other young people who lived nearby who had been involved. One mother in Battersea was told that she and her eight-year-old daughter now faced eviction from their council house because of her eighteen-year-old son's conviction. Punishing whole families for the crimes of a relative is the practice of fascist dictators. The Nazis called it *Sippenhaft*. North Korea calls it 'three generations of punishment'. The Conservatives of Wandsworth Council called it 'being fair to neighbours'.

Perhaps this story upset me so much because he could have easily been one of our students. We had had our fair share of challenging kids at Lambeth Academy, and no amount of idealism was going to resolve the problems they presented. I had gone into this project thinking that our school would never need to permanently exclude a pupil, that we would find a way to help seriously disruptive or damaged children within the nurturing environment of our academy. And then all the bunnies would hop around playing with the soldiers who had thrown away all their guns. The reality is that governing a school forces you to confront every social problem you can imagine coming through the school gates. 'Every child has the right to a good education.' I had once thought that this was an argument against expelling any pupil. But then I came to learn that there are some individuals so destructive and in need of very specialized help they deny their classmates *their* right to a good education.

Sometimes, as an alternative, we arranged 'managed moves' between neighbouring schools, where we would swap students in the hope of giving both a fresh start. And we created a protocol in which parents of students threatened with permanent exclusion had the opportunity to make their case directly to the governors and sometimes, you saw the problem right there. 'Don't talk to me about children!' shouted one angry mother to me. 'I know more than anyone about raising children. I've had eight.' There should be a special award for governors who refrain from saying what they are thinking.

There were one or two occasions where I overturned the recommendation of the leadership team and gave a student one more chance but, more often, the student would have to go, no matter how much I hated it. Wielding power in a situation like this is the part of the job that I think some on the left might recoil at, being the authority figure who sits in judgement on others, and quite possibly changes an individual's life for the worse. But it is a grim and necessary part of defending the right to education for many hundreds of others.

And I think this shines a light on the biggest difference between the campaigning left and the governing left, between Labour in opposition and Labour in power, between idealists and realists. If you're serious about changing the world, eventually you have to be prepared to take control and make some really shitty decisions. The same political values that made me campaign for this school for local kids now made me believe that one particular child should no longer be allowed to come here. I had fully transformed from campaigner into authority figure, although I would maintain that, in fact, we are all on the same side. Because we do need both; we need people peacefully camping outside St Paul's to make us stop and think about how global capitalism is failing us all, and we need people prepared to give up the second Monday of each term for a Curriculum and Standards sub-committee.

Like the Occupy protestors in Wall Street and London, I too had been trying to change the world, except that my meetings came with tea and biscuits. Also, I didn't fancy being baton-charged by the police and having my tent dragged away. I would have been too anxious that the riot squad were not folding up the tent correctly; as they were beating me with truncheons, I would have been trying to tell them that the groundsheet only fits in the bag if you follow the exact instructions.

Both my children were leaving Lambeth Academy in the same summer. My daughter wanted a new challenge and was attracted to the huge Graveney sixth form down in Tooting, while my son was heading off to university. In September, we loaded up the car with all the things he needed and a few things he didn't and, outside the front door, his younger sister gave him a farewell hug and said, 'Don't drink too little.' Then we drove him up the motorway and carried his stuff into this little room, and found a picture that his sister had placed in among his stuff of the two of them sitting in a bouncy castle aged five and seven. I wasn't crying, I just had something in my eye.

In a flash, they had gone from those innocent little kids to these young adults making big choices. They had come through a non-selective inner-city state school and, in my not-very-neutral opinion, had emerged well balanced, happy and really well educated, in every sense of the word. Although being in a school with so many languages and nationalities had provided my daughter with something of an identity crisis when it came to performing at the academy's International Evening.

'Dad, everyone is doing songs from their family culture, and I don't know what to perform. Are there any, like, Irish songs or anything you could teach us?'

'But you're only a bit Irish, you're English, really, you're from here; from Clapham.'

'So what do I sing?'

And so at International Evening at Lambeth Academy, after

all the songs from all over the world, my two kids finally got up on stage, him on guitar and her on vocals, and my daughter said, 'This is a song about where we're from,' and she sang 'Up The Junction' by Squeeze, and they got huge cheers from all their classmates which seemed to say, 'Yeah – that's cool! You're from right here!'

Damn – that thing in my eye is a really recurrent problem. As I sat there in the audience, watching so much talent and enthusiasm on stage, I couldn't help feeling it had all happened too quickly. My kids have grown up, my life is flying by so fast that before I know it, I'll be ninety years old and it will be time for my middle-aged children to have that difficult talk with their father.

'The thing is, Dad, we think it's time you went into a residential home where you can get full-time care.'

'Well, my dears, I'm sure you only have my best interests at heart. Which home did you have in mind?'

'Well, there's that expensive private one up the hill?'

'Oh yes?' I stammer hopefully.

'Or there's that very popular one where your brother went.'

'Oh yes, that was nice.'

'But we're not sending you to either of those. We are going to campaign for a brand-new old people's home and we will send you there. You can't look round it because it hasn't been built yet. And there are no staff so far, no residents, no routines and no way of knowing what the hell it is going to be like. That's where you are going to spend the rest of your life. Oh, and if it goes horribly wrong in the first couple of years, we're going to keep you there anyway, because we believe it's important that the community keeps faith with this brand-new, experimental old people's home.'

That would bloody well serve me right.

The Sickest Man in Politics

Eastleigh By-election – 28 February 2013

I joined Twitter. My publishers said it would be a useful tool in promoting my books. And then I stopped writing books because I was constantly checking Twitter. It was like a sort of existential drug, as if you were standing alone in some vast mountain range shouting, 'HELLO?' Then you waited for just one person to shout back 'Hello!' but sometimes there was total silence and you felt certain you were the last person alive on earth and the future was blank nothingness for ever. Or sometimes you heard dozens, sometimes hundreds, of people confirming that you existed, and you felt vindicated and popular and then, five minutes later, you felt the need to check again in case they had forgotten all about you. The whole thing was basically an online shallowness test, and I have to say I was pretty pleased with how well I was doing.

When seeking to make political points on Twitter, I learned quickly that uncertainty is a low-scoring emotion. Ambivalence or even-handedness is just wasting everyone's time. Anger! Certainty! Blame! These are the primary colours on your palette, this is how you get yourself noticed in the constantly churning grey crowd. And because 140 characters may not always be quite sufficient to drill down through all the levels of complexity that surround a particular issue, now the news I received first on social media was presented to me as one simple FACT that was either GOOD or BAD. There might be other people who had a different take on the news to me, but I didn't follow them, and so I could be increasingly certain of the only truth and feel reassured that the rest of my world seemed to agree with me. Jonathan Swift said, 'It is the folly of too many to mistake the echo of a London coffee-house for the voice of a kingdom.' But I had more followers than him, so what did he know?

Twitter provided the focus for our Two-minute Hate. Whether it was about George Osborne cutting the top tax rate or the *Daily Mail*'s focus on the dress sense of female politicians, there was always something to react to and be offended by. Part of the fun was wondering who we would be hating tomorrow. British society had always been one massive Venn diagram but, without us quite realizing it, the overlapping sections were rapidly pulling apart, until the circles were completely separate; now, we were just a collection of isolated bubbles: loving Clarkson, hating Clarkson; supporting Miliband or trolling Miliband; watching anger against the Coalition reach fever pitch or watching a kitten stuck in a tissue box. Even when the whole country tuned in to respond to a shared national experience like the opening of the London Olympics, we could all agree it was a witty and stirring portrayal of a forward-looking modern Britain or 'leftie multicultural crap'.

The gap between the 2012 London Olympics and the 2016 referendum was a mere four years, and yet the two moments seem like the self-expression of two completely different countries. To me, 27 July 2012 seemed like the definitive final word on modern and inclusive Great Britain, with its industrial heritage and its Sergeant Peppers and its NHS and the World Wide Web. Everyone had wondered how we could possibly improve on the spectacle and scale of China's opening ceremony four years earlier – and this was the perfect answer: be funny. We don't have thousands of gymnasts dancing in perfect synchronicity, but we do have Mr Bean getting bored playing the theme tune to *Chariots of Fire*. We have hundreds of kids bouncing on NHS beds, we have the queen parachuting into the stadium, we have David Beckham looking slightly embarrassed as he holds the Olympic torch aloft on a speedboat. A few days earlier, that flame had come through Clapham, and Jackie and I had followed it on our bikes, past cheering crowds, all the way to Chelsea, where the stars of *Absolutely Fabulous* took the sacred Olympic flame and used it to light a fag. I'm pretty sure that would never have happened in China. Here was the little island that had exported the Industrial Revolution and liberal democracy and so many inventions and writers and values, and what did we do with our moment in the global spotlight? We made them laugh. I loved that. It was just so fantastically confident. God, I miss that relaxed, humorous Britain.

Even the Mayor of London was a novelty comedy act. How many foreign politicians would see their ratings improve after getting stuck on a zip wire, and dangling there forlornly waving the national flag? In this atmosphere of national unity and good-will, I tried not to be too open about my resentment that the Conservatives were the ones parading on this global stage built by Labour. But then I have never been one to put old rivalries behind me. If it had been up to me, the official name for the 2012 games would have been the *London (not Paris) Olympics*.

I relished the fact that this global event was happening all around us. I directed some lost Russian athletes on the South Bank, I took a break from writing in the London Library to watch the cyclists come down the Mall, and then Jackie and I got tickets to the Paralympics, where we marvelled at the urban redevelopment and the scale of the stadium and watched a bit of sport, and then realized we don't like athletics very much so we came home again. But it all felt great, a massive national party that could make us all proud of inclusive, welcoming Britain. And I think I presumed that everyone else felt the same way. But the thing about the London Olympics was that they mainly took place in London, maybe I should have spotted that in the name. Elsewhere in our dis-united kingdom, many people, understandably, felt a little less thrilled about this great big party they had not been invited to. They should have closed the roof on the Olympic Stadium, they should have put the whole Olympic Village in a massive glass dome so it could have been even more like a bubble.

I appreciated that my privileged life was very different to those of most people around the country, and I hoped I got the occasional sharp dose of reality when dealing with some very disadvantaged families at Lambeth Academy. But what I hadn't quite grasped was the *scale* of hostility from those outside the bubble, the sheer weight of numbers beyond the M25 who had grown to despise all the politicians, the bankers, the phone-hacking journalists, and the rest of the 'metropolitan élite' who both ignored them and judged them at the same time. It was at this point that the great electoral gods decided I should be whisked from London to an unremarkable English town to ask them all to vote for me.

Eastleigh was billed as the most important by-election for decades, although its deeper political significance would only become apparent after the result. It presented itself as a Liberal/ Tory marginal at the unique moment when the two parties were in coalition together but suffering increasing tensions. The Tories had to retake Stephen Milligan's old seat if they hoped to win an outright majority in 2015; while, if Nick Clegg lost here, he might lose leadership of the Liberals after his humiliation over student loans and the AV referendum. So Clegg and Cameron had to throw everything into this fight, while pretending they were still in perfect agreement in government. It was like some surreal satire of politics: all this effort and money was being expended by two parties fighting each other for the right to vote for exactly the same policies.

The Labour vote had been squeezed over the years as people voted Liberal to keep the Tories out, but now the Liberals had kept the Tories *in*, so who were these people supposed to vote for now? This is where I rode into town on my white steed, tipped my hat at the townsfolk and said, 'Howdy, I hear you good people are in need of some political representation in these here parts.' In fact, the idea that I should be the Labour candidate in a high-profile by-election did not come from me but directly from Ed Miliband's office. They wanted someone that people had heard of, but it turned out that Fiona Phillips was far too sensible, so they asked me. I fear that Ed Miliband may have had the idea that I was more of a public figure than I really was. Hardly anyone was recognizing me in the street any more, although one woman on a demonstration had recently said to me, 'Excuse me, you look just like an *older version* of John O'Farrell.' Little did I know that, soon, I would be all over the *Mail* and the *Sun* and the *Telegraph*. But guess what? Not in a good way.

Two weeks before the by-election was called, David Cameron had made the dramatic announcement that, if a Conservative government was re-elected, there would be an in–out referendum on Britain's membership of the European Union. I think, in his own mind, he believed that this was some sort of courageous masterstroke that would reunite his party and kill off UKIP. But the thing about bold gambles is that they only look bold when you win them. In another universe, David Cameron was an impoverished working-class bloke talking to his wife about their imminent eviction. 'My brilliant idea is to take out a massive loan from Wonga and put all that cash on a horse. Then, when the horse wins, all our problems will be over.'

'Yeah, but Dave, what if the horse loses?'

'*Look, I know what I am doing, all right? God, you're so negative sometimes!*'

There is a certain kind of alpha male who believes that they are completely invulnerable, and there are far too many of them in British politics. The Eastleigh by-election had been caused by another one who thought he could cheat and lie and never have to face the consequences. Chris Huhne was the Liberal Minister for Energy and had burnt up quite a lot of it speeding down the M11. He was charged with perverting the cause of justice and was forced to resign his seat. There's a lesson here; if you're caught speeding and persuade your wife to take your penalty points, do not become a Cabinet minister and then run off with another woman.

So it was that I was sitting at my desk on a bleak Thursday morning in February trying to get started on a new book, when my search for avoidance was helpfully assisted by a surprise phone call from the Labour leader's office.

'John, how would you feel about going down and campaigning in Eastleigh?'

'Er, maybe. Which day do you want me to go down there?'

'Every day. We were wondering if you would be the Labour candidate?'

I have a very tried-and-tested system for how to solve difficult life questions like this one. Ask Jackie. Frankly, the problems of this world would be a lot fewer if international leaders down the decades had had this resource.

'Jackie, our imperial Japanese government is so angry about American naval power in the Pacific that we are going to bomb Pearl Harbor. What do you think?'

'Look, before you do that, why don't you take the rest of the day off and just go for a swim at Tooting Lido? It's a lovely day, and you might just feel differently when you get out.'

My wife was of the opinion that I should definitely go for it. We both had strong views on this appalling government and on taking a stand when necessary. Eastleigh was only an hour and a half from my house – or an hour, if Chris Huhne was driving.

'Besides, what else are you going to do for three weeks? Sit at your desk farting around on your computer?'

'Um, well, I was starting a novel—'

'Exactly!'

I rang Ed Miliband's office back and said, yes, I would do it. I would completely dedicate the next three weeks to making a really good impression upon the voters of Eastbourne.

'It's Eastleigh.'

'I knew that. Eastleigh. In Dorset.'

'Hampshire.'

'Got it! Tell Ed he can rely on me.'

Given the timescale, they proposed imposing me as a candidate. Labour's National Executive Committee would ratify it and I could be in place and campaigning before you could say,

'Parachuted in.' But this set alarm bells ringing for me. I said I'd much rather be selected properly, by the local party. We were unlikely to win this by-election, so it seemed foolish to risk a story of undemocratic high-handed Westminster fixers ignoring local wishes.

So over the weekend, I announced my interest in becoming a candidate in the way that politicians have down the centuries – I did a tweet. Everyone thought I was joking. So I did another tweet and confirmed that, yes, if I won, I would take the job seriously. There'd always been a bit of me interested in being a politician for part of my life, and you have to give the dice a chance to roll that way.

On Sunday, I went down and campaigned as an ordinary volunteer, meeting a couple of other people who'd expressed an interest in being the Labour candidate. There was lots of firm shaking of hands, and 'may the best candidate win' and 'we all want the same thing' and frankly, it was all very British and embarrassing. On Monday, I was interviewed by a panel from Labour's National Executive Committee to check that I was a suitable candidate for their shortlist. They asked me if there was anything in my past that might come out and embarrass the Labour Party. I told them I once wrote for *Hale and Pace*. In fact, I did mention that there were lots of things I'd put in my political memoir that could be used against me, but they were confident that anything that was already in the public domain was not an issue. I'm not sure the *Daily Mail* ever got that memo.

The following night, I prepared to address a packed meeting of Eastleigh Labour Party members, trade union affiliates and one noisy baby on why they should adopt me as their prospective Labour candidate. It was a big night – it might even be the lead story on Radio Solent local-news round-up. I spoke of my experience in standing for elections. I spoke less about my record of losing elections. Then, during the question-and-answer session, the three candidates were asked to name the worst thing Labour had done during their thirteen years in government. The moderator came to me last, and I was surprised that the other two had not chosen the blindingly obvious thing that was always going to be my answer. Iraq wasn't just the elephant in the room, it was a whole herd of woolly mammoths in the room – woolly mammoths with Attention Deficit Disorder.

After the votes were counted, I wished the other two well and called home, shook a few hands then tweeted, 'Honoured to have been selected as Labour's candidate for Eastleigh. There is a lot of very hard work ahead. But first I am going to the pub.' It turned out there was so much admin and completing of official forms, I never got to go to the pub. My first campaign promise was already broken.

The press reaction to my selection was fairly positive, with even Tory commentators saying it made things a bit more interesting. A couple of journalists added that it might be fun to have someone with a sense of humour in the House of Commons. The papers were really building me up. I was trying to remember what usually comes next.

I had learned from my extensive research that Eastleigh is a former railway town in Hampshire, between Southampton and Winchester, and that Wikipedia needs your donations now. Famous people from Eastleigh seemed to be limited to Benny Hill, so bad luck to those residents who had their address changed to 'Benny Hill Close'. Eastleigh landmarks included the Swan shopping centre, the railway sidings and the site of the old Mr Kipling factory. To be honest, there were not many views of Eastleigh where you thought, *Do you know, I could easily be in Florence!* It wasn't especially ugly, but it's hard to think of a reason anyone would ever visit except to fight a by-election, and that doesn't seem enough of a basis for a local economy. Like so many English towns, it offered the same soulless chain shops interspersed with the Save the Children shop and the British Heart Foundation shop, and then the opportunity to bet on a horse, have your nails painted, drink a cappuccino, buy a greetings card, watch Sky Sports with a pie and a pint and get a tattoo. I don't want to get all Marxist about this, but how exactly were the workers here supposed to create surplus value? What is Eastleigh for? None of this is the fault of the good people of Eastleigh, it's just that we seem to have lost what defines us; our identikit high streets signify a wider post-industrial identity crisis and loss of purpose. Once England was a nation of shopkeepers. But they're all charity shops now.

The first question I was asked by the local press was 'Will you move to Eastleigh if you win?' In this situation, the ideal candidate is not supposed to dry-heave, laugh, shake their head incredulously then pass out. Already, I was making basic mistakes. On day one, I spotted the Liberal candidate in the high street and so went over to shake his hand. 'Oh, you're down from *London*, are you?' he said, cleverly emphasizing my lack of local credentials.

'Er, yes, that's where I live. Where the Parliament is that we're trying to get elected to?'

Soon after, one of the Liberals' entourage shouted, 'I expect you'd rather be in London?' And, slightly undiplomatically, my dear wife replied, 'Well, yes. *Obviously*,' and gestured around her. I struggled with the idea that people should vote for candidates because they are local rather than for what they stood for. 'Well, I've always been a great believer of the economic theories of John

Maynard Keynes, but then the BNP candidate lives in Station Road, so I'm switching to the neo-Nazis . . .'

In fact in this election there was no BNP candidate, which was indicative of the fascists' implosion since the General Election and which I counted as a victory of sorts before we'd even started. However, there was a UKIP candidate and, based on activists of theirs I'd met in the past, I was expecting some swivel-eyed loony. But, much as it pains me to admit this, the UKIP candidate was very impressive. Diane James was a good public speaker, well briefed on all the issues, quick and confident, and in fact was the only opponent who I thought looked like potential Westminster material. The role of the off-message, ignorant right-wing amateur was therefore adopted by the official Tory candidate, who had been selected after Alf Garnett turned out to be a fictional character. Maria Hutchings was against gay marriage, anti-abortion, anti-European and rather bizarrely asserted that she had to send her very clever twelve-year-old son to private school because that was the only way he could become a surgeon. Of course, I had no particular opinion about her having to go private because her son was bright. Nope, nothing to see here, move along, please . . .

The Tory leadership denied they were embarrassed by their candidate and she avoided further gaffes at the BBC hustings and the debate organized by 38 Degrees by cunningly not showing up at either. Over at Eastleigh Conservative Club, a woman's faint voice could be heard from inside the stationery cupboard, shouting, 'Let me out!'

By way of a contrast, I discovered that I was being painfully on-message when I glanced at my own Twitter feed. I had given the Labour Party my log-in details so my Twitter feed could be synchronized with a Tumblr blog, or my Ceefax page, or whatever it was they were setting up, and saw that I was apparently tweeting things like 'Great canvass at Hedge End today! Voters switching to #OneNationLabour #Eastleigh #LabourWinningHere'. Underneath were lots of responses, like 'John O'Farrell tweeting like an MP' or 'Oh no, the body snatchers have got him.' That was the only time during the whole campaign when I said no. When it came to writing anything, I wanted to do it in my own voice. I tweeted a suggestion that people come to Eastleigh to canvass for Labour. Someone responded, 'I'd rather shit in my hands and clap,' so I replied, 'I'll put you down as "maybe",' and the screenshot of this exchange went viral; so at least I was getting some sort of message across.

Twitter was like this fourth-dimension communication channel. The traditional media would interview me in Blenheim Road, and I felt like I had to be all serious and on-message, but then, on social media, I felt able to be myself, taking the piss or saying what I really thought. Of course, most of the people I reached were not Eastleigh voters, but by-elections are about more than just the one place they are happening in. When the big news story was that Findus 'beef' lasagne was 100 per cent horsemeat, we mocked up a yellow microwave carton with 'Lib-Dem lasagne' on it, and a blue sticker that read '100% Tory'. The canvassers would come back to the office saying, 'Not many Labour promises in Botley today,' and I'd say, 'Never mind that – look, our lasagne gag got a thousand retweets!'

The experience of being a candidate in an important by-election campaign was so utterly different to standing in Maidenhead. I didn't decide what I ate for lunch for the entire three weeks. A sandwich would just appear in front of me as I was driven from one event to the next, and my minders tried to get me up to speed with local issues, the layout of the constituency and the current form of Eastleigh FC: 'Currently tenth in the Southern League, manager's name is Richard Hill – that's the Ford Factory there, closing next year with three hundred job losses . . .' My minders were Labour MPs, and splendid people they were, too. John Denham and Alan Whitehead were both Members of Parliament for Southampton, and Toby Perkins came down from Chesterfield to add some blunt northern pragmatism to the scene. (Chinese waiter: 'Are you all right with chopsticks?' Toby: 'Yeah, we're not UKIP.')

There was no time for me to stand back and say that perhaps we should focus on this, or maybe I could write a piece about that; I was being whisked to a sixth-form college to answer questions alongside Harriet Harman, or be off to Southampton Airport with Chuka Umunna, reciting a business-regeneration plan for Eastleigh John Denham had written for me and which I'd learned off by heart by setting the alarm for five thirty that morning.

In between time, it was just the old-fashioned business of knocking on as many doors as possible, albeit reinvented to feel more dynamic and visually impressive. A dozen canvassers would blitz the same street, with one team leader directing us and collecting the data. Twenty-five years I'd been doing this, and I still felt that same fizz of nerves as I walked up to that first door. And at the next house I could hear one of our canvassers saying, 'Would you like to meet our candidate, John O'Farrell? No? Oh, okay.'

Credit where it's due, though, I was good with people's dogs. No matter how huge the hound jumping at me and barking and snapping at my leaflets, I could pat it on the head, identify the breed and start a conversation.

'Oooh, what a lovely dog. Chesapeake Bay Retriever?'

'That's right, well spotted!'

This is going well, I think. *I am bonding with this voter's dog.*

'What's his name?'

'Bobby.'

'Oh, same as Peter Mandelson's dog.'

Doh! Another vote lost right there. Volunteers poured in from across the country; coachloads of Labour activists kept on turning up to support our campaign – or perhaps because they had always had a burning desire to visit Eastleigh. When Eastleigh food bank was running out of supplies, we put out a tweet asking people to come with donations, and the response was amazing. And so many people donated money to the campaign I was told that this became the first by-election in Labour's history to actually make a profit. The odds on Labour winning had started out at 100–1, then they shrunk to 20–1, then 10–1 . . . and now were down to 8–1 as punters saw that Labour were making a real effort in a seat where the two front-runners represented the same government.

Eastleigh was not a prosperous place and, if it had been in the north of England, I think it might have been a Labour seat.

'But we always vote Liberal, just to keep the Tories out,' a voter explained to me on my first day of canvassing.

'Right, yes, I see,' I said, all excited about being able to produce my trump card. 'But of course, this time if you vote Liberal, you'll be keeping the Tories *in.*'

'What?'

'Well, now that the Liberals are propping up a Conservative-led coalition, a vote for the Liberals will *keep the Tories in.*'

'What do you mean?'

'Well, because Nick Clegg did a deal with David Cameron to support the Conservative government, a Liberal MP for Eastleigh would vote for all the Tory policies. That's why I'm asking you to vote Labour this time.'

She looked at me a little dubiously for a second, like I was trying to play some sort of clever mind-game with her.

'No, we always vote Liberal, just to keep the Tories out,' she repeated, and the front door closed in my face.

To try to draw attention to the fact that the other two main parties were representing the same government, my campaign managers organized a press stunt with two inflatable horses – an attempt at a visual representation of our belief this was a two-horse race between the Opposition (the red inflatable horse) and the Coalition government (the blue-and-yellow inflatable horse). I was active in politics because I wanted the world to be a better place. I wanted everyone to see that we could be so much better than this, we could create a more empathetic and compassion-ate society. And because of that, here I was in Eastleigh High Street, beside a pair of comedy inflatable horses gamely ridden by two of our young activists, as the press pack took photographs and nodded patiently as I gave my stump speech explaining the political symbolism. 'You see, there are only *two* horses in this race!' I shouted, as if they hadn't got it within the first half a second. 'The Government, represented by the blue-and-yellow horse . . . and then Labour – the red horse . . . So the Liberal candidate and the Tory candidate – they're basically *one horse*, not two horses . . .' I'm losing them now. They've stopped writing things down; they've got their photo. It is then that I become aware of Toby Perkins MP pacing up and down behind them, making an urgent call back to headquarters.

'One of the horses has a puncture!' he reports anxiously.

'Which horse is it?'

'It's the red horse! The Labour horse is deflating!'

The very horse that is supposed to represent the next party of government is going all soft and floppy, right in front of the national media. That is when he gets the message from HQ. 'Puncture the blue horse!'

'What?!'

'Puncture the blue horse, so the Labour horse looks less floppy than the Tory one.'

'Actually, it's a Coalition horse, blue *and* yellow, that's the whole point – 'cos, you see, it's a two-horse race.'

'Yeah, whatever.'

This episode struck me as something of a metaphor for modern politics. I could just picture myself at a press conference afterwards, saying, 'Yes, I will concede that the Labour horse was more deflated than we would have liked. But I think if you look at the *government* inflatable horse, then ours was nowhere near as soft and floppy. And that's why Ed Miliband should be the next Prime Minister.'

Cherie Blair came down, and we went to Southampton General Hospital together and were photographed with some poor baby with bandaged legs suspended in the air while me and Cherie looked on. This picture then popped up in my inbox, sent by my football team, who had supportively organized a caption competition. Winner – Cherie to baby: 'No, I don't know who he is either!'

I did a press event at a car dealership with Ed Balls and, as we chatted with a mechanic, Michael Crick barged in with his cameraman and asked the mechanic what he was voting. 'Conservative,' said the mechanic. Great, thanks a lot. That's the last time I do my 'looking concerned' face. I did a poster launch with Yvette Cooper, and even though Ed and Yvette were in town on the same day, they weren't going to have time to meet up, which I think I was more concerned about than they were. In addition to this, over a hundred Labour MPs came to support me and I felt bad that I never got to see them to say thank you. Dennis Skinner arrived at the same time as Polly Toynbee, but I decided against sending them out together. Alf Dubs rolled up with a posse of Labour lords, and another old friend, Fiona Mactaggart MP, was also in town with a delegation from Slough Labour Party. There were so many people I would have loved to stop and have lunch with, but there was never any time.

Whenever I watched professional politicians talking to the media, I was struck by what a ridiculous charade this had become. All the reporter wants is one off-message gaffe or admission of failure; all the politician wants is their campaign message broadcast. Neither wants a genuine conversation about what needs to be discussed.

'You can't deny that this latest opinion poll is the clearest sign yet that Labour picked the wrong leader?'

'One Nation Labour is making great progress in the south of England and we expect to do very well here against the Conservative-led Coalition, whose cuts are really hurting hard-working families.'

And they would ask a different very rude question and the politician would be very rude back by completely ignoring what they had just said and repeating the one soundbite they wanted on the news, and I would just stand there, feeling embarrassed and wishing everyone could just talk normally. Also, why did we only stand up for 'hard-working families'? Maybe I could be the politician who stood up for the lazy ones?

Jackie had given me some sage advice about how to respond in the face of aggressive media questioning. 'Just pause and then tell the truth,' she said.

'Admit it, you've never been to Eastleigh before, have you, John?'

'Er, yes, I've visited the harbour at Hamble.'

'What, on a yacht?'

You know, you really don't need to work that hard to catch me out. I've got a huge back catalogue of inappropriate quotes for you to draw on if you just did five minutes' research.

Over at the *Mail*, at least somebody was taking the trouble. On Wednesday, they ran a story about my opposition to the Falklands War, as recounted in my political memoir. They were obviously very slow readers at the *Mail*, because it wasn't until the weekend that they had managed another forty pages and got to the bit where I recounted my reaction to the Brighton bomb. You know that thing I had told myself after the AV referendum, about always stopping and preparing for the worst thing the right might throw at you? I really should have taken my own advice.

When I was twenty-two years old, in the middle of the Miners' Strike, the woman I hated more than anyone else in the world was nearly killed by an IRA terrorist attack. And I had confessed that my first reaction back in those angry, divided times had been regret that Thatcher had survived. I admitted this dark thought as part of a wider point about political hatred. 'I hated her more than was healthy' were my exact words; surely the *Mail on Sunday* would explain this if I read to the bottom of the article. Oh, apparently not, who'd have thought it!

I was out canvassing with lots of volunteers when the call came through. Our campaign's press secretary told me the *Mail* were running this story tomorrow and he read me the sensible-sounding quote he had come up with for me to say in response. I said that was fine and went back to canvassing, thinking that, if I just ignored this problem, maybe it might just go away. The next morning, it was like I'd been exposed as the senior commander of the IRA's Derry Brigade. All the other papers and news bulletins were running with the story, Sadiq Khan was having to defend me on national television, and this outrage became the defining issue with the now massively tainted Labour candidate. 'Is he the one who planted the Brighton Bomb or something?' Some people on Twitter noticed I had an Irish surname and, frankly, what more proof do you need? It was freezing cold in Eastleigh, but I thought I'd better leave the black balaclava at home.

The next day, the local rag, the *Southern Daily Echo*, cut and pasted the story on to its front page, with a big picture of the bombed Grand Hotel and me laughing in front of the rubble, and disappointingly I found that this did not improve my appeal among the 'Don't Knows'. Now, my efforts to appear charming and responsible to the local voters were made a tiny bit more challenging by having passing motorists shouting, '*Terrorist!*' at me. I was with Labour front-bencher Rachel Reeves, who'd made the effort to come down and support me despite being eight months pregnant, so I felt especially embarrassed that she should have to witness all this anger and hatred rather than listening to whale song and doing yoga. The two of us were scheduled to visit a florist's to chat to the owner about business rates or something. To be honest, it was a bit hard to concentrate with a one-man lynch mob shouting at me from his car outside.

'This is a lovely florist's you have here—'

'*You traitor!! You should be shot at dawn!*'

'Yes, I love flowers . . .' My concentration was struggling in the face of this onslaught. I was trying to make floral-based chit-chat, but it just wasn't happening 'Um, I like the way you can put them in a vase . . .'

'*Traitor! You should hang – I'd pull the lever!*'

I definitely couldn't hear anyone outside, you could tell by my completely relaxed conversational style. 'Flowers, yes, and they come in all different colours, don't they?'

'Er, yes. They do.'

'IRA supporter! Falklands traitor! Socialist scum!'

And there it was. Now, the focus of the Two-minute Hate was *me*! It's a rather unsettling experience to have doors slammed in your face and strangers screaming at you, to have your Twitter time-line clogged up with threats and bile and bad spelling – it's an education on the human psyche. Should I read the comments thread under the original *Mail* article? Hmm, maybe not. Now I wished I'd kept that glowing review the *Mail* had given *Things Can Only Get Better*; this might be a good time to tweet it.

But to be honest the thing about this scandal was that, actually, I didn't really mind. On a personal level, I didn't feel that I'd been caught doing a bad thing; those doughty investigative reporters at the *Daily Mail* had unearthed a secret I had hidden away in a bestselling memoir. There wasn't a single person I cared about who thought any the less of me for what I'd written; it wasn't some shameful revelation or embarrassing scandal. On the contrary, suddenly becoming the number-one bogey figure of the *Daily Mail* seemed to be a feather in my cap in Labour circles. Having wished death on Margaret Thatcher appeared to make me some sort of revolutionary hero for people way to the left of me, as if I were some modern-day Che Guevara (which I so clearly was not).

What I did feel sad about was how the story made the job of the Labour team in Eastleigh so much harder. Young volunteers who had felt optimistic about Labour making a breakthrough here now knew their task was reduced to damage limitation because of all the baggage the candidate had brought with him. That was the worst thing about it. I felt that Labour might have done better without me, that this brilliant campaign team were working fourteen-hour days for something they really believed in, and now their hopes were shot.

I was also a bit disappointed that this issue became the default challenging question from every single news source, including the ones I respected. The BBC and others lazily took their cue from the *Mail* instead of deciding themselves what the important issues were. And so I was forced to explain at length in every interview that of course those weren't my feelings any more and that I had just tried to write an honest book about my youth. Then, when I knocked on one door, one old Labour voter said to me, 'Oh, I heard what you said, and I completely agree with you!'

'Oh, good, thank you. I think a lot of people were presented with something out of context—'

'I wish the IRA had killed that bitch, too!'

'No, no . . .' And suddenly I'm backtracking and explaining all over again.

I had always known that Labour was very unlikely to win in Eastleigh and that my main task had been to make sure Labour didn't disappear in all the media coverage of the by-election. In that sense things were going splendidly. The *Mail* did a follow-up piece under the headline 'Is ED's PAL THE SICKEST MAN IN POLITICS?' That's me all over.

'Do you know John O'Farrell?'

'What, Ed's pal? The really sick one?'

'Yeah, that's him. Sickest man in politics, he is.'

When my pal Ed faced Cameron at PMQs, the Prime Minister actually read out extracts from *Things Can Only Get Better* in the House of Commons, which was not something I ever foresaw when I was writing it. The end result of the whole thing was that the book went shooting back up the Amazon charts and my publishers had to do a reprint. Cheers, Dave, thanks, *Daily Mail*, much appreciated.

In truth, I had known quite early on in the campaign that we weren't getting the protest votes. For some reason, that seems counter to the democratic way of doing things: lots of the early postal votes are counted long before polling day, and the campaign agents are present at this early indicator of the political weather. My agent came back to our campaign offices shocked at the number of UKIP votes and a little depressed by the number of votes for us. The bookies must have had someone in that room as well, because the odds on Diane James immediately shrunk dramatically, while, in a flash, I was back out to 100–1. I had already sensed on the doorstep that the voters of Eastleigh were not expressing their opposition to the government via the opposition to the government. The protest votes were going to UKIP, an all-powerful tide was overwhelming this coastal seat and I was Cnut, powerless to hold it back. At least, I think that's what that voter shouted.

It's a curious thing a bandwagon; many people join it without quite knowing why. A Polish woman told me she was voting UKIP because everyone else seemed to be. Of course, lots of people were voting UKIP because they believed in what the party stood for, but I think lots of their other voters didn't. It made me realize just how many votes Labour must have gained the previous decade just because we'd been so fashionable.

But there was no doubt that immigration had become a huge issue. And I learned at first hand that, just because the left feels uncomfortable talking about an issue, it doesn't make it go away. In terms of pure numbers, more people had arrived in the United Kingdom in the previous decade than at any time in our history, and it is a huge credit to this country that they were assimilated without riots or racial violence. But voters in Eastleigh talked about the struggle their grown-up children had finding employment and asked me why everyone serving in the coffee shops was Eastern European, and I didn't have a simple answer.

The Tories started doing leaflets in UKIP colours, and I was keen to attack the UKIP vote head on, but the professionals said we had to focus on just getting to our own core vote. When I was spending too long trying to talk round a UKIP voter, Kevin Brennan MP said 'Come on, John, stop flogging a dead horse. Leave that to Findus!' At some point, I came to realize that, if UKIP were doing as well as it seemed, I'd be pushed into fourth place. That would be the headline; this by-election would be all about Labour's failure!

So that was the only suspense on polling day. Could UKIP actually win the seat? Or did the Liberals have enough postal votes locked down that local councillor Mike Thornton would be forced to leave Eastleigh to spend some time in 'that-there London'?

I had presumed that I would pass the entire evening at the count as I had at Maidenhead, standing behind the tellers, watching them sort the votes into their various piles, most of them higher than mine. But once again, a by-election is different. With lots of media attention, the entrance of each candidate is stage-managed and its timing agreed between the parties. So we waited for much of the evening back at the house of one of my favourite local activists. Finally, we were told that it was time to go, and Jackie and I and my two grown-up kids squeezed into a car to get there at precisely the right moment. But after we had been driving for a few minutes we got another message that this wasn't the right time to arrive – we might overlap with one of the other major candidates. *Does anyone care?* I was asking myself. But we turned off and parked in a dark country side road, switched off the headlights and waited. And waited. Then another text to the lead driver in our convoy . . . was that the signal to go? No, that was about something else; maybe he'd been miss-sold PPI. We seemed to be there for ages. It was just as well no police patrol car happened to pass by.

'May I ask why are you all sitting here in this parked car in the middle of the night?'

'Well, I am a by-election candidate, and we are hiding in this dark country road so that we can make a dramatic entrance at the count at precisely the right time.'

'Right. And you expect me to believe that, do you? You are aware this is a popular dogging spot?'

At last, we arrived at the historic setting of the Fleming Park Leisure Centre. John Denham was waiting for us and told us how we should line up to walk past the TV cameras. My daughter had wanted to walk in proudly holding my arm, but it was explained that the Labour Party might not want to give the impression that their fifty-year-old Labour candidate had just picked up some eighteen-year-old blonde.

My agent told me I had indeed come fourth, but it looked like the Tories had come third, so at least I had dodged a bullet in terms of the next morning's headlines. In fact while the Liberal and Tory votes had dropped dramatically, Labour's share had gone up a little, so we had held our own, even though the pie was now cut four ways instead of three. But there was no escaping that this was not the result of a political party that was going to form the next government. There had been no enthusiasm for Labour or Ed Miliband or John O'Farrell; just 'I'm not voting for any of you' or 'I'm voting UKIP just to shake things up a bit' or 'You're all the same, except only one of you is an IRA terrorist.'

It became apparent that the voters of Eastleigh had voted Liberal to keep the Tories out, or keep them *in*, depending on how much interest they took in politics. The candidates gathered beside the stage, ready to be invited up to hear the official result. But the council officer started without us and I thought, *Well, this isn't right. We're supposed to be up there behind him, with our big rosettes and the loony candidate with a giant cowboy hat and flashing bow-tie.* 'Go on, Mike,' I said to the Liberal. 'You've won! Get up there and enjoy your moment.' And he climbed up and we all followed to stand in the traditional self-conscious row, me in a red tie, him choosing yellow. But even though the status quo had apparently been maintained, the cameras were all pointing at the runner-up – the big story was just how close UKIP had got to winning. They got the most votes cast on the day, and might have won if the campaign had been longer than three weeks. David Cameron's EU referendum pledge had failed at the first hurdle, and the UKIP breakout began right there in that hall.

Mike Thornton made a suitably modest speech. 'I'd like to thank the police,' he said. And down in the crowd, Neil Hamilton quipped, 'Yes, or else there wouldn't have been a by-election.' Once the three main contenders had finished their speeches, the press all disappeared from their space below the stage and went off to do their reports. It was as if the very act of me stepping up to the microphone was enough to make everyone vanish. But there was also a bit of jostling going on at the back of the hall, as the humiliated Maria Hutchings was bundled out of the building by her Tory minders and prevented from saying anything to the baying press pack. Just in case anyone was still listening, I tried to emphasize that this was a very bad result for the Conservatives; 'Tonight, it has been *beastly* in *Eastleigh* for David Cameron.' Look, it was late and I was tired, okay?

I woke up in the hotel the next morning to see Jackie putting a cup of tea on the bedside table. 'Morning, loser,' she said affectionately. We sat up in bed together, reading my emails and messages and all the kind things people had said on Twitter. 'Aah, everyone loves you,' she said. And then a pause. 'Except the voters of Eastleigh.'

I got a thank-you call from Ed Miliband, we had breakfast with the kids and got in our car to head back home.

'Do you know something?' I said to Jackie. 'I leave Eastleigh feeling very positive.'

'Yes. Because you're leaving Eastleigh.'

After three weeks of neglect, I went to see my old mum, who was starting to suffer from memory loss.

'You were very busy with something, weren't you? What was it?' she asked.

'I was standing for Parliament.'

'Oh, that's right. You won, didn't you?'

'No, I lost.'

'Oh. That's not very good. Why did you lose?'

'Because most people in Eastleigh voted for the other candidates.'

'Oh, well. They're silly.'

I'm sorry, Eastleigh, but you can't argue with that. My mother thought you were silly.

Mike Thornton lost the seat at the subsequent General Election; Eastleigh was won by the Tories, although Maria Hutchings would not be their candidate. Eastleigh Conservatives did at least cut a little flap into the door of their stationery cupboard to pass her food, liquids and any *Daily Express* front pages about migrants (i.e. all of them). Diane James, on the other hand, rose rapidly through the ranks of UKIP, becoming party leader in

October 2016. She managed to keep UKIP in the news by resigning again eighteen days later. She'd taken the party as far as she could, it's always better to quit before people feel you've clung on for too long. So there was a brief point in my life when I had lost elections to both the Tory leader and the UKIP leader – I clearly have a fetish for being beaten by right-wing women. Ten days after the by-election, both Chris Huhne and his ex-wife went to prison for eight months. I wonder if she had ever heard the ancient Chinese proverb 'Before you embark upon a journey of revenge, dig *two* graves.'

Eastleigh itself was destroyed by a meteorite, but nobody noticed.

Better Together

Scottish Independence Referendum –
18 September 2014

Lady Thatcher died. It was natural causes, *I* didn't do it. In fact, in a perverse way, her death made me vaguely depressed. All that hatred I had wasted on her in my twenties, all that impotent rage I'd expended; and then the decades had flown by and the invincible political colossus of my youth had withered and died. Thatcher had been my anti-mother; all I'd wanted was to be the opposite of everything she stood for. Perhaps I felt melancholy because the last flicker of my youth died with her.

I closed myself away in my office and tried to get on with some work. When I eventually opened the door, the life-size *Spitting Image* puppet of Maggie Thatcher had been retrieved from the loft and was standing there on the landing grinning at me. Clearly, my daughter was the second sickest person in politics.

I tried to avoid the news as the tributes poured in and history was rewritten. We were informed that Margaret Thatcher had apparently won the Cold War single-handedly, had invented ice cream and had a number-one hit song with 'Don't Cry For

Me, Argentina'. The Speaker of the House of Commons recalled Parliament to allow Conservative MPs to compete with each other for who could give the most gushing, distorted tribute. Meanwhile in *Viz*, Johnny Fartpants tried but failed to disprove the theory of nominative determinism as his family paid their respects at her funeral. This was despite being urged to do what he did best by 'Arthur Scargill, Tony Benn, Derek Hatton, John O'Farrell and all the rest'. I choked on my tea when I saw this; that I should be included on such a list of leftie impossibilists. Perhaps that was always supposed to be the gag.

On the day of the funeral I tried to block out the noise of the helicopters hovering over London and felt generally grumpy about the excessive cost, the one-sided coverage and the enormous respect being accorded to someone who had shown such contempt for the poorest and weakest people in a society that she didn't think existed. I had thought I was over it. But she was my first hate, and first hate never, ever dies.

My kids were now the age I had been when Maggie was at the peak of her powers, but their attitude to politics seemed so much more nuanced and constructive than mine was back then. My son was studying history and politics at university and suddenly seemed to know a lot more than I did. He got involved in specific causes, gave up his holidays to volunteer; he was making so much more difference than I had when I'd gone around my university town spraying left-wing slogans all over the banks.

My daughter's confident and glamorous feminism seemed a world away from the stringent 1980s version I had needed to get my head round as a young man. And now I struggled to square my puritanical gender politics with her confident, sassy version of a twenty-first-century woman. A generation earlier, fathers hadn't wanted their daughters going out in short skirts because they thought it was indecent and unladylike. Now I attempted to claim that I didn't like my daughter looking too immodest because of the, er, objectification of women by the patriarchy and stuff.

In September, our daughter started at university and suddenly it was just the two of us again. On the drive back, Jackie and I attempted to pick up the conversation where we'd left off in 1992. '. . . So, what was I saying? Oh yes, do you think this "internet" thing will take off?' or 'I can't believe John Major won the election' and 'I am *never* getting a mobile phone . . .'

Back in the family home, we looked at the space in the middle of the sofa where we had placed our first baby after we brought him back from the hospital.

'Well, that went by quickly,' I said. Now, there would be just two of us in this echoey house; no interesting new music playing in the kitchen, no line of slipped-off shoes in the hallway when all their friends came round, no hilarious interrogations over dinner on the burning issue of 'Shag? Marry? Kill?'

I remembered asking my dad what had been the happiest time of his life, and he answered, 'When all you kids were at home, when we were all together,' and that had stayed with me. 'Better together' was unveiled as the 'No' slogan in the Scottish referendum, but I felt it could have easily applied to my own family. But the anticipation of my children leaving home was far worse than the reality; it was great to see them thriving with new friends in new towns, and Jackie and I took the chance to take holidays out of term time to travel to exotic, far-off places, like the garden centre and Balham.

Oh, and I bought a narrowboat. It wasn't a mid-life crisis, I just felt the need for that rush of adrenalin you get as you chug along the canal at four miles an hour, the G-force testing your senses to the max. I would go and stay on it for days at a time, supposedly writing, but mostly making tea and staring at the wood-burning stove. I had grown up beside the Thames, and felt myself drawn to it once again – in a very direct, gravitational way, whenever I misjudged the jump to the slippery bank.

On the way home, I would call in on my mum, who I was gradually losing to vascular dementia. It is one of the cruel ironies of middle age that when the generation below finally becomes self-sufficient, the one above can no longer cope. My mum now needed full-time care, though there were still visits to various clubs, where she would be wildly inappropriate and people who hadn't known her before presumed that this must be a symptom of her condition. They played a word game where they went round the group:

'Agnes, what begins with a D?'

'Dog!'

'Good. Now, Peggy, can you give me something that begins with E?'

'Egg!'

'Super. So, Joy, now can you think a word that begins with F?'

Later, the care worker told me, 'Joy won't be attending the word-game session any more . . .'

I was sad that she wouldn't be able to share in the excitement of a new writing project that had just got the go-ahead and I felt guilty that I would have to leave her for long periods while I was away working on it. Back when Karey and I had been writing *The Film That Won't Get Made*, he had pitched another idea to me that he suggested we co-write.

'A musical?' I said incredulously. 'Who the hell for?'

'For Broadway,' he said, with a straight face.

'Oh yeah, like we could ever get on Broadway!' I blurted,

displaying that unstoppable British can-do attitude. But this turned out to be completely unlike every speculative script I had written before; traffic lights kept turning green, rival projects fell away as money was raised and talented people jumped on board. Suddenly I found myself in a mirror-lined studio on 42nd Street, with lots of people in leg-warmers who hugged you the first time you met them, watching them rehearse our all-singing, all-dancing musical comedy *Something Rotten!* I had to pinch myself: I was working in showbiz in New York, New York! If I could make it there, I could make it anywhere. Except Eastleigh.

I had been my usual nervous self before I'd got on the plane across to America. I know all the experts say that, statistically, it's extremely unlikely to happen, but there was still that irrational fear that I might just bump into Louise Mensch. I spent months in midtown Manhattan, where my corner shop was the M&Ms megastore and as you headed across Times Square every morning you were nearly accosted by a grubby Smurf. I lived on my own in a twenty-seventh-floor apartment, Skyping Jackie when I could, microwaving meals for one and, for some reason, listening to the albums that had first kept me company as a slightly homesick eighteen-year-old in my first few weeks at university. Looking back, I realized why I'd never felt like I really fitted on that intense English and drama degree course. The earnest theatre of Brecht and Grotowski is all very well, but those guys never put in enough gags or tap dancers for my tastes.

Our Renaissance musical set in Shakespeare's London was about as apolitical as it was possible to be, save for a comically over-optimistic feminist expecting full equality by the year 1600 and a sub-plot about oppressive Puritans trying to close down the Elizabethan theatre scene. You presume America is this unregulated capitalists' paradise but, bizarrely, the world of

Broadway theatre is one of the most strictly unionized industries I have ever encountered; we couldn't carry our own keyboard into the theatre without a couple of stagehands being paid a full day's wages (in fact, two days' pay, totalling $2,000, because this was a national holiday). I reported this to Jackie in the sense of 'Isn't that ridiculous?' and she just said, 'Good!'

'Good?!'

'Yeah, good. How often do you hear that the balance is too far in favour of union members? When was the last time the workers were too powerful and not the management?'

And I thought, *Yeah, she's right. Good on you, Broadway unions!* And I fantasized about Arthur Scargill leading the great Tap Dancers' Strike of '84: 'Henceforth, my members will be working to rule, and our lads will only do ball-change, ball-step, shuffle and heel step, but absolutely no double pull-back or kick line with or without jazz hands and spangly gold tights.'

I was in the United States at the time of the Scottish independence referendum and felt vaguely guilty for leaving my country at such an important time. As I had flown out and looked down on the shrinking landscape below, I hoped they'd take good care of the United Kingdom while I was away; I didn't want to come back and find it broken in two. There was too much change happening for me already: my kids had left home, I was losing my mum and now it seemed possible that the very country I had grown up in might be about to fragment. Were the Mum and Dad of Great Britain going to get a divorce as well as everything else?

I watched from afar as the 'Yes' vote for independence briefly went ahead in the polls and then Gordon Brown made a powerful intervention which helped pull things back. David Cameron asked the 'No' campaign whereabouts in Scotland he could be of most help, and they told him: 'England.'

Most Americans I spoke to about the situation in the UK were romantically in favour of the notion of Scottish independence. A short conversation usually revealed that this position was based on the fact that they had seen *Braveheart*. Occasionally, I was personally lumped in with George III and Lord North: 'Well, we fought you guys for our independence, so stands to reason they should, too?'

I felt instinctively against the notion of Scottish independence, but I think my opposition had many layers. The thinnest was perhaps some conservative nostalgia for Britain staying the shape I had always known. It had been bad enough when my 'counties of England' wooden jigsaw became out-of-date, but now that big blank bit above Cumberland had got fed up with being ignored and wanted a jigsaw of its own.

My next layer of opposition was a narrow political one: Labour held forty-one of Scotland's fifty-nine parliamentary seats; getting rid of the Tories was hard enough as it was; without Scotland, it looked virtually impossible. (None of the advertised options mentioned Scotland staying in the UK but Labour losing all those MPs anyway.) However, my fundamental reasoning behind hoping Scotland would remain in the United Kingdom was a broader, philosophical one. I just don't see how you can base an interpretation of society, economics and human inter-action on a place. The basic philosophy of the Scottish National Party is 'Scotland' and, somehow, that just doesn't seem enough. I'm originally from Maidenhead, but that has never been my guiding political credo.

'How can we create a society that enjoys maximum social inclusion while granting the greatest possible individual freedom?'

'Well, I think the answer to that is clearly "Maidenhead".'

'Eh? How can Junction 8/9 off the M4 help us find the greatest happiness for the greatest number?'

'Well, if only Maidenhead wasn't part of a royal borough with Windsor, then all our problems would disappear . . .'

Whenever any politician tries to tell you that all your troubles *here* are all the fault of those people over *there*, you can be pretty confident that such a simple answer is always going to be the wrong one. Of course, there have been many times in history when people have been exploited and oppressed for who they were or where they came from, and the causes of nationalism and liberty could be conveniently conjoined. But in twenty-first-century Europe, the problem for Catalonia isn't Madrid, the problem for England isn't Brussels and the problem for Edinburgh isn't London. For all those places, it's the same old basic problem of the distribution of power and money. As multinationals get stronger and ever more pervasive, finding new ways to squeeze every last penny out of us, they are definitely not thinking, *Smaller nation states with less leverage; that's what we fear the most*. Nationalism is generally the enemy of progressive politics, and I say that as someone who is irrationally proud to be from England, from Britain, and rationally embarrassed to be from Maidenhead.

Although I didn't realize it at the time, the surge in support for the SNP wasn't just about nationalism, it was part of the same anti-politics-as-usual movement that had seen UKIP push me into fourth place in Eastleigh and was now seeing old political loyalties evaporate right across the Western world.

On Election Night itself, I took advantage of the five-hour time difference to watch the results coming in through the night in Edinburgh and, by the time I went to bed, I felt reassured that the threatened political earthquake had not occurred. It was the highest turn-out for any vote in the United Kingdom since the advent of universal suffrage, but the people of Scotland had voted to keep the status quo by a margin of over 10 per cent. I breathed a sigh of relief that Labour would still have those forty-odd Scottish MPs at the next election.

I think the result in Scotland gave me false hope that, despite the widespread disillusionment, it was still politics as normal. I arrived back in the still-United Kingdom to see that Labour was ahead in the polls and, in the approaching General Election, I looked forward to Ed Miliband becoming the Prime Minister, probably at the head of some sort of coalition. But I could live with that; we might get Proportional Representation and the Tories could be kept out of power for decades. No more bedroom tax, no more benefit cuts, no more talk of a ridiculous Euro referendum to patch up the Tory Party, no more cuts to legal aid, no more £9,000 student fees, no more failed austerity, no more bloody free schools diverting millions from communities that genuinely needed extra student places.

Finally, when we had at last secured enough secondary-education provision in our part of south London, a new Catholic free school was created down the road from Lambeth Academy by a journalist from the *Spectator*. Jackie and a friend had taken him to the pub to try to persuade him to get behind our local secondary school, but to no avail. I was angry that he got a new school where a school wasn't needed and, when I thought of the battles we had fought, I was probably jealous that he got it so easily. They got £18 million from the government and attracted seventeen students in their first year. Remember that when you are next doing a Where's Wally Fun Run to buy essential equipment for your kids' primary.

By now, I had stepped down as chair of governors of Lambeth

Academy, after twelve years of close involvement with the school: four years of campaigning followed by eight years as chair of governors. Stephen Potter had retired, as he always said he would, once the school was thriving, and I had overseen the appointment of our third headteacher and found a suitable successor for my own role. I felt the school needed someone with new energy and ideas, someone who didn't use the template of the last meeting's agenda without remembering to change the old date at the top.

My involvement with that school had been an emotional roller-coaster; in fact, it was more than that, it was an 'emotional Big Thunder Mountain Railroad Ride', surging daily from enormous worry to immense pride. I remembered one moment which had sort of encapsulated the extreme sensations of the whole decade. I had been walking down a busy corridor as the students were heading to their next lessons when I became aware of a commotion up ahead. I got closer, and I saw there was police crime-scene tape across the classroom door, there was someone in a white forensics suit, my heart was in my mouth: something really serious had happened. Then I recognized the voice of one of our young English teachers from inside the suit.

'King Duncan has been murdered! "Bodyguards to blame," says Macbeth!'

Her students weren't even in the classroom yet, but my god did she have their attention! I so miss those wonderful, creative, dedicated teachers; their energy and enthusiasm, the spell they cast on teenagers whose lives could have so easily gone in another direction without them. They worked so hard that many of them were exhausted by the time they reached their thirties, but they genuinely transformed some lives inside that building. I recognize young people walking around Clapham today who have confidence and potential and opportunities because of those teachers. So, my apologies to Lily Allen for that time I heckled you at the Hammersmith Apollo, when you were having a go at teachers in front of my young daughter and her classmate. I'm sorry you had some bad ones, Ms Allen, but Lambeth Academy wasn't open when you were young. Teachers are the best, and so many of those teachers I got to know at Lambeth Academy were the very best of the best.

But now it was time for me to leave that phase of my life behind. I gave a farewell speech to the entire staff, and some local councillors and local primary heads came along to wish me all the best as well. I was presented with multiple and generous gifts, as well as one of those old shit-brown sweatshirts introduced by the academy's first headteacher, which I accepted with a good-natured laugh and disposed of as soon as possible. And then I walked out of the school gates, stopped and turned to have one last look and carried on home.

I had found myself slap bang in the middle of a radical new approach to education, introduced by the political party I had always campaigned for; I had seen the academy policy in action from the inside from infancy to its domination of secondary pro-vision, I had sat on the board of the largest academy chain in the country – and here's the thing: *I still didn't know whether I thought it worked or not.* What was clear to me was that you can't turn a bad school into a good school just by rebranding it as an academy; the girls of St Trinian's don't suddenly stop being twenty-seven and revert to being studious teenagers just because their school got a sponsor and a specialism in business and enter-prise. Lambeth Academy had been turning into a bad school under our first headteacher, and then became a much better one under successive leaders. Decent funding, strong leadership, good teachers and a balanced intake – these are the things that make a good school, whether it is a comprehensive, an academy or a school for witchcraft and wizardry (which I have to say seemed to go a very long time without an Ofsted inspection). It's easy for governments to change structures or labels; it's much harder to find the serious money that actually makes the difference.

I got quite a lot of flak for being 'a supporter of Tony Blair's academies', which I suppose I was, given that I worked very hard to make Lambeth and other academies work the best they could. But I still wouldn't call myself a convert to the policy of taking schools away from local authorities and giving them to private sponsors. Maybe, one day, political fashion will swing back the other way, and the job of selling carpets will be taken away from Harris and be entrusted to Hackney Council.

Having been at the centre of Lambeth Academy for so long, I thought it would be best if I didn't keep coming back for events, like Banquo's ghost. (Anyway, that English teacher probably already had a Banquo ghost hologram organized for her next lesson.) So I kept well away, declining invitations and getting my substitute school fix by volunteering at another academy as writer-in-residence through the literacy charity First Story.

Sometimes, I drove past Lambeth Academy and glanced through the gates, wondering how it was all going. Finally, I relented and made one visit to my old second home to play in an evening game of five-a-side football. Inside the gymnasium that I had watched being constructed, I ran up and down and chased the ball, but I found it was hard to concentrate on tight man-marking while you are also thinking. *Why are there no nets in these goals? That doesn't give a very good impression to the local community . . .*

'*John! Get goal-side!*' shouted a team mate, as an attacker ran straight past me because I was standing still, tutting to myself,

'Oh, I wish the architect had listened when I asked if we could have the changing rooms open directly into the gym.'

On the way out, I hoped I might catch up with David, the world's friendliest security guard, who I'd got to know quite well down the years. But there was somebody new on the desk. Instead of heading straight outside, I went the other way, towards the internal glass doors, to have a peek through at the artwork on display in the atrium.

'Excuse me, you can't go in there!' shouted the new receptionist.

'Oh, sorry, no, I was just having a quick look—'

'That area is not open to members of the public!' he said firmly.

'Oh, it's just that I used to . . . um, no, okay, sorry.'

'We can't let just anyone wander in and look around after hours.'

'Yup, fair enough. I'll be on my way then.'

And then I headed out of the door and past the beds. *They're still not watering that bloody bamboo*, I thought.

#Milifandom

General Election – 7 May 2015

It's the hope that kills you. That un-suppressible bastard optimism, the stupid dumb hope that springs eternally from the darkest cave of electoral impossibility; you squint and stare into the blackness, and look, there's a tiny chink of light – we're not lost in a cave, it's just a tunnel! And then you rush in that direction, and it's getting brighter and brighter and your hope builds and your morale surges – and then you get there on Election Day and you feel like your insides have just been ripped out. That light you were rushing towards? It was just your iPhone; you must have dropped it when you were celebrating how many people supported Labour on Twitter.

Every election, I told myself I wasn't going to fall for it this time, and then Labour would creep ahead in the polls and I would read that we were doing particularly well in the key marginals and would add that result to the forecast for the SNP and, look, we might be able to form a progressive coalition government! And then, damn it, they've got me yet again! Those siren voices of optimism, they are luring me towards the rocks of false hope.

'Oh Jo-ohn,' they sing. 'Look at that lovely Panelbase poll, go on, you know you want to . . . Labour two points ahead . . . Imagine a Labour victory, John. It could happen, you just have to put all your faith in it and it will definitely come true . . .'

When Ed Miliband first became Labour leader, he had an operation on his nose to fix a deviated septum. 'Typical Labour leader, as soon as they get elected, everything moves to the centre.' I wrote a version of this slightly obtuse gag for him at the time, which made one or two broadsheet diary columns, even though I think the essence of it was untrue. Ed Miliband did not immediately abandon everything he had stood for; he attempted to win over the British electorate with perhaps the most openly left-wing mood music that Labour had presented for a generation. It was great; I felt unembarrassed, I felt uncompromised. And then I felt really, really devastated and stupid when the electorate threw that all back in our face and elected the Tories with a working majority.

Why can't there be a satnav for politics? Why can't we know for certain where each road ends up before we choose it? Was it always obvious where the path marked 'Ed Miliband for Leader' would lead? Should we have spotted the signs that read 'Banking Crash Ahead, Turn Off Now'? Should Gordon Brown have been challenged before 2010? Should Tony Blair have brought in PR from a position of strength? Would a more radical Labour government in 1997 have made the Tories irrelevant for a generation?

After Labour's devastating election result of 2015, lots of people seemed very confident that they had known the answer to all these questions all along – but if you can be absolutely certain where unexplored political paths might have led, then you're a much smarter person than I am. Perhaps this was the best that the British Labour Party could ever hope to do, just

Tony Blair three times and that's your lot; perhaps there was nothing Labour could have done to reshape the historical setting in which it had to operate, in a world where social-democratic parties everywhere were losing traditional support and faith in democracy seemed to be at an all-time low. All that said, I still really wish Ed Miliband hadn't eaten that bloody bacon sandwich.

After the Eastleigh campaign, Ed Miliband had invited me into his office for a one-to-one talk about how I had found the experience and how Labour could do better. I thought quite hard about this opportunity beforehand, and what I should focus on for my brief audience with the man who carried all our hopes upon his shoulders. And my headline note to Ed was quite personal; it was about how he should present himself in the face of so many pressures to be different. I was flattering and rude at the same time. 'You are clearly highly intelligent and I think the people grappling with how to present you should head directly into that. "Geeky", "nerdy", "swotty", "geeky" – oh, sorry, I already said that one – don't worry about those jibes, just roll with them and turn them into a positive. Because you can't hide who you reallyare, and Ed Miliband being smarter than David Cameron might be the only trump card we have.' So that's all I said to the leader of my party. Hang on to who you really are. Don't let them try to make you something you are not. I certainly did not advise him to say, 'Am I tough enough? Hell, yes, I'm tough enough!'

The job of party leader involves a hundred different skills and character traits but, tragically, in our shallow, brand-led world, being good on television is right up there in the top three. If there ever is a Second Coming, I hope Jesus Christ comes across well on the BBC Breakfast sofa, because saving all mankind will be a lost cause if he doesn't. Nigel Farage was wrong about pretty well everything but said it with confidence on camera with that 'man of the people' act he learned at Dulwich College and when trading commodities in the City. Gordon Brown was right about most things but terrible on television, while that little voice in his head kept saying, 'Remember: big smiles at random moments!' Now Ed headed into a series of TV debates which could decide the balance of power after polling day and, though I was nodding emphatically at every word, I fear I was in the small minority of viewers who was listening to the lyrics and not the tune.

The brutal national focus group that was *Gogglebox* watched him trip on the edge of the stage after one of the TV debates, and you didn't get the sense they'd just had their prejudices challenged. Since the 2010 election, the format of the debates had evolved – or, rather, 'mutated horribly' – so that now we had various combinations of multiple leaders standing behind hi-tech podiums where you were half-expecting Ann Robinson to shout, 'Nick Clegg, you *are* the Weakest Link – Goodbye!' In the *Challengers Debate*, Clegg and Cameron were allowed off the hook, and the Leader of the Opposition was lined up against leaders of all the minor and nationalist parties, which just reduced the status of the alternative Prime Minister and made you think how good it would be to have a few more women at the top of British politics.

Meanwhile, over at Labour Party HQ, they were concerned that not enough was being done to embarrass Ed Miliband. 'How about we get him to unveil a huge plinth, with a list of empty platitudes carved in stone?'

'Oh, yeah, but with really meaningless phrases. Like *A strong economic foundation.*'

'Oh, that's good. What else will make people shrug and go, "Meh"?'

'Er, how about *An NHS with time to care?* And *Motherhood and apple pie* and all the lyrics of "Wouldn't It Be Nice" by the Beach Boys?'

'Great. Let's call it the "Ed Stone". Because that sounds like "headstone", thus associating this election with our leader's funeral.'

The most positive stuff in support of Labour came from outside the party machine. Over in my online bubble, Ed Miliband had become the pin-up of *#Milifandom*; his head on the body of Superman, his tousled hair garlanded with crowns of flowers – perhaps the unlikeliest teenage heart-throb of the decade. Labour had gained Twitter North, there was a massive swing to Labour on Facebook Central; it seemed picky to ask if we were making any headway in the actual constituencies. Late in the day, Russell Brand urged his zillions of YouTube followers to vote for Ed after an illicit-looking meet-up at Russell's east London home, but since Brand had spent years saying, 'Don't vote, they're all the same,' it was all a bit late in the day to make any difference. I think Brand believed for a moment that he possessed the power to swing the result, but then Russell's bubble only had him in it.

Because Labour were ahead in the polls but not enough to win outright, the spectre of Scottish Nationalists holding the balance of power in Westminster was dangled over English voters as this terrifying scenario in which we would all be forced to use Scottish banknotes and listen to The Proclaimers' later work. But stirring up prejudice was having some effect; English people were turning away from Labour for anti-Scottish reasons, Scottish people were turning away from Labour for anti-English reasons and 4 million people were turning to UKIP for anti-everyone-else reasons. Oh, and if you typed, 'Is Ed Miliband . . .' into Google, no, it's too depressing even to report what was the most popular search, unless that was just Ken Livingstone googling over and over again.

My own efforts during this campaign involved a lot of leaf-letting in our own patch, which I did listening to high-energy jogging playlists which I had previously compiled for Jackie, causing me to slam voters' gates too hard and leap over walls with more gusto than was probably advisable. And then up came the theme tune to Benny Hill that I'd stuck in there for her as a surprise joke, but no scantily clad lady voters chased me back down the street again.

Jackie and I were full of admiration for all the hard work being done by our local organizer, so neither of us ever had the heart to say no if he brought around more leaflets. The problem was that whoever answered the door was then the one lumbered with the job. So the bell would ring on a Saturday morning and, guessing who it probably was, we'd shout to each other, 'Can you get that?'

'Er, no, can you go? I'm a bit tied up here, reading this – er, newspaper . . .'

I did some proper canvassing down the road in Battersea, which was apparently marginal on paper, though I think that paper may have been more like ancient papyrus with hieroglyphics drawn all over it. Canvassing at election time is like cold-water swimming: you always dread it, but you always feel better afterwards. I was pounding the very streets where I used to live, except now they were full of obtrusive new bin sheds and over-large BMWs. In fact, if someone had invented a 4x4 wheelie bin, I'm sure some of these Tory voters would have paid the extra.

Battersea's young Labour candidate had worked so incredibly hard over the previous few years and it seemed so unjust to me that it would all be for nothing. To be honest, I saw a bit of myself in him: dedicating so much time and effort to this noble cause, only to have the voters of Battersea throw it all back in his face. It's why I'd ended up putting my efforts into something I could quantify: a school I could see; students I could watch grow. And yet I was full of admiration for all these Labour activists who just keep pushing that Sisyphean rock up the hill, who knew we would probably lose here but couldn't see any alternative to working very hard to give ourselves the best possible chance.

Alf Dubs came door-knocking, too, and I watched him with a sense of wonder. Eighty years old, but so much younger than me; no less energetic or positive than when I'd first met him thirty years earlier. As I was standing at a front door, taking slightly too long to decide that a voter wasn't in, I could hear Alf on the other side of the street, unrelentingly cheerful in the face of rude voters recoiling at his red rosette, and I wanted to cross the street and say, 'How dare you talk to him like that! Do you know who this man is? This is Alf Dubs! Lord Dubs of Battersea – this man is a Labour legend. He came to England as a Jewish child escaping the Nazis and then dedicated his whole life to helping others; so don't sneer, "Oh, you're all the same!" to Alf Dubs, because while you were sat on your arse watching telly, he was going to Calais to help refugees, he was organizing food convoys and challenging government legislation in the House of Lords while constantly apologizing to us for being a Lord and explaining that he thought the Lords should be elected.'

Revisiting those streets off Queenstown Road made me melancholy and nostalgic for *les temps perdus* and so many *élections perdues* as well. And then on the last sheet I'd been given, at the bottom of the list was my old flat where I had lived during my twenties. As I got closer, I could see a huge hedge of ivy growing over the front wall where I had planted two little strands. When I rang the doorbell and heard its familiar sound, I half-expected my long-dead Labrador-cross Bowie to start barking in response.

Rather wonderfully, the lady who lived there recognized me and invited me in. She and her husband were Labour voters so I started to tell her all about the Labour history of her home, the election campaigns run out of that front room, the polling-day hub, the endless branch meetings held there – but the words were dying in my mouth, it sounded so boring. 'And I remember I was sitting right *there* when we proposed shortlisting our conference resolutions to the Local Government Committee.'

When it came to Election Day itself, the only thing I did was sit on a polling station for a couple of hours collecting numbers. That was a job I used to give to the older volunteers but, obviously, things had changed in the last three decades. Oh no, hang on . . .

It was now thirty years since I had first moved to this part of south London. I used to walk across the common and inhale the malty scent of the brewery on the breeze from Wandsworth. But that had long since closed down and now I could smell the coffee beans wafting from the Costa roasting plant as I set off to vote. My son was the age I had been when I moved here, and May 2015 was the first vote in a General Election for both my kids. In a poetic piece of symmetry, our polling station had been moved to their former primary school. This time, neither of them wanted to hold my hand across the road on the way there. I looked around the school hall and remembered Christmas nativity plays and parents' evenings and hugs in the playground at picking-up time. And now here they both came, towering adults arriving to cast their votes, giving their names to the election official, going into the booths to do their civic duty: the next generation of Labour voters. Well, I'm presuming they both voted Labour. If they voted 'Cannabis is Safer than Alcohol', they certainly didn't tell their father. (In fact, the Cannabis candidate ended up with only 164 votes in Vauxhall. I think they may have had a bit of trouble motivating their supporters.)

This year, there would be a change of tradition in how we would watch the results come in. Jackie and I had received an invitation to go round to the house of some friends who were having an Election Night party. I have to admit I wasn't entirely comfortable with this. With the exception of when I was a candidate, I have watched every Election Night at home, surrounded by maps of target seats and complex lists of projected regional swings, with left-over piles of 'Vote Today' leaflets still in the hallway and exhausted door-knockers flopping down after their final push and one elderly volunteer phoning up at half past ten, saying, 'The instructions say, "Stay at the polling station until you are relieved," but it's all closed up now and everyone's gone home.'

I'm afraid our friends threw a very disappointing election party. I mean, there were lots of nice people there, and the food was great and there was plenty to drink, but the upbeat and optimistic atmosphere suddenly soured at ten o'clock, when the BBC announced the result of their exit poll. Suddenly, I didn't like my friends' party at all. Their television was awful, I wanted one with much better results.

The thing about really bad news like this is that it happens in an instant and yet hits you in a series of unrelenting waves of realization: of the lost years looming ahead of you, the unwinnable battles piling up, the damage that has yet to be done. David Cameron is Prime Minister again, Labour has been defeated again, and by now a leaden depression is pulling down the pit of your stomach as you grasp for some crumb of comfort, but there is none.

I said it felt just like 1992, and the young people present looked at me as if I was describing the Crimean War. But the sensation was just the same: the cruel trick of months and months of tantalizing polls, the elaborate promise of change, the psychological preparation for victory and then that brutal split second when the rug is pulled away and you feel stupid and angry for ever daring to hope for a positive future.

And just like in 1992, the pollsters were still predicting a hung Parliament after the exit poll, and we were told to expect a continuation of the Conservative–Liberal partnership, but as the night wore on, the Liberals almost completely disappeared from the electoral map, the Conservative results just got better and better and the only aspect of the polls that had been correct was the Labour wipe-out in Scotland. At about half past four in the morning, I decided it was time to go to bed. And maybe stay there until the year 2020.

When the dust finally settled, David Cameron had won an outright Conservative majority of twelve. His tactics had been vindicated, he had exceeded everyone's expectations; finally, his self-confidence must have got that little boost it so badly needed. Labour had managed only a dismal 30.4 per cent of the vote, with twenty-six fewer seats than the disastrous result of 2010. We had lost Ed Balls, Douglas Alexander, Jim Murphy and many other great talents. Ed Miliband resigned the following morning, declaring that the fault for losing this election was his and his alone, which is one of those daft things defeated politicians often say, although it's nearly always rubbish. I dropped him a line because of that, perhaps more for my own benefit than for his, as I tried to make some sense of the election outcome and find some positives to take from the previous five years.

But the sickening disappointment didn't go away; in fact, it grew with each day. I watched David Cameron putting together the first Conservative majority government for a generation. It was their lack of surprise, their comfortable entitlement that I found so galling. You just knew that when George Osborne or Jeremy Hunt walked up Downing Street, they were thinking, *Well, naturally . . .*

They thought they were so highly educated, so intelligent, so sophisticated, and yet they could behave like the worst kind of thugs with a casual stroke of the pen. But we had failed to oust them, we had let them tighten their grip on the levers of power. Labour had botched the election and its five years in opposition, with all the terrible consequences that would flow from that. Now, more than ever, we needed to get it right. Now, our side really needed to be smart and strategic and pick a leader and a direction that could make us serious contenders for power. And, literally nobody said, 'Well, obviously it's going to be Jeremy Corbyn.'

'Jez We Can'

Labour Leadership Election – 12 September 2015

It is said that one butterfly flapping its wings can trigger a chain of events causing a hurricane a thousand miles away. But in the Labour Party, beginnings tend to be a little less dainty and poetic than that. In February 2012, Eric Joyce, the Labour MP for Falkirk, got pissed in a House of Commons bar, head-butted a Tory MP, punched some more Tories and a Labour whip for good measure, and as a result later resigned his seat.

When allegations were made that local union officials were attempting to fix the nominations for his successor, Ed Miliband brought in a radical reform of the Labour Party membership and its system of selecting MPs and leader. Now, you could become a registered Labour supporter and get a vote for just £3 and the five seconds it took to send a text (or five minutes if it was me writing a text while my kids were watching). Everyone thought this was a bold and democratic reform. No one said, 'In three years' time, you are really going to regret this.' No one thought that this would bring chaos and division to the Parliamentary Labour Party, bring in a leader who was ambivalent about the coming

EU referendum which meant the Brexit vote would be narrowly lost, that Europe would start fragmenting and Scotland would look set to the leave the UK too. Eric Joyce broke a window when he got drunk in the House of Commons bar. And a lot more besides would get broken further down the road.

In the summer of 2015, I had not quite grasped how much politics was changing, so my reaction to the disaster of the General Election was to scan the horizon for the next ship's captain who might possibly sail to our rescue. But there was no one obvious choice whom we could all get behind. Alan Johnson might have seemed the most statesmanlike, but he had a quick look at the job spec and decided he didn't fancy it: 'Tabloid punchbag required for five years of impossible slog ending in humiliating defeat. Must have harmless family we can set out to destroy.' Chuka Umunna announced his intention to stand and then withdrew five minutes later. They were like me at school when I was forced to play rugby: 'No, please do not hand me the ball! I do not want a load of thugs jumping on my head and stamping it into the mud!'

I admired the remaining three contenders, they were all very smart and sincere politicians, but none of them felt like John Smith or Harold Wilson, the obvious choice who instantly passed the Downing Street Wave Test. Labour's Socialist Campaign Group met to talk about fielding their own candidate, but since Diane Abbott had scored a measly 7 per cent last time and John McDonnell had failed to get on the ballot against Brown, it now fell to veteran left-winger Jeremy Corbyn. This was a little annoying for everyone involved, because at some point it had become illegal to say his name without the prefix 'veteran left-winger'.

'You'll have to do it then, veteran left-winger Jeremy Corbyn.'

'But it's going to be such a mouthful for the media, listing all the Labour candidates and then having to end with "and veteran left-winger Jeremy Corbyn".'

Under the rules, VLJC would need to be nominated by thirty-five Labour MPs, but that was way beyond the number who would ever vote for him and the deadline was approaching fast. He appealed to his comrades on the Labour benches and they blushed to hear the words 'comrades' after so long. With only a couple of minutes to go until the noon deadline, he was still just short of the total. Which is when a couple of Labour MPs went, 'Oh, go on, then! I mean, what harm could it possibly do?'

And then something happened that absolutely nobody had foreseen, least of all the man himself. His candidacy caught fire. It became the focus for all the pent-up frustration on the left about our endless compromises and failures. The 'anti-politics-as-usual' revolution that had transformed Scotland and given rise to UKIP now overwhelmed the Labour Party membership and all the people who were jumping on board for three quid and the cost of a text. Corbyn's rallies were attracting thousands, which was a bit of a shock to all the long-standing Labour members, who were used to setting out eight chairs for their local ward meetings. He came across well in interviews and the candidates' debates, exuding a certain gnarled integrity that looked vaguely heroic after decades of politicians who knew how to wear a tie.

At the curry after my weekly football match, a Conservative voter called down the length of the table, 'So, John, is the next leader of the Labour Party going to be Jeremy Corbyn?' and I rejected this with a dismissive laugh. 'No, that is never going to happen!' I said, and my team mates probably thought, *Okay, well, John seems to know what he's talking about.*

But then I was shocked to read that veteran left-winger

Jeremy Corbyn had actually gone ahead in the polls. Could it really happen? Could he really change his prefix and become '*Labour Leader* Jeremy Corbyn'? How the hell was this going to work – having a Labour leader who had rebelled against the Labour leadership 617 times? Was he going to rebel against himself? Maybe Ed Miliband could try that Nigel Farage trick, and *un*resign as leader of the party?

I felt fairly instinctively that electing Jeremy Corbyn as the leader of the Labour Party would be a very bad plan. In fact, I thought it was up there with some of the all-time bad plans, like when England was being ravaged by the Black Death and the Scottish army thought, *Well, now would be the perfect time to invade.* I saw the excitement and the enthusiasm of the Corbyn campaign, the way it energized people and brought a huge influx of new members to the Labour Party. I wish I could have got swept along in all that excitement, and shared in the certainty that, finally, we'd found the simple answer to Labour's existential inner struggle between socialist principles and electoral pragmatism. But, for me, it felt like we were casting ourselves straight back to the 1980s, when Labour made itself unelectable and divided and Jeremy first bought that linen jacket.

In all the zealous certainty of Labour's reincarnation, I confess I felt nervous of making my negative feelings public. Better-known voices than mine were making their opposition to Jeremy Corbyn known, and they were shouted down as traitors and Tories, while Tony Blair was called a Blairite, which was going a bit far. In any case, I had always tried to avoid taking sides in internal Labour Party fights; I felt a deep-seated irrational kinship with the Labour Party and, right now, I felt like a child hiding in his bedroom, covering his ears because he hated hearing his parents fighting.

The atmosphere was turning increasingly bitter as newly signed-up members were denied a vote if it was deemed they did not share the 'aims and values' of the Labour Party. Those 'aims and values' currently seemed to centre around losing elections and pissing off as many potential recruits as possible, so if that wasn't their thing, they just weren't welcome. I couldn't help feeling that a party that had let Shaun Woodward switch from being a Tory MP to a Labour minister and fixed him up with a safe Labour seat could probably find room for that bloke who used to stand outside Woolworths selling *Living Marxism*, before they abolished Woolworths (and Marxism). So, if people wanted to join the Labour Party because they genuinely thought Jeremy Corbyn could re-energize the British left and oust the Tories, then all respect to them (and all Respect's members back to the Labour Party, God help us).

However, I did develop a strong antipathy for a very different group of Corbyn supporters whose vocal support for this revolution was about something much less valid. It was all about themselves. 'Yeah, well, I'd rather have a genuinely socialist Labour Party in opposition than endorse some wishy-washy Tory-lite Labour in office.' I encountered many versions of this terrifying notion during that surreal summer and I was struck with how fantastically self-serving this position was. It translates as 'I'd rather have the Conservatives be allowed to do whatever they want in government than for me personally to feel uncomfortable or embarrassed about my tiny association with Labour.' This left-winger's position is incredibly *right-wing*, because it's all about how *he* appears, how comfortable *he* feels, not about what might be achieved for the greatest number. It's posture politics, the perennial bane of the left. Adopting political positions as fashion accessories is nothing new, and there have been times when the left has combined well with musicians and designers to back a worthy cause, even if Trident missiles somehow managed to survive being criticized on a Katharine Hamnett T-shirt.

I was becoming a militant convert to a really unfashionable concept in left-wing politics: *compromise*. It's perhaps the most fundamental principle in a democratic society and yet the word is imbued with notions of weakness, lack of principle and, worse, Liberal Democrats. No one ever went on a demo and chanted, 'What do we *want*?!'

'Compromise!!'

'When do we want it?!'

'Well, when's good for you?'

In fact, compromise is how you get things done; it's how you achieve change in a democracy, it's how we negotiated a new school in Clapham, it's how every advance was ever achieved, from universal suffrage to the creation of the NHS. Because if you want to change things, it's always going to be step by step; if you want to be effective, you're going to join forces with lots of other people – energetic, interesting people who have ideas of their own and may find fault in some of yours. People are always calling for unity on the left, and unity and compromise are an inseparable double act, the Marx and Engels of Left politics. No, that's too uncompromising: they are the Marx and Mandelson.

This, I concluded, was why I could not vote for Jeremy Corbyn: because there was no meeting the electorate halfway. I personally believe in unilateral nuclear disarmament, a universal basic income, the abolition of private education, the renationalization of all the major utilities and a special £1 million windfall tax on men who go to feminist book events and dominate the questions. But I wouldn't suggest putting any of these things in the next Labour manifesto. It's okay for us as Labour supporters to separate out what we ourselves believe in from what we think Labour should advocate as a party. It's just compromise. We do it in every other aspect of our lives. Try doing away with give and take at home and see how long your marriage lasts.

So I voted for Yvette Cooper, and not just because I thought it was high time Labour had a woman leader. Maybe Corbyn wouldn't quite reach 50 per cent in the first round, and one of the others might win it on the second-preference votes? But when the result was announced on 12 September, we didn't need to bother with all those second choices; the man who had started out as a 200–1 outsider won the first round by a landslide. Perhaps that had always been the plan: bet all Labour's savings on Corbyn and then get Tony Blair to say don't vote for him.

It wasn't just the new £3 registered supporters who had swung it, Corbyn had also won a majority from ordinary Labour members and affiliates (though I doubt that his support would have snow-balled in the way it did but for the new system of electing the leader). Hundreds of thousands of people were jubilant. Once upon a time, I would have been jubilant. But I wasn't, I was really depressed. I didn't dislike Corbyn personally or disrespect him or think he was insincere, it just felt like my student daughter had just married a very unsuitable older man and, while every bone in my body was telling me this was going to crash and burn, all I could do was hope that I was completely wrong and maybe it would all work out somehow.

As the year wore on, I became increasingly worried that 'a new way of doing politics' might just mean 'being very bad at doing politics'. Labour disappeared from the news, except when Corbyn made gaffes by walking into great big elephant traps set by hostile journalists. Seumas Milne, my old boss at the *Guardian*, had been hired as Corbyn's press secretary, perhaps more for his political zealotry than his ability to put Labour's message at the top of the news agenda: 'Tonight on the BBC news: concerns are growing for the Leader of the Opposition, who has not been seen now for six weeks. Friends have begged him to contact the media, even if it is a capitalist cartel totally biased against the working class and international socialism.'

Instead, the job of appealing to wavering voters was handed over to the pantomime villains previous Labour leaders had always tried to keep out of the public eye. John McDonnell waved his copy of Chairman Mao's Little Red Book around the House of Commons. Diane Abbott kept appearing on telly even when it wasn't time to go to bed. Ken Livingstone continued to star in the long-running panel game in which you had to talk for a whole minute without repetition, deviation or mentioning Jews and Hitler. Corbyn's campaign manager set up Momentum as a mass movement to support the new leader of the Labour Party. I thought we already had one of those – it was called the 'Labour Party'.

Labour's poll rating was plummeting, but no one could agree if that was the fault of the leadership or the Parliamentary Labour Party, who so obviously could not get behind their new leader and were being threatened with deselection by members of Momentum. The general sense of incompetence spread across the whole movement. I got an email from the Labour Party that began 'Dear *FirstName*'. I have to say I was a little taken aback by their over-familiarity; I told them, 'Excuse me, Labour Party, but it's *Mr LastName* to you.' Every week, it seemed we'd hear about another stupid cock-up or confused squabble over party rules: 'Oh, look, I've got an invitation from the Labour Party about a piss-up they are organizing in a brewery. Hang on, they've put three different dates and, anyway, that brewery was knocked down ages ago.'

All of this might have been tolerable if we'd been five years away from our next important test and Labour had time to sort itself out. But the shock result of the General Election meant that David Cameron was now obliged to hold the EU referendum which he had recklessly promised during that period when he believed himself to be a political and tactical genius (October 1966–June 2016).

Nine months after Corbyn became leader, the United Kingdom had a massive decision to make, and detailed polling on the issue showed that it could be a much closer result than everyone had presumed. This referendum would be won or lost in the Labour heartlands. The Leave Campaign would paint their bus red for a reason, they would make their slogan on the side about the NHS for a reason. The people who identified as instinctively Labour had suffered most under austerity and globalization, and their ears were open to anyone who could put a half-decent case for staying in or getting out.

'Okay, pass me my coat!' said Jeremy Corbyn, suddenly looking resolute. 'I'm off to the Tolpuddle Martyrs Festival . . .'

Breaking Point

EU Referendum – 23 June 2016

My mum died. It was probably a wise move, given what was coming.

I had thought she might carry on for another decade, but I visited her on a Thursday and mentioned to Jackie that she'd had a bit of a cough. By the weekend, it was pneumonia, she fell into a coma for a week, and we were told she wasn't going to come out of it. It was unlike my mum to take so long to go, she was normally in such a great hurry; when she was late for her speed-awareness class she got done for speeding on the way there. In her honour, we really should have got the hearse to jump the lights, do a U-turn on a one-way street then park in that private space clearly reserved for the estate agents.

In fact I had already lost my mother incrementally over the previous five years, there had been fewer and fewer flashes of the outrageous, hilarious Joy, until finally there were none. I was sad that the staff at her care home had no idea what a bold, hyperactive, talkative, glamorous, generous, eccentric woman she used to be. 'Fearless' is the word my daughter used in her powerful eulogy in Cookham church; I had never thought of my mum as a feminist role model, but now, at her funeral, I got a full sense of the enormous impact she'd had on everyone she'd met. From the midst of my mum's scatterbrain chaos she'd suddenly hone a laser-like focus on what was morally right and pursue that path with obsessive determination.

The church was packed with family and friends, fellow volunteers and activists, all of whom had had their lives enriched by her infectious enthusiasm and enormous sense of fun. After the service, I walked across the churchyard to look over the wall at her former home. The slightly bonkers garden where she'd planted carrots in between the azaleas was now a churned-up muddy building site; the dining room where she had welcomed visitors from around the world was a half-demolished shell. Maybe her spirit would live on here. Maybe she'd come back and haunt her old cottage, and in the middle of the night there'd be a mysterious smell of burning toast and a bowl of milky tea made for the dog, and all the toffees would be missing from the second layer of the chocolate box.

So, of course I was sad when David Bowie died, and when Victoria Wood died, and so many wonderful famous people died, in that grimmest of years. But I suppose you respond to news of celebrity deaths a little differently when you have just lost a parent. I thought it was unlikely I could ever feel genuine grief at a piece of news. I had been saddened by news, appalled by news, and depressed by news, but never *bereaved*. That is, until the morning of 24 June 2016.

I don't wish to sound over-dramatic, but the shock decision of the British electorate to leave the European Union really did feel like some sort of death. When Jackie woke me at five o'clock in the morning, saying, 'It's Leave!' I was incredulous; bereft, angry, stunned, there must be a way to undo this, it can't be true, what have we done, this can't have happened . . . Both of us were in shock, so much more upset than I ever imagined I could be about something so abstract.

Why did I feel so distraught? In my teens, I hadn't fallen hopelessly in love with the concept of a European Parliament setting universal safety codes and environmental standards. I didn't have pictures of customs-and-trade agreements pinned up over my bed. I'd never queued all night to get a chance to watch the stars of the European Parliament discussing fishing quotas.

I think perhaps it was because of all the politics that had led up to this day. I wasn't sad about Europe, I was sad about England. I hadn't wanted to confront my own patriotism but, ironically, now it had been forced upon me, I was grieving the eclipse of the nation I had thought we were by somewhere much darker and meaner. It turns out I really did love my country after all. I thought I cared about 'society' and 'community' and 'humanity', but all that time I had loved England, and now the plastic patriots of UKIP had turned it into something nasty and stupid and small. My mother made me, then she lost her mind and died; but I could accept that. My country also made me, but then lost its mind and jumped off a cliff – and that I just could not come to terms with.

Whatever happened to tolerant, gentle England? Of course, British politics had always had a sinister side lurking under the surface, but never before had it prevailed. The referendum campaign was like being forced to read all the comments under the article. It stirred up all the poisonous creatures that normally stay out of sight in the dark, dank spaces at the bottom of the internet; the psychos with no picture and no followers who troll you and then do it again under another anonymous, number-heavy username. The language, the tone, the atmosphere of British politics fundamentally changed in 2016. Racists were given permission to abuse foreigners, Polish people were called 'vermin', xenophobic graffiti appeared and the police recorded a sharp increase in the levels of hate crime. Then, in the final days of the campaign, when Nigel Farage unveiled his poster of hundreds of men with dark skin apparently walking right towards *your house*, I felt a visceral revulsion that a new low had been reached in British politics, certain that physical violence would flow directly from this one poster.

It's an impossible thing to measure, of course, but when Indian restaurants are firebombed, or mosques have their windows smashed, or when an Asian man is set upon by a group of young white men, there will always have been some warped propaganda that led these attackers to think that such behaviour is acceptable. 'Breaking Point' said Farage's poster; it was almost inviting people to snap. A few hours after it was unveiled, Jo Cox MP was attacked in the street by a deranged white supremacist shouting, 'Britain first!' He stabbed and shot the Labour MP for Batley and Spen as she was heading into the local library to help her constituents. Whether seeing that poster is what finally tipped the attacker over the edge it's impossible to know; he had already been researching Cox's movements and acquiring weapons – but it felt like this deeply shocking murder was the uncontrollable eruption of all the hatred that had been deliberately stoked up over the previous months.

The more we got to know about Jo Cox, the more she contradicted the lazy stereotype of grabby politicians in it just for themselves. She had spent a decade working for Oxfam, putting herself into some of the world's most dangerous war zones, and she saw Parliament as the logical next step in how she could make a difference. For a brief moment, the media acknowledged the dutiful, public-service ethos of our MPs. Campaigning in the referendum was suspended. And then it was back to the ugly business of trying to turn people against the 'Westminster élite' by lying to them and blaming European co-operation and immigrants for all their problems.

And all this could have so easily stayed in the bottle; this referendum was so unnecessary and irrelevant to anyone looking at the real problems facing Britain in 2016. We should have been talking about economic injustice and low pay and housing shortages and food banks and all the other appalling things for which the government was taking no responsibility. Instead, the whole country was being consumed by an exercise to try to patch up the divisions within the Conservative Party, and it didn't even succeed in that.

David Cameron had already been on the winning side of two referendums since he'd become Prime Minister and presumed that he would easily win a third, a straightforward In/Out referendum on Britain's membership of the European Union. There were many around him (including his Chancellor) who thought his decision to make this promise was a dangerous and unnecessary risk. But in the script Cameron had written for himself, he would go to Europe and secure major concessions from our European partners and, off the back of this diplomatic triumph, he'd easily win the referendum, particularly after Dave had done lots of straight-talking to groups of ordinary voters with his jacket off and his sleeves rolled up. The disparity on the graph between Cameron's self-confidence and his self-awareness had to end in some sort of crash, the growing gap between his ability and humility was unsustainable.

Cameron tried to pretend that he had secured fundamental

changes in our relationship with Europe but was utterly bewildered when all the newspapers who had always slavishly backed him against Labour now started being really mean to him. 'This must be what it's like being Labour in a General Election,' remarked one of his astonished aides. Things started to go wrong for him quite quickly. Michael Gove came out for Leave, despite the deal-clinching fact that Dave had specifically asked him not to. Now came a crucial decision for the Mayor of London. He had to choose between the interests of Boris Johnson or the interests of Boris Johnson. The reaction of most observers was that Johnson cynically backed Leave while expecting Remain to win, thinking his stance would eventually secure him the Tory leadership. Actually I think his motivation may have been even shallower than that. I think Boris just wanted to be the star of the show. He would have always been Best Supporting Actor to Cameron's leading man in Remain, so at some level he found himself drawn to the bandwagon where he would be top of the bill. Still, it was only our entire futures you were playing with, guys; don't worry about it too much. For the likes of Cameron and Johnson, politics and government were just a game, a traditional pursuit they'd been born into – a country sport using a real country.

With all of them presuming that Remain would win, everyone in the government was only pretending to fight a referendum campaign: they were actually more focussed on that other vote over the next hill, the one for the leadership of the Conservative Party. The unpopularity of the Remain case with the swivel-eyed Little Englanders who made up the Conservative membership led to some embarrassing silences when Cameron asked for volunteers, 'Who's doing the next Remain press conference? Theresa – how about you?'

'Oh, er, I would . . . obviously . . . but Thursday's my zumba class.'

'What about Friday?'

'Well, Friday is the hard sudoku in the *Telegraph*, which always takes me ages to finish.'

Theresa May's strategy was to be like the quiet one on *Big Brother* who just keeps their head down and so manages to survive right until the end. Only George Osborne resolved to tie his political fate to a victory for the Remain camp, which led me to experience the uncomfortable sensation of catching myself emphatically agreeing with the Tory Chancellor. 'Oh, well said, George. Good point!' I exclaimed at the television, and then felt disgusted with myself, running upstairs to the shower and putting all my clothes on a boil wash.

This would end up being the election I cared most about, but the campaign in which I did the very least. In May, the sum total of my efforts was to go to the front window and take down the poster that had read 'Sadiq Khan, Labour' and turn it around because on the other side, it read 'Labour IN for Europe'. Well, I say I made no effort – in fact I had to find a new bit of Sellotape, the old strip couldn't be re-used.

I had done some leafletting for Sadiq Khan's mayoral election (the only bright spot in a very dismal year) and perhaps because that was specifically a Labour campaign, I had not hesitated when asked to do my bit. Plus, there was the extra motivation of beating Zac Goldsmith, entitled son of Sir James Goldsmith, the bloke who had originally planted the referendum seed nineteen years earlier. Labour performed very well in that election, despite one friend of ours voting for the Women's Equality Party because her husband told her to. But when the EU campaign came along immediately afterwards, there wasn't the same sense of urgency or resolve. Perhaps if I'd seen the Labour Party nationally getting really stuck in to this battle, I might have felt prompted into going out and doing something. Yes, that's it: it's Jeremy Corbyn's fault I was so lazy – I'm going to stick with that.

In fact, the election of Corbyn as Labour leader the previous autumn was one of the significant factors in the historic decision of British voters to leave the European Union. I don't think it's unreasonable to assert that if just one of those thirty-five Labour MPs who nominated Corbyn had not done so, then the United Kingdom would still be in the EU. Because the big percentage shift to Leave over the course of the campaign happened in Labour constituencies, when all the traditional Labour voters ever heard was a Posh Tory Prime Minister telling them that if they didn't do what he told them the economy would crash, and they looked at their boarded-up high streets and thought, *Well, we're not bloody listening to you . . .*

If only we'd had a Labour leader telling them not to trust the lies about the £350 million that would go to the NHS every week; if only Labour had been forcefully putting the case that Europe secured them employment rights that the Tories couldn't wait to tear up; that jobs depended upon trading with our nearest neighbours; that Brexit would not magically stop immigration and that the work of immigrants actually boosted our economy; that the pressure on jobs and services stemmed from Conservative austerity and underinvestment and decades of policies that had been insufficiently left-wing so, whatever you do, don't think the solution will come from following the hard right. We completely understand that you want to give the establishment a bit of a kick, but you can't get much less anti-establishment than Boris Johnson and Nigel Farage.

All these lines were offered to Jeremy Corbyn, as shadow

ministers and Remain HQ desperately tried to get him involved.

'So what is it we are protesting against?' he asked them.

'No, you're campaigning *for* something, Jeremy.'

'How do you protest *for* something you already have? I don't understand. Are they closing Islington Library? I'm definitely against that.'

'No, it's bigger than that, Jeremy. It's about this country's place in the world, it's about Britain being open and tolerant, it's about nation states working together to tackle climate change and to combat the power of global corporations.'

'Okay, leave it with me! I'll order some little enamel badges.'

There was a strong suspicion that Jeremy Corbyn privately wanted to leave what he used to call the 'Capitalist Club' of the Common Market, and he wasn't much good at pretending otherwise. Meanwhile, Labour Party members were working hard knocking on doors, running street stalls and certainly giving it more than the 'seven out of ten' which Corbyn unhelpfully said was his level of enthusiasm for the EU. But the Labour Party as a national organization was actively prevented from throwing its full weight behind the Remain campaign by the leader's office, where a combination of outright hostility and sheer incompetence changed British history and which I dearly hope will not end up being the most significant legacy of the leadership of Jeremy Corbyn.

The polls got narrower as 23 June approached; there were ridiculous rogue polls showing Leave going ahead, and then sensible, reliable polls confirming that Remain was well in the lead. I felt confident that, just as in Scotland, the vote would swing back towards the status quo on the day. The consensus was that the Remain camp had won the argument on the economy, and that was always the clincher, wasn't it?

The European Union had played an integral part in British society for over four decades without us ever being very well informed about how we benefitted from its existence. Whenever I'd travelled around Ireland or continental Europe, I had seen the EU flag on signs, explaining the European grants that had been allocated to a certain project or region. In the UK, we saw the National Lottery logo everywhere, but European funding was always done in secret. So many things had quietly improved, from our rights at work to product safety standards . . . I mean, had people really forgotten just how disgusting wine in pubs used to be?

You tried to focus on the complex arguments and not on the celebrities taking sides, but then you learned that Brexit was supported by Vladimir Putin, Jim Davidson, Marie Le Pen, ISIS, Joan Collins and Ian Botham, though, hopefully, they didn't agree this stance together at some weird private meeting. I have to confess I didn't know a single person who was voting Leave, and I am someone who is proud to have a diverse set of friends from all walks of life, from writers of fiction to writers of non-fiction. Oh, in fact, I did know one Leave supporter: my local Labour MP was Kate Hoey, who had last been spotted on a boat on the Thames, posing next to Nigel Farage. I had hoped for more from my elected representative. Like pushing him overboard.

Jackie and I took the dog with us to the polling station and I stuck my now slightly ragged Remain sticker on to her name tag, so that any waverers approaching the gate would see how cute she was and might feel bad about disappointing her. I tweeted a picture of her and she made the front page of the *Evening Standard* website. She looked so happy outside that polling station, wagging her tail and panting and smiling, trusting all the humans to do the right thing when they headed inside.

And then we went home and tried to treat it like any other day. But when I went downstairs to make a cup of tea, I wondered for a moment why there was no one here on this most historic of days. There were no Labour activists rushing in and out with lists of voters to knock up, no one arriving with boxes of last-minute leaflets to deliver, there was just the barely audible tick of the kitchen clock as we waited for it all to be over.

Jackie and I went to bed and switched on the radio. We listened with the light on, and then tried to stay awake, listening with the light off. At midnight, we heard the first result come in from Newcastle. 'Remain win!'

'Well, that's a good start,' I said, knowing that Jackie would be wide awake.

'Yeah, though they're saying that Remain should have won by more there.'

The pollster Peter Kellner was still predicting Remain would get 55 per cent of the vote, then Nigel Farage seemed to con-cede victory and I must have decided it was safe to nod off. The radio stayed on all night as I drifted in and out of sleep, some-times half-hearing cheering noises from the radio but never quite awake enough to grasp the context. Hours later, the jumbled voices from the bedside table prompted a nightmare that Leave was actually winning, but dreams are always nuts; I was in a shopping centre in my pyjamas, my teeth were crumbling, the country had listened to Nigel Farage, it was all classic nightmare nonsense.

But that is sort of how the United Kingdom left the European Union; half-asleep, in a haze, not quite aware of what any of it meant. The next morning, the country really was in a job interview we hadn't prepared for, we really were falling from a great height, we really were standing naked in public. At around

5 a.m., Jackie shook me, in the way that you might if the house was on fire.

'It's Leave!' she exclaimed.

'Leave are winning?' I mumbled.

'No, Leave have won. It's Leave!'

They say grief comes in seven successive stages, but I think in that moment I went through most of them at once: shock, denial, anger, blame, guilt, bargaining and then an extra wave of shock for good measure. (Acceptance still hasn't turned up to this day.) We sat up in bed for a while, listening to the commentators, who sounded every bit as stunned as we were. Jackie talked about our kids and what this meant for their future, wondering what sort of country they would be living in in ten years' time. Then she got up and, fifteen minutes later, she was swimming up and down Tooting Lido, to the astonishment of the ducks, who weren't used to being disturbed that early.

Donald Trump flew into the country to congratulate us on our decision. 'Oh, cheers, Donald, great to have you here, thanks for the compliment.' The markets tumbled and the pound fell but, of course, the real economic cost of Brexit would take years to be felt. The poorest parts of Britain had angrily lashed out against the political establishment, but guess who would end up suffering most under a weaker British economy? I had the strong sense that there'd been some sort of seismic shift in British politics. I'd been on the losing side in elections before; that was not a new sensation. But the sensibilities of this referendum were different from anything I had known in four decades of being consumed by democratic politics. Before, when a lie was exposed as a lie, it was the liar who was put on the defensive, not the person pointing out the truth. People had always been entitled to their own opinions, but not to their own facts. When Michael

Gove was unable to name a single economic expert to say that Britain would be better off outside the EU, he declared that people in this country had 'had enough of experts'. Suddenly, being well read on a subject meant you were 'out of touch', being educated made you part of an élite.

When the news came that David Cameron was to make a statement outside Downing Street, I switched from the radio to television. The lectern was placed out in the middle of the street, which, when you think about it, is a weird way to make a historic announcement; you'd have to be pretty confident the Ocado van wasn't due to turn up in the middle of it all. And then out of that famous front door came David Cameron – and Samantha as well, and as soon as I saw her I thought, *Oh wow, he's resigning.* She wiped a tear from her eye, and his voice cracked as he said that he loved his country, but I felt no sympathy whatsoever. He had taken an insane gamble with Britain's future and got it completely wrong; we had cut ourselves off from our own continent, and Scotland looked likely to be lost, too. Already he was being compared to Neville Chamberlain and Anthony Eden; the only difference was that neither of them swanned off to give after-dinner speeches about it all, at £100,000 a time. When he was first asked why he wanted to be Prime Minister, David Cameron said, 'Because I think I'd be rather good at it.' Well, it turns out you weren't, David.

The following fortnight had the writers of *Game of Thrones* tearing up their scripts and going, 'No, this is nowhere near dramatic enough! We can chuck in as many tits and dragons as we like, we're still less outrageous than *Week in Westminster.*' Cameron had resigned as Prime Minister, Farage resigned as leader of UKIP, the Labour front bench resigned; it didn't feel safe to leave the news for five minutes in case the queen resigned and declared a republic under Len from *Strictly Come Dancing*. Oh no, can't be him, he's just resigned as well.

The morning after the Brexit vote, Boris Johnson and Michael Gove appeared at a press conference with their heads hanging low and their hands clasped in front of them, looking like 'a couple of teenage arsonists', according to one Tory Remainer. Johnson's cunning tactic of backing Brexit to give himself a long-term advantage in some future Tory Party leadership race had been rather more effective than he had planned. 'You were only supposed to blow the bloody doors off,' said everyone, doing their best Michael Caine impression. Suddenly, Johnson was way out ahead in a race to become the next Prime Minister, with 'The Gover' as his campaign manager. The dream team looked unstoppable.

There are a range of things you are expected to do as campaign manager. But quite a long way down the list is stab your candidate in the back, declare that he should never be Prime Minister and stand against him yourself. Boris discovered that this was exactly what Gove had done to him on the very morning of his big launch, and Boris's grand speech declaring why he should be the next Prime Minister was hastily rewritten to announce that he would not be running after all. Boris's shambolic 'making-it-up-as-I-go-along' act now had a new authenticity to it. The shock reversal stunned the assembled journalists and Tory MPs as phones buzzed and lit up with news of Gove's own audacious bid for the crown. He had sprung the greatest treachery in modern party political history, and destroyed his own reputation at a stroke. In fact, I think Gove made a moral and patriotic choice. At the very last minute, he had looked at the imminent prospect of Boris Johnson becoming Britain's Prime Minister, and he realized this absolutely must never happen.

In contrast to all this drama, Theresa May looked like a cool head in a crisis. Being a vicar's daughter from the Home Counties doesn't automatically mean you must be very boring, but Theresa showed it was still an odds-on bet. Her big pitch for the leadership was that she didn't gossip about people over lunch, or stay late drinking in bars, and I thought, *Hang on, those are my favourite pastimes you're dissing there!* She helpfully explained that 'Brexit means Brexit,' which certainly cleared up all those difficult questions about how years of negotiations were going to pan out. Today, if you go to the *Oxford English Dictionary* and look up the word 'Brexit', it just says 'Brexit'.

With Johnson gone, May took a huge lead in the first round of voting, with Gove a poor third to Andrea Leadsom, who I have to confess I'd never really heard of until now. Maybe I wasn't going to enough Business for Britain luncheons. One thing was immediately certain, Britain was going to have its second woman Prime Minister, and it pained me that she would be a Tory again.

To make a point about how dignified and statesmanlike her team were, Andrea Leadsom's supporters marched on the House of Commons, chanting, 'What do we want? Leadsom for leader! When do we want it? Now!' They looked like the Surrey Amateur Dramatic Society attempting some play about the Miners' Strike. It's against the law to organize spontaneous marches outside Parliament but, disappointingly, the Tory right-wingers were not kettled by police and kept there for six hours until they wet themselves or passed out. Enduring the first serious public scrutiny of her life, Leadsom came under fire for exaggerating her responsibilities in her business career and then spoke very carelessly to a journalist about Theresa May being childless. She did this interview alone, without an aide or a minder. It is one of the first rules of politics that Mouth should always be accompanied by Brain. The resulting furore lost Leadsom further support in the party and, two days later, she announced she was withdrawing.

Thus Theresa May became Prime Minister without ever having to win a mandate from the British electorate or even from Tory Party members. (In fact, the only votes she'd ever got were from the residents of Maidenhead, and we know what poor taste they have.) Back at home, Michael Gove must have been thinking, *Hang on. If Leadsom's withdrawn, doesn't that put me back into the members' ballot?* but nobody asked him, and with everyone congratulating the new Prime Minister, it didn't feel quite like the moment for Michael to go, 'Hello? We could still have a vote between me and Theresa, maybe? No? Hello?'

Despite being the authors of this immense crisis, the Conservative Party had miraculously sorted itself out in under three weeks. The Labour Party, meanwhile, was looking like it might remain in crisis for the next three decades. The morning after the Brexit vote, there was a palpable anger within the Labour Party, the strong sense that this catastrophe could have been avoided. Then, to make matters worse, Corbyn went on television to demand that Article 50 be invoked immediately, which was not something even hard-line Brexiters were demanding.

Hilary Benn was the first to resign; there was some symbolism that he was the son of the man Corbyn had followed for so many decades. Then Labour front-benchers were resigning faster than you could remember which one was which. Almost the entire shadow Cabinet quit in one dramatic day; it was a nightmare trying to organize all the different leaving cards. These actions provoked fury among the large numbers on the left who still had faith in the Corbyn project, and any Labour MP checking their Twitter feed may have read some strongly worded messages, things like, 'I think it's a dashed shame, and really not on at all. #nuisance.'

I had tried to keep an open mind and had never criticized the leadership in public, but I thought it was pretty clear that Jeremy Corbyn had no understanding of how to lead, of how to shape policy, engage with the media and influence the news agenda, or reach out to any voters who didn't already agree with him. I was frustrated that so many of his supporters were determined to stand by him, whatever the polls were telling us. You hear about children developing Oppositional Defiant Disorder, but never an entire political party.

In the end, sixty-five shadow ministers and junior ministers resigned their positions. What the Parliamentary Labour Party needed was a unity candidate to stand against Corbyn. So, to make doubly sure, they came up with two unity candidates. Eventually, the fact that Owen Smith had not been in Parliament to vote for the Iraq War seemed to make him the best person to try to win over the fundamentalist Labour membership, and Angela Eagle's leadership bid was over almost before it had begun. But the so-called coup was doomed to failure the moment Labour's NEC ruled that Corbyn didn't need to be nominated by MPs again to defend his position as leader. A staggering 180,000 new members had signed up so that they could vote, and Corbyn won even more support than he had done the year before.

I really could see no way forward for the Labour Party or the country; it seemed like we had given the worst kind of Tories a free pass to Downing Street for a decade, at least. And much as I wanted to bury my head in the sand, all anyone was ever talking about was bloody Brexit. It was like I turned on the weather forecast and all I could hear was 'A lot of Brexit across the country tomorrow, a bit of Soft Brexit in these eastern areas, turning to Hard Brexit later, and then, as we head into the weekend, it's pretty much Brexit, Brexit, Brexit.' I'd attempt to start yet another *Guardian* front page about the aftermath, and Jackie would laugh to see me cast it aside after ten seconds and reach wearily for the sports section. In the entertainment pages, there was a feature about who the BBC would choose as the next Doctor Who. Maybe they should have David Cameron; then he could travel back in time and not hold a fucking referendum.

What I thought this period of history had taught me was that you must never offer some token idea on a ballot paper if it absolutely must not happen. Cameron never dreamed Britain would choose to leave Europe, he was just holding a vote as a cunning ploy; those Labour MPs who had nominated Corbyn were just making an empty political gesture, and yet in both cases the tactic blew up in their faces, with disastrous consequences.

Jackie ripped up her Labour Party membership card. Then she remembered that our local councillors would need nominating in a couple of months so she Sellotaped it back together again and postponed her resignation for a couple of months. The next time she had to present the card, it was all skewed and the words didn't line up – it seemed weirdly appropriate.

I was clear that I would not be resigning. I still believed that the Labour Party would have to be part of the eventual solution. But later that summer a terrifying thought popped into my head. I was walking my dog one morning on Clapham Common when I stopped and just stood still. My dog looked at me as if to say. 'What is it, what's the matter?' I had just realized that if there was a General Election now, I wasn't sure if I could bring myself to vote Labour. Could I really go down to the polling station and put my cross next to the name of Kate Hoey, who had campaigned so hard to take Britain out of the EU and posed beside Nigel Farage on that boat, despite her being MP for the most pro-Remain borough in the whole country?

In previous elections, I had tolerated our maverick local MP, despite disagreeing with her about fox-hunting and gun control and various local issues, because when I voted for her I was also voting for the Labour leader, the front bench and their policies. But who would I be voting for now? Pro-Brexit Kate Hoey and a leadership team of Jeremy Corbyn, John McDonnell and Diane Abbott? My dog was barking at me now for standing still for so long, but I was stunned by the very thought of not voting Labour, for me, it was like suddenly deciding, *Ooh, I think I might change gender* or *I've decided to become French.*

I had always felt a fierce certainty that anti-Tory voters who supported minority parties were simply helping the Tories by other means. And not voting was also a massive cop-out. I'd maintained a very low tolerance for the excuses other socialists gave for being unable to get behind the biggest party on the left. Of course, I would vote for Sadiq Khan again in a flash, I would campaign for our local Labour councillors. But something I never could have imagined happening was looming up ahead of me. Come the General Election, this lifelong Labour activist would be standing in the booth staring down at the ballot paper and thinking, *I really don't know . . .*

Love Trumps Hate?

American Presidential Election –
8 November 2016

And then things got even worse. I'd thought Brexit had to be the low point, but no, they thought this might be a good time for politics to take a darker turn. On 8 November, the entire world had a bad-hair day, and the hair wasn't even the worst of him.

It was all the fault of one British TV producer. Mark Burnett transformed Donald Trump into a national celebrity when he cast him as the presenter of *The Apprentice*. Without that hit show, Trump would never have gone on to become President of the United States of America. If only that producer had chosen someone else to front his show, say Timothy West and Prunella Scales. I could definitely live with a White House where the most alarming rhetoric was about the hazards of a narrowboat trip up the Oxford Canal.

'Later today, I will give my State of the Union address . . . Ooh, careful, Pru! Overhanging branch!'

'Whoops, lost my hat! Never mind, let's open a bottle of wine!'

I kept finding myself doing this. Looking back at seemingly tiny moments in history and wishing that a different choice could have been made. If only the FBI director hadn't done that last-minute press stunt about Hillary's emails; if only that final Labour MP hadn't nominated Corbyn; if only Boris hadn't backed Brexit; if only Nigel Farage's plane had crashed directly on to Donald Trump and Marie Le Pen and whichever overprivileged git decided that the weather forecast should include snow conditions for skiers headed to the Alps.

Donald Trump knew how to talk to angry people, probably because he was one. No matter how big his name was on those skyscrapers, no matter how many products bore his name, no matter how much twinkling wealth he paraded, he could not hide the boiling fury that left him feeling so empty inside. Who knows what sort of childhood produced such an insecure narcissist. There are certain occupational therapies that can assist deeply damaged individuals. But making them President is not one of them.

When Trump announced he was running for President in June 2015, the late-night comics rejoiced. This was going to be hilarious, this will be the comedy gift that keeps on giving. And then he started to win some of the Republican primaries and people stopped laughing. I was spending a lot of time in America in the run-up to the election, and my colleagues there were still confident that Trump would crash and burn. 'My father is a life-long Republican,' said one of the actors in our show, 'but he says he could never vote for Donald Trump.'

But then I would get out of New York City, into the small towns and the countryside, and I would be reminded that there's a whole other America which has 70 per cent of the population (and 95 per cent of the body weight). A village where I stayed had one little store that sold only the bare essentials: food, drink and ammunition. The sign on the wall read 'USA – Love It or Leave It!' Several big men on Harley-Davidsons pulled up outside in studded leather jackets with Stars and Stripes and skulls and not one 'I'm with Her' Hillary T-shirt anywhere to be seen. I thought to myself, *Do you know, it's possible that I've got a false impression of the demographic of the United States. Not all of them are gay musical-theatre actors with small, fluffy dogs.*

For months, I watched the two main parties going through their bizarre ritual of spending millions to attack their own front-runners in public before turning their attention on the other side. Hillary Clinton had faced a strong challenge from Bernie Sanders, but Democrat supporters were persuaded that the left can win only when it moves to the centre. That was just one more injustice to add to the list: left-wing radicals were apparently still unelectable, but now the right could be as extreme as it liked and voters would line up behind demagogues like Farage or Trump. Just one of Trump's gaffes or scandals would have been enough to sink any other candidate. Donald could mock a disabled reporter, he could deride former Vietnam veteran John McCain for being taken prisoner, he could call Mexicans 'rapists' and make up policies that collapsed under any sort of scrutiny, but enough people were so utterly disillusioned by Washington politics that they thought this rule-breaker offered something new. The day we heard an old recording of Trump boasting how he grabbed women 'by the pussy', I got into a conversation with an American military wife who was still determined to vote for him. No attempt by me to talk about Trump's attitude to women cut any ice with her; I had to stop myself being the sort of man who might try to put a woman straight on her lack of feminism. She kept saying 'those emails', but she couldn't tell me what, exactly, the problem with the emails was. The hatred for Hillary was a big factor in this election: it seems a man can be forgiven everything, but a woman will be forgiven nothing.

Finally, Tuesday, 8 November arrived. My son's American girl-friend was with us; she is from Minnesota, the only consistently Democrat state over the last forty years. She was in London doing a Master's degree in migration studies and learning Swahili; it was always a long shot that Trump would have won her over. And now she watched the election coverage through her fingers, sitting cross-legged on the floor, rocking back and forth, she was too tense to sink back into a sofa, as if her body language might suggest to fate that she really wasn't that bothered. As a good host, I tried to reassure her, but I understood that the stakes were bigger even than anything we had gone through five months earlier.

We started watching the BBC but, entertaining though it was to see Jeremy Vine leaping around a floor map of the United States, it was insufficient consolation for having to listen to Andrew Neil taking five minutes to explain that, in America, Democrats are blue and Republicans are red ('Yes, you said, Andrew. We get it!'). We switched to CNN for the microdata on the colonial-sounding little districts – which the presenter might have made up, for all we knew – but he said it with confidence so we took him at his word.

'That is an interesting figure from William County.'

'I'm confused. Is William County a man or a place?'

'A significant gubernatorial contest there today as well.'

'Oh, come on, now you're just making words up.'

It was weird that the night seemed to have exactly the same shape as 23 June: cautious optimism and official reassurance as we headed into it – 'Look at the polls', 'The voters would never be that reckless', 'There's an 85 per cent chance of a Hillary victory'; and then the first few indicators not as reassuring as they should have been. I would have said I had a terrible sense of déjà vu, but we weren't allowed to use French words any more. As soon as Hillary won Florida, it would all be over. Oh, but it seemed Trump had edged slightly ahead in Florida. They assured us that the blue counties had yet to be added to the tally. 'Blue counties? If only Andrew Neil were here to explain which party that was . . .' We cut to North Carolina: it was slightly too close for comfort but still nothing to worry about. After all, Hillary had been ahead in every single poll since the whole thing began. I went to bed after 1 a.m., still refusing to countenance the possibility that the world's greatest democracy could basically give up on the idea.

But, in the early hours, I was aware of Jackie going downstairs to talk to my son and his girlfriend, and I could hear her tears and disbelief at what had happened to her country. 'Trump's won,' said Jackie, coming back. 'She's really upset.' And I lay awake in bed for hours, becoming convinced that it was taking much longer to get light than usual. Eventually, I got up and gazed down on to our street. A couple of early risers were heading off to work under the glow of the streetlights. Life would carry on. Everything would continue as normal.

But then I stared a little harder at my street, and I looked at the new blocks stuck in between the Victorian terraces, marking where the original houses had been destroyed in the Blitz. That's what happens when politics goes badly wrong: it starts with lies and appeals to people's worse instincts and blaming innocent minorities and it ends with one group of people dropping bombs on other people's homes. Who knows where the twenty-first-century version of broken politics would take us now. *I don't know how we get out of this mess*, I thought. *I don't know how we can turn it around.* I was so sure I had it all figured out, but it turns out mine has been a long journey of seeing everything less clearly, of gradual obfuscation. I wish I could agree with the notion that love is the most powerful human emotion, but I'm not convinced any more. Sometimes, anger is stronger than reason; sometimes, our dark side comes to the fore. 'Love Trumps Hate' – that had been the optimistic message from Hillary Clinton in response to all the bile spewing from the other side. Except whoever runs her Twitter account put an errant apostrophe in there, so the message from Hillary about how she was feeling read 'Love Trump's Hate!'

Jackie went off to work, and I took my son and his girlfriend out to a local café and didn't attempt to find any silver lining on the huge cloud that was hanging over this day. I had no more answers than the twenty-something students. Later, they would go and demonstrate against Trump and everything he stood for. I particularly liked the historical erudition that went into her banner: 'Make America Mexico Again!'

For the benefit of the cameras, the outgoing president was obliged to welcome his successor for talks at the White House. Obama's attempt at a well-mannered smile was like that of a child who had just tried one of Grandma's pickled herrings and wasn't allowed to spit it out. Trump's success was all the more galling because he had received 3 million fewer votes than his Democrat opponent; he had no mandate, it was just America's bizarre electoral college system that had cheated the nation's voters out of their rightful president. But this didn't alter the grim fact that the way the votes had fallen on 8 November meant that the world's most powerful man would soon be a deeply unstable, lying, racist demagogue. I read that, on the same day, three Democrat states voted to legalize recreational marijuana. *Yeah,* I thought. *Well, they're going to need it.*

274

There was one guilty consolation I felt about the election of Donald Trump: I was slightly mollified that it wasn't just the UK that had gone mad, it wasn't just mistakes by the British Labour Party that has led us here, there was some global fault line in democracy and politics that had caused earthquakes on both sides of the Atlantic. Trump and Brexit were obviously related, though I could have done without the picture of Donald and Nigel giving us a cheery thumbs-up from his golden lift to really ram that home.

When Bill Clinton had been in the White House and Tony Blair was in Downing Street, life had improved for most of the poorest, as the economy boomed and unemployment fell. But lifting millions out of poverty can't just be a temporary bonus when there is spare cash available. It has to be embedded in the system. So, when the financial crash came along and the poorest were made to pay for it, it's no surprise that poverty pushed people towards extreme solutions. When Britain's former industrial heartlands voted for Brexit, and the rust-belt states turned to Trump, they did so because they were desperate and angry.

So, mock me if you wish, Conservative commentators, but I would assert that the underlying reason people turned to the right in 2016 was a historical lack of socialism. Or call it 'government intervention' if you prefer, or 'investment', or 'economic justice'. But in a volatile global economy, right-wing governments in Britain and America left it up to the unfettered free market to decide the fate of millions of their citizens, and guess what – the free market didn't give a toss about them.

Many of the new Labour members voting for Jeremy Corbyn hoped the party could make a more meaningful and permanent change. But I sensed that many others were swept along by the same phenomenon that caused Trump and Brexit, the 'oh-fuck-it' politics that gives up and says none of it seems to make any difference so we might as well chuck a grenade in there and see what emerges from the rubble. But nothing ever 'emerges' from rubble. You can't replace European co-operation with bindweed, you can't just give up on Washington politics and replace President Trump with some stinging nettles and litter . . . actually, bad example, that would be an improvement, but democracy, the Labour Party – these are very precious things which we should handle with the utmost care and respect, not press the big red destruct button simply because it's so complex and difficult to see the right way forward.

Any Labour government is better than any Tory government, and I was infuriated by the nihilists who said, 'They're all the same,' because, if they really believed that, then they were extremely privileged not to have experienced the difference for people on the lowest incomes between the first decade of this story, and the second. Does that make Tony Blair in power more left wing than Jeremy Corbyn in opposition? I don't know, try suggesting that on Twitter; I'm sure it would prompt a very thoughtful and well-reasoned discussion.

So toxic had the debate become within the Labour Party of 2016 that Theresa May was able to flip the soundbite that made her name back on to us. 'Do you know what some people call them?' she said. 'They call them the Nasty Party.' Ouch. People who had given their lives to fighting the Tories were dubbed Tories; vitriol was heaped upon anyone questioning whether the best launchpad for the next General Election was a Labour leader scoring a negative rating with every single age group, every social class and *most Labour voters*.

By the end of the worst year of my life for left-wing politics, there was no longer any effective opposition to challenge the excesses of the Tory Party. Theresa May could appoint Britain's most undiplomatic man, Boris Johnson, Foreign Secretary, she could ignore a major funding crisis in the NHS, she could impose a 'Hard Brexit' that no one had voted for, and still the Labour Party was twenty points behind in the opinion polls and managing to lose a safe Labour seat in a by-election.

And then the government abandoned their pledge to take more unaccompanied child refugees, reneging on the commitment that Alf Dubs had worked so hard to secure, and I felt sick that even this small but significant victory had been snatched away. Perhaps because I had known Alf for so long and was so proud of what he had achieved against all the odds, this felt like the last straw. We were utterly defeated. They had won. We had lost.

I was sitting on a bench in St James's Square, eating a sandwich with a friend. 'So, what do we want to happen now?' she asked me. 'Who is good? Who should I get behind for the next Labour leader?'

'No, we have to stop thinking like that now. It's over. There is no hope any more. See that tiny little fragment of hope on the ground?' And I stamped my foot five times, very hard. 'There. It's gone – hope is dead, crushed, obliterated! That's our lives now, for ever!'

She was laughing or maybe crying, or possibly both. 'No, John, you're the one we turn to when things like this happen, you're always so optimistic! You can't be like that.'

But, for the first time in my life, I really couldn't see any light at the end of the tunnel. At least, under Neil Kinnock, we'd been cheered up between election defeats by poll leads and council victories; under Ed Miliband, we'd had the double bonus of gaining Louise Mensch's seat in a by-election *and* the fact she was leaving the country. But now the future looked unremittingly bleak, regressive and illiberal; always winter, never Christmas.

Jackie got a standard letter from the Labour Party expressing sadness that she was resigning her membership after twenty-six years, and she filled out the section asking why she was leaving. She nearly needed an additional piece of paper. Before, I would have tried hard to persuade her to cling on until things improved, but now my response was a passive, defeated shrug. It wasn't a conscious decision, I think I had reached a place where I didn't want to think about any of it any more. Turn off the news; it's too depressing, I don't know how to process that stuff any longer; my remedy has been proven not to work. 'Despair is not an option,' said Bernie Sanders. 'Speak for yourself, Bernie. Despair is the only option, despair is *in*, it's all the rage. *Despair is the new hope.*'

Is this who I am going to be from now on, someone who has given up on trying to change the world, someone who shuts out nasty things and cares only about having an easy life? And then, late one night, alone in front of my television, I realized I had reached rock bottom. I caught myself and thought, *Wow, I think I may have sunk to a new low.* I was lying on my sofa, chuckling away at *Comic Relief,* which I'd recorded earlier. And I was fast-forwarding through all the bits from Africa.

Things Can Only Get Worse?

General Election – 8 June 2017

'So – did things get better?' I was always asked after my first book was published, and I can't believe I used to be so equivocating and mealy-mouthed with my answers. Yes! Definitely! Labour in power was infinitely better than what had come before and what was to follow; just look at all the things that were achieved – it's like 'What did the Romans ever do for us?' Just writing off the debt of the world's poorest countries would have been enough on its own, or transforming the NHS by trebling health spending and massively reducing waiting lists, or halving the UK's nuclear missiles. Any one of those would have kept me delivering leaflets for years.

But I'd also like to raise a glass to the minimum wage, and pensioners getting free TV licences and the winter fuel allowance, and let's drink to peace in Northern Ireland and beating the Kyoto target on greenhouse gases, and equality for the gay community. Let's drink to all the new schools that were built or refurbished and the huge improvement in education standards, let's drink to sixth formers receiving the Educational Maintenance Allowance;

to free nursery places for three- to four-year-olds, to free entry to museums and galleries. I've raised a glass to quite a lot of things now – my speech is starting to slur and I'm getting a bit over-emphatic – but here's to the massive expansion of university places, to paternity leave and the Equality Act, to devolution, to long-term youth unemployment being slashed, to falling crime, to homelessness being reduced by over 70 per cent. Let's drink to free school milk and fruit, to the European Social Chapter (whatever the hell that was) . . . I'm swaying now, but let's drink to the ban of those bastard cluster bombs, yeah! Bloody hand-guns banned, stupid fox-hunters stopped. Sorry, am I shouting? To the ban on the testing of cosmetics on animals – that's so cruel, how could they do that to bunnies? I feel dizzy. I need to sit down. Oh, hang on, I forgot to mention two thousand Sure Shtart centres . . . I can't even say it; but let's drink to winning the 2012 Olympics, YEAH, GO TEAM GB! Excuse me, I think I'm going to go and have a lie-down on that carpet over there. No wonder Labour never tackled binge-drinking: there was a lot to celebrate in those thirteen years.

And all that would have seemed like some fantasy wish-list when I'd first joined Labour, right after its catastrophic wipe-out in 1983. I don't know what I was thinking then, because all the commentators were telling us that Labour was finished as a political party. I read a hundred articles on how the decline in traditional industries meant that class-based politics was a thing of the past and Labour would never form a government ever again. And then, the following decade, Labour won the greatest election victory in the history of British democracy; the first of three wins that saw the longest-ever period of Labour government.

So, although it felt like we were back in the 1980s and as far from power as it was possible to be, I had come to understand that nothing is for ever in politics, not even the Tories holding Maidenhead. Oh, no, actually, that *is* for ever. I may have become exasperated with the Labour Party, but there were many fronts on which to fight the good fight, and I learned that the antidote to my political gloom could be found through getting involved in other campaigns. I joined Alf Dubs to chair the launch of Wandsworth Welcomes Refugees, and I could feel my morale climbing again. I did a film for a union campaign here, an event for the National Literacy Trust there; I accepted an invitation to a day promoting diversity in publishing, being, as I am, a great role model for Somali women poets.

Maybe it had been a cop-out to keep out of the ugly battle for the soul of the Labour Party, but I reasoned that it was okay to take a back seat for a while, as long as I directed some political energy elsewhere. Any talk of a new party seemed ridiculous to me. We already have this huge party on the left, which has a long-established voter base across the country, so many great MPs, thousands of local councillors and a large supply of tatty red rosettes in the store cupboard. A new party would face all the problems Labour has endured if it grew large enough to be a serious contender, in which case it would be further splitting the progressive vote and only helping the Tories. You can be idealistic *and* pragmatic; in fact, that is the only way to be. Pragmatism without idealism is just political management, and idealism without pragmatism – well, it's good for badges. The difficult balancing act is to try to be sufficiently socialist that we fundamentally reverse the injustice and suffering in this world but not so socialist that we start crying with love when Kim Jong-un visits our tractor factory.

So though I understood why Jackie resigned, I remained convinced that, however the Tories ended up being defeated, Labour would be a central part of that, and I was going to keep on supporting it and be there to give it a tiny nudge in the right direction whenever there was a chance. Also, I wouldn't want to miss the local Labour karaoke nite and that retired councillor's heartfelt version of 'Imagine'. Oh, no, I've just checked my diary; seems like I'm going to have to miss that evening anyway.

I hoped we might be able to limp through the next few years and slowly start to sort ourselves out, as long as Theresa May didn't suddenly call a snap election. I was quite surprised that she had categorically ruled out going to the country – it seemed it would be such an easy win for her, she had a massive opinion-poll lead and a tiny majority, and lots of difficult back-benchers, and an impossible negotiation ahead, and an easy chance to assert total authority over party and Parliament by wiping out the opposition.

The Easter break was all quiet on the political front. The Prime Minister made one minor intervention in support of some Christians who were annoyed that chocolate eggs weren't being called Easter eggs. Then, on the Tuesday morning, it was announced that Theresa May would be making an important statement at 11.15 outside 10 Downing Street. Was she going to say that chocolate bunnies must have the word 'Easter' on them? There was even speculation that this might be nothing to do with chocolate at all.

The moment the newsflash 'PM calls General Election' popped up on my computer screen I swore so loudly that my daughter had to apologize to the stranger she was speaking to on the telephone. Renegotiating her phone contract was made impossible by the fact that her father was pacing up and down right behind her shouting, 'FUCK!' over and over again. This was a disaster! Labour were going to be wiped out! My daughter told the bloke from the call centre the breaking news. He said the closest that he was allowed to say to 'Fuck!'

The 2017 General Election was the fourth major electoral event in as many years and, frankly, I wasn't sure I could take much more of it. As we headed into the seven-week campaign, I felt like I was living in some dystopian future in which there was a permanent election/referendum campaign but we never ever got to polling day. It pained me to admit it, but I thought Theresa May's surprise had been cleverly sprung. A decade earlier, she had watched Gordon Brown overhype the idea of a General Election during his first few months in Downing Street and seen how that had blown up in his face. So May had kept her snap-election plan a total secret, not giving the slightest hint even to anyone in her Cabinet. And I felt sure Labour were going to be wiped out. The Tories had millions more than us to spend on advertising and targeted social-media campaigns, they had virtually all the press on their side, and the referendum campaign had exposed Labour's chronic deficiencies as a campaigning organization. 'Crush the Saboteurs' read the front page of the *Daily Mail*. Well, it was always a long shot that they were going to switch to Labour.

Theresa May began by saying that the Tories offered 'strong and stable' government in the national interest. And then she said it again. Then she said it eleven more times and she hadn't even got out of bed yet. Poor Philip May had only offered her a cup of tea, but she just kept repeating the line about the choice between 'strong and stable government' or the 'coalition of chaos'. Her confused husband just kept nodding and wondering if Coalition of Chaos was that punk band he'd seen supporting The Clash back in the '70s. Given that Theresa May had only the one line to repeat over and over again, it was perhaps not surprising that she announced she wouldn't be doing any TV debates. She had nothing to gain by putting herself on a level playing field with Jeremy Corbyn, and her huge poll lead allowed her to ignore all the usual democratic niceties, like talking to voters or taking unvetted questions from journalists. All questions had to be submitted and approved in advance and her inquisitors weren't even allowed to hold the microphone themselves; a Tory aide would hold it to their mouth and it would be whisked away before they could attempt a tricky follow-up question. It couldn't have been more fixed if she'd only taken questions from a Sooty puppet on her hand that whispered them into her ear. 'What's that, Sooty? Describe my next government with two words beginning with S?'

It infuriated me that the press pack wasn't challenging her on the notion that the Conservatives brought 'strong and stable' government; as if this was just something widely accepted as fact. Oh, apart from the Tories taking us crashing out of the European Union by accident, and watching helplessly as the pound plummeted and Britain lost its influence and alienated its closest allies. Oh, and then changing the Prime Minister one year after the General Election, that bit wasn't very stable, but at least the new PM promised not to hold a General Election, until she changed her position and announced a General Election, before anyone realized that the Tories had no idea how to negotiate Brexit, or who we would trade with, and what would happen to our economy and all the treaties and travel agreements which had been carefully built up over the decades, but *apart from all of that*, the Tories gave us really strong and stable government. Theresa May was about as strong and stable as a jelly in a microwave.

But all the polls confirmed that the new Prime Minister was still enjoying a honeymoon with the voters. Since she was way more popular than the party she led, the new blue banners behind her urged people to vote for 'Theresa May's Team', as the

Conservative Party had now been rebranded. The Tories were taking the bold step of building the cult of personality around somebody with no personality. She toured the country in the 'Theresa May Bus', asking for a strong mandate for her hard Brexit, in the very same vehicle which, one year earlier, had toured Britain, urging everyone to Remain. Like Theresa May's views, the bus had had something of a makeover.

The Labour leader was on the move, too, but while the news showed Theresa's sleek coach whizzing down the motorway, it then cut to the car carrying Jeremy Corbyn running over the foot of a BBC cameraman. It felt like a foretaste of the calamitous campaign that everyone had been predicting from the hapless challengers. Corbyn was generally visiting Labour seats; this election was clearly about trying to cling on to what we already had. The local elections fell early in the campaign and were disastrous for Labour; we lost hundreds of council seats and the Tories' share of the vote reached its highest percentage in years. The BBC extrapolated that Labour was on course to getting 27 per cent of the vote in the coming General Election, which would be close to our all-time low. Theresa May's snap election was looking like a political masterstroke.

Perhaps the other reason that I'd sworn so loudly when the election was announced was that I had hoped to avoid having to make my own local choice quite so soon. I thought I'd have three more years to grieve about Brexit, but they wanted my response right now. 'Come on, come on, do you forgive Kate Hoey or not? We need a decision right now!' Labour's leading voice for Leave had been reselected in my constituency, despite her also supporting grammar schools and fox-hunting. Every Liberal leaflet featured the same picture of Kate Hoey, side by side with Nigel Farage on the bow of that boat, like Kate and Leonardo in

Titanic, except in this version the whole country hits the iceberg. For the first time in my life, there was no Labour poster in our front window. I was an undecided voter and I hated it.

The antidote was to go and work for great Labour candidates in other constituencies. In Brentwood and Isleworth, we all got a free tub of 'red rose ice-cream' created especially by a local café to help Ruth Cadbury defend a majority of 465. In Tooting, they gave me free curry after canvassing; basically if you're ever peckish during election time, go and volunteer for the Labour Party, because there's always lots of sandwiches and home-baked cake and generous treats laid on for all the volunteers.

In Walthamstow, I foolishly agreed to host a Labour Party Family Fortunes fundraiser. Unfortunately, I had never seen *Family Fortunes*, so I kept doing it wrong and Stella Creasy had to keep leaning in and whispering, 'No, John, now you offer the question to the other team.' Frankly, I think I did an excellent job of making all the politicians look slick and competent. Wherever I went canvassing, I noticed Labour volunteers who were meeting for the first time engaged in carefully coded conversations to work out where everyone else stood on the highly divisive issue of Corbyn's leadership. It was a timid, well-mannered dance, treading carefully, no one stepping too far out of line. Because, above and beyond our differences, we all shared an unspoken understanding that this was a General Election and we had to focus on simply winning, for any type of Labour candidate. After we'd lost, well, then we could all rip the shit out of one another.

Once or twice, I tweeted pictures of myself out campaigning, which I worried might be more the point of the exercise than the canvassing itself. And sometimes, the local party tweeted a picture of me campaigning for them, which I never seemed to retweet straight away. If you find yourself in two different pictures, it's always worth leaving the second one a few hours and retweeting it when you're back at home with your feet up, then it looks like you've been out door-knocking the entire day. If you follow a lot of Labour people, like I do, your election-time Twitter feed will be almost permanently clogged up with photos of motley canvassers standing around a sign saying 'Station Road' or whatever, which must serve some sort of purpose, though no one has worked out what this is yet. I think, next election, I may just take the one selfie then Photoshop in a different street name every day, just to save myself a lot of wet walks and unanswered doorbells.

The presumption of incompetence surrounding the Labour campaign was reconfirmed when news broke that the party manifesto had been leaked. I read the news with a weary sigh as each wing of the party blamed the other. God, we can't even control when we announce our policy of building a hundred thousand homes a year, oh, that's a good pledge; and we shouldn't have the papers announcing that we're abolishing university tuition fees, blimey, that's bold; and ending the freeze on benefits; and guaranteeing thirty hours of free childcare to all two-year-olds – wow – that would be amazing; and banning zero-hours contracts, quite right, too; and taking back state control of the water companies and the railways and the Royal Mail, yes, yes, yes! *This is a great manifesto*, I thought, *I agree with nearly every word of it*. And so did millions of others, as it turned out that, deliberate or not, the leak had given these popular policies much more press attention than they might otherwise have received. Suddenly, it felt like there was a real sense of purpose and optimism to the Labour campaign, even to suggest such things were possible felt like a big step forward.

Then came the Conservative manifesto. The clever chaps at

Conservative Central Office looked at their most reliable demo-graphic, the elderly *Daily Express* readers who always vote for the Tories in elections and against any Muslims or gays on *The Great British Bake-off* and thought, *How can we really piss off the grey vote?* They considered banning Werther's Originals or putting ejector seats on Stannah stairlifts, until one genius working late into the night came up with a brilliant new idea: the 'Dementia Tax'. 'Under the next Conservative government, if you develop Alzheimer's disease, then we reckon you won't even notice that we've sold your house to pay for your care.' The Tories were so supremely confident of getting a massive majority, they thought they might as well get all the bad news out of the way at the same time. It was a spectacular own-goal; Theresa May attempted the first ever manifesto U-turn during an election campaign and was then greeted with more scorn when she tried to claim it wasn't a U-turn. I was actually starting to enjoy this election.

Then Corbyn announced that he would be debating with the other party leaders on television after all, and May was caught between doing another U-turn or seeming remote and cowardly. Political journalists challenged her on why she wouldn't appear in the television debates, and the entire nation watched Theresa force a phony laugh, pull a weird face, give an unconvincing answer then make a bad joke that just hung there awkwardly. And we all thought, *Oh, that's why she's not doing the television debate.*

If this had been the West Country Gurning Championships, Theresa May would have been easily ahead, but everywhere she went she looked wooden and awkward and a little bit weird. It turned out that she was rubbish at this. And then it dawned on me that Theresa May had never really had to campaign for anything. She had a safe Tory seat (with one particularly easy-to-beat opponent), and she had walked into the Tory leadership without any sort of battle, stepping over the corpses of her kamikaze opponents and thus the person who'd actually initiated this unnecessary contest had never been properly road-tested on the campaign trail. You presume that top politicians just have this in their DNA but, as I had witnessed in Maidenhead, Theresa May just wasn't able to think on her feet, take on opponents or engage with ordinary people without sounding like a 1950s B-movie robot.

In contrast, Jeremy Corbyn had spent his whole life campaigning and looked in his element as he addressed thousands of people at a time, all enthusiastic and optimistic and singing his name. Corbyn was transformed from the brittle politician who, only a year before, had seemed like a condemned man, chased down the street by reporters he refused to acknowledge. Now, he was relaxed and comfortable in his own skin, he refused to get ruffled or annoyed, no matter how many times he was interrupted or insulted, which, in the case of the Jeremy Paxman grilling, was the entire interview, barely leaving Corbyn time to say anything.

The Liberal Democrats really should have been doing much better. There was a massive vacuum in the middle of British politics, and only one major party was speaking directly to the 48 per cent who had voted Remain. Unfortunately, that party seemed to be led by Tintin. Whatever that magic quality it is that you need to look like a statesman or top party leader, Tim Farron didn't have it. He was failing to make his voice heard, except when he denied that he believed gay sex was a sin, which he managed to say in such a way that you were pretty sure he thought gay sex was a sin.

A Liberal canvasser came to our door, and Jackie told him she was furious with our Labour MP but said she'd always found the Liberals a bit wishy-washy. And as if to prove a point, the Liberal said, 'Oh, okay then,' and went on his way. She wanted to call him back and say, 'No, this is when you're supposed to try and persuade me,' but I don't think he was quite as experienced at this as she was. It's weird being on the other side of the canvassing conversation. When the Tories came round and asked me if there were any issues particularly bothering me, my head nearly exploded with the number of things I wanted to scream at them all at once. But you have to stay polite, you take a leaflet and promise to read it, and only after you have closed the door are you permitted to draw on a little Hitler moustache and devil horns and then tear it into a hundred pieces.

Because it is a very civilized thing we do when we discuss politics on the doorstep; there is a respect for one another implicit in the way we accept our differing beliefs and give our consent to the winners at the end of it all. As if to emphasize the fragile humanity of liberal democracy, there were two horrific terror attacks during the campaign. Tragic, pointless acts of random murder, of ordinary people, which left you feeling numb and powerless and groping for some sort of meaning. We desperately want everything in our world to make sense, that's partly the purpose of politics: to analyse and explain our problems and their causes and to suggest courses of action that might improve things. But what can you do when one deranged man sees virtue in murdering lots of young concert-goers in Manchester, how do you apply reason and logic to the act of driving a van into pedestrians on London Bridge and leaping out and stabbing passers-by, how do we stop people thinking that this is a worthwhile thing to do?

The only way I can see of retrospectively imposing any meaning on to it is by vigorously reasserting what is right and humane about our own way of life. This election that we were all currently involved in – democracy – that is the defining hallmark of an enlightened culture. Freedom of speech, a free press, the rule of law and religious tolerance; these are precious, hard-fought rights on which we shall never compromise. The only thing of which I think we should be aggressively intolerant is intolerance itself, whether it is hate preachers perverting the teachings of Islam or far-right commentators trying to tarnish all Muslims with the stain of terror.

After the attacks, all the major parties agreed to suspend campaigning for a day. Instead of doing anything political, Theresa May made a statement outside Downing Street, repeating her manifesto commitments on policing and security. I feared that two terrorist outrages during a campaign might make voters swing to the right, but in fact some of the anger coalesced around the fact that Theresa May had overseen large cuts in police numbers while she was Home Secretary. We were reminded that she had told the Police Federation that it wasn't the number of police you've got that mattered, it was how you deploy them. Theresa May had operated under the radar for most of her time in the Cabinet, but now she was asking for re-election she was being intensely scrutinized for the very first time, and people were rapidly becoming less willing to give her the benefit of the doubt.

A lifetime's experience had taught me that campaigns make only a tiny amount of difference in the polls; the trench warfare of intensive electioneering usually leaves the parties pretty much where they were before it all began. But this election was different in so many ways. Suddenly Labour had apparently halved the Tories' lead; there was even a rogue poll predicting a hung Parliament, which I dismissed out of hand. 'Oh, look, it's that familiar old imposter "electoral optimism" turning up at my doorstep again. Go away, hope, be gone positivity, there's no place for you here.' But Labour seemed to be the only beneficiary of the support that was seeping from the government, despite all the propaganda the voters had been fed about Corbyn's extremism, now that they finally saw him for themselves, they quite liked what they saw.

With just a few days left till polling day, I was still undecided about how I would vote in Vauxhall. I desperately wanted to vote Labour nationally, but I was really struggling to endorse my local candidate. It was just that image of her smiling beside Nigel Farage that made me wince at the idea of putting a cross by her name. Jackie caught me reading about our local Green candidate a few days before the election.

'Why did you slam your laptop shut? Why was your office door closed? Why are you looking so guilty?'

'Nothing, I was only looking, I thought everyone was out.'

I wondered what all those Labour activists I had met around the country down the years would do. The local councillors I had sat next to at fundraising dinners, the branch secretaries, the union conveners – would they always vote Labour, whatever the circumstances? What would Neil Kinnock do? Oh, there he is, I'll go and ask him.

I'd been invited to a lecture being given at the BBC, and Neil and Glenys were at the drinks reception beforehand. I had joined the Labour Party just as Kinnock became leader, and I never dreamed that, one day, I'd be asking him whether it was okay to vote for another party. But they were very understanding and sympathetic about my dilemma; in fact, Neil apologized for imposing Kate Hoey as the Labour candidate in the 1989 by-election. They were in no way judgemental or critical of my reservations, but Neil said he could simply never vote anything but Labour. He had just been out canvassing in his local constituency.

'Who's your Labour candidate?' I asked.

'Jeremy Corbyn,' he said with a wry smile. We agreed that none of us could remember an election quite like this one. Neil Kinnock said that he could always predict every election to within ten seats, but with this one he had absolutely no idea what was going to happen.

I completely understood what he had meant when he said he just couldn't vote for anyone else. I try to tell myself that voting at election time is a purely rational, intellectual exercise, and maybe I would have voted Liberal if I lived in Richmond Park and that was the only way of keeping Zac Goldsmith out. And sure, I agreed with much of the Green Party's manifesto, even if I thought they split the progressive vote, which only helps the right. But here's the thing: *I love the Labour Party*. When people say unfair things about Labour, I get irrationally defensive and a little angry: hey, watch it, that's my family you are slagging off there! I am married to the Labour Party, for better for worse, in sickness and in health, in Kinnock and in Blair. And sometimes they drive me mad, and I feel embarrassed and ashamed. But much more often I feel proud, deeply proud of that picture with Nye Bevan and the first little girl treated under the NHS, or Barbara Castle welcoming the Dagenham strikers and forcing through equal pay for women, and yes, that picture of Jeremy Corbyn being led away by police for demonstrating against apartheid. These are photos from my political family album, they help me understand who I am, but now I want us to add new pictures, I don't want the battle against inequality to be stuck in black and white. And the thing about being in a great big political family is that there is something that runs far deeper than its individuals. All right, so Kate Hoey is that auntie in Kettering who got crossed off the Christmas-card list; she's my nutty cousin who got drunk at the wedding and took a swing at the vicar. But she is still related to me (twice removed, maybe), and would be voting for most of those policies in our manifesto in the unlikely event of us winning this election.

I woke up on Election Day, and I was suddenly absolutely clear in my head what I was going to do. I was going to vote Labour. Durr! Just like Jackie and my kids said I would all along, even though I thought I'd been grappling with a difficult decision. Note to self: never attempt to write political thriller, the plot would just be 'Man who always votes same way feels uncertain, then votes same way again, the end.'

As I was walking home from the polling station, a jogger stopped to ask me what I thought was going to happen. Most of the experts were predicting a Tory majority of around sixty, but I told him I thought it might be a lot worse than that. He thought so, too. This was why I wouldn't be watching Election Night with anyone I didn't know very well. I worried about how they might react to me lying on the floor in the foetal position, sobbing quietly. Our household was planning a small private funeral, as we laid to rest our dear old Labour Party, which had done amazingly to get to 117 years old but had finally passed away after a short illness. However bleak the exit poll, I still resolved to stay up all night; I was surprised that Jackie was making plans for the following morning. 'But there might still be results coming in, are you saying you don't want to watch twelve whole hours of jubilant Tories pouring champagne on each other's heads?' The verdict of the exit poll approached; I was dreading the next few hours, the next five years, the next decade. Silence in millions of homes as Big Ben struck ten o'clock. I felt a heavy churning in the pit of my stomach . . . Here it comes, tell us the prognosis, Doctor, don't hold back.

It didn't quite make sense at first. I didn't quite grasp the enormity, the wording was too vague. 'And the Conservatives are to be the largest party . . .' but that didn't do it, that didn't convey the magnitude of this news! Dimbleby should have looked directly into camera and said, 'And as a result of our exit poll we can now reveal that Theresa May is totally fucked!' with a range of other evocative swearwords flashing in capital letters diagonally across the screen. It was only when he added the detail that they were predicting a hung Parliament that the penny dropped and I found myself standing up, punching the air and shouting, 'Yes! Yes! Yes!' provoking our dog to bark, grab her toy and excitedly tear it apart in socialist solidarity.

My phone started dinging with shocked messages, there was no app for this, no user group created for fatalistic Labour supporters suddenly being amazed and delighted! I saw my son and his girl-friend rushing up the front path, and I ran to open the door for them. I think they could tell by my groovy dad-dancing that it might be good news. Was it really possible that Theresa May's cunning masterstroke had backfired so spectacularly? Could millions of people really have switched to the Labour Party over the past few weeks? All those people who had been repeatedly told that Jeremy Corbyn was a dangerous terrorist-sympathizing extremist – thirteen whole pages in yesterday's *Daily Mail* – and now the British people were saying, 'Sorry, we just don't believe you any more.'

The BBC had projected their exit-poll graphic on to the side of

Broadcasting House, complete with a giant picture of the Prime Minister. Jackie's old office window was right under Theresa May's left nostril. This prediction just didn't feel like it fitted with everything that had gone before, and yet, given the shocks of Brexit and Trump, it sort of did. Finally, the rejection of old politics was in favour of something positive, something constructive and hopeful. Ah, but, I'd been tricked too many times before, I was still paranoid it could happen yet again. The info bar scrolling underneath read 'Majority possible but not certain,' and I worried that we had celebrated too early. 'Let's just wait until we see some actual results,' said every single Tory interviewed down the line. I'm not sure why they sent cameras all over the country to record them all saying this; they could have easily used the same clip from previous elections and no one would have noticed.

Now I had to pass a couple of hours perched on the edge of my chair, a cocktail of hope and anxiety spinning around my head. The first few declarations seemed to show only tiny swings to Labour. But then the Tories failed to take their first target seat of Darlington, and I took some encouragement from this, even if a former industrial town in the north-east sort of sounds like it should be ours for keeps. The first really big cheer in our house went up when Labour held previously marginal Tooting with a huge majority of 15,458. If it hadn't been for all the work I'd done there, it could have been as low as 15,457. The reason I'd gone to places like Tooting was because I had completely given up on our chances of regaining Battersea, where I usually helped out. But now Labour took Alf Dubs's old seat on a 10 per cent swing – the place where I'd had my political heart broken in my youth had embraced us once again. 'Labour Gain Battersea': I think those might be my favourite three words in the English language. I don't need Jackie ever to say, 'I love you'; she can just meet me at the airport and whisper, 'Labour Gain Battersea,' and that would do me.

It was a miracle, this election really was going our way. Labour was making serious, surprising gains in what I had feared might be our worst-ever night. Labour gained Croydon Central; and so the Tory MP who wrote 'How to Win a Marginal Seat' duly lost his marginal seat. There was news of a recount in Kensington – Kensington? Is that what happens when you leave your domestic staff to cast your proxy vote for you? Now even the *Daily Mail* would have a Labour MP – how very satisfying. The London results were looking spectacular for Labour; the supposedly endangered Kate Hoey won Vauxhall with twenty thousand votes to spare; all that soul-searching and hand-wringing by anti-Brexit lefties like me looked sort of ridiculous now.

The Lib Dems were confirming their indecisiveness by alternately losing and gaining seats across the country. Vince Cable regained Twickenham but just over the river in Richmond, the Liberals lost by a galling forty-five votes to Zac bloody Goldsmith. The former deputy PM Nick Clegg was ousted in Sheffield Hallam, which got far too much sympathy for my liking, considering it had been Clegg who'd made the Tories' austerity measures possible. Meanwhile, recounts in Westmorland suggested that Clegg's successor might also be in trouble. Tim Farron was losing votes in all directions; to the Conservatives, to Labour and to a man in a giant fishfinger costume. When he finally squeaked home after a recount, Farron politely thanked 'Mr Finger', who seemed outraged that the Liberal leader had got his name wrong and the rest of his acceptance speech was completely upstaged by Mr Fishfinger mouthing the correct name and doing a fish mime behind him.

Although the results were erratic and unpredictable, the general direction of the night seemed to be getting closer and closer to that elusive promise of Theresa May losing her majority. But then came a series of Conservative gains from the last place anyone expected: Scotland. The Tories had begun the night with only one MP in Scotland, the most they'd had in the previous twenty years. But now they were making gain after gain north of the border, defeating the SNP's former leader Alex Salmond and their current Westminster leader What's-his-name, and for a while this looked like it might be the cruel twist of Election Night: how Theresa was unexpectedly saved at the last minute by a dozen Tartan Tories riding south to the rescue.

Labour gained Canterbury and lost Middlesbrough South, the Conservatives gained Stoke but lost Stroud. These election results were nuts; it was as if someone had just thrown all the cards in the air to see how they might land. With a certain amount of cosmic justice, the author of the Tory manifesto lost his seat. The next day, one of his giant blue campaign posters was graffitied and, instead of claiming, 'Ben Gummer delivers on jobs in Ipswich,' it read 'Ben Gummer delivers *kebabs* in Ipswich.' Tough, but fair.

In Newcastle under Lyme, a large number of students had registered online and received a polling card for Election Day. But one polling station did not have the updated electoral register, and so some of them were denied a vote. Perhaps, in another age, they might have given up and left it at that, but soon it became clear that there was a serious problem in a key marginal. The council was alerted to its mistake, social media went into overdrive, urging the students to go back to cast their vote, and Labour ended up winning the seat by thirty-five votes. Thank you, Twitter, thank you, Facebook, I always said what a great help you were to the Labour movement.

I can pinpoint the exact moment on Election Night when the anxiety lifted from my shoulders and at last I felt euphoric about the result of the 2017 General Election. I think, on many levels, I knew that there was hope for our dear country when the cameras cut to the Magnet Leisure Centre, Maidenhead. It was the combination of that grim look of defeat on Theresa May's face and the bizarre row of loony candidates standing on stage alongside her that made me think that Britain was going to be okay. All right, we might be about to lose our trading partners and our influence in the world, and we were heading for economic disaster and we hadn't quite thrown out the Tories, but we got pretty damn close and, right now, the image of the humiliated Tory leader on stage with a parade of joke candidates in outlandish costumes filled me with an enormous sense of pride in British democracy and culture. Stupid jokes, that's always been what keeps us all going; Boaty McBoatface or Premiership mascots fighting each other, or those police officers who had a special mug made after the election that read, 'Theresa, it's not the number of MPs you've got, it's how you deploy them.' I'm actually a little disappointed in myself that I didn't bribe someone in Maidenhead to play 'Boogie Nights' at full volume over the PA system. But to see our Prime Minister patiently standing alongside a giant red Muppet and an intergalactic space ranger, it sent a message around the globe about the correct level of respect to be afforded to world leaders. My American friends struggled to understand this photo when I showed it to them later.

'So that's Theresa May?'

'Yes.'

'And that's Elmo from *Sesame Street*?'

'Yes.'

'So the head of your government has to be there to listen to how many votes were cast for Elmo and that crazy guy with a massive white cowboy hat?'

'Oh, that's Howling Laud Hope – he stood in Eastleigh; charming chap – Official Monster Raving Loony Party.'

'The *Official* Loony? So that weird guy in black is not an official loony?'

'No – that's Lord Buckethead.'

'Lord *Bucke*thead?' Their emphasis made it seem that this was not the sort of name they were used to encountering within the American political system. 'He's not an actual British lord, is he?'

'Oh, no, he wouldn't be allowed to stand if he was. But he's a space-lord – so it's fine.'

Conservative candidates generally attempt a fake, patronizing smile at the antics of the novelty candidates, but by 3.30 a.m. Theresa May's smile was looking more than a little strained. Like the rest of us, she knew that her political reputation had been utterly destroyed in a few short hours and that she alone was the architect of her own humiliating downfall. She had had perfectly adequate power, but wanted much more, and now had ended up losing it all. Oh, how utterly satisfying; what an Aesop's fable of an Election Night, what an apt illustration of how greed and power corrupts and leaves you grasping at the watery reflection of what you've just lost. During the campaign, one interviewer asked her what was the naughtiest thing she had ever done. It turns out there are a lot worse things than running through fields of wheat. Her speech from the stage was faltering and weak, simply reciting the official line that had been emailed to all Conservative candidates. 'No, Theresa, you're supposed to be the leader, this might be a good time to come up with something inspiring of your own!'

I felt euphoric and incredulous. Labour had won an astonishing 40 per cent of the vote share, that's more than we had got since I was standing on that stage next to Theresa. Labour might not have won this election, but it felt like the Tories had just lost the next one (provisionally booked for next Thursday). In the split second of that exit poll, my entire world view had changed, forty years' experience had been turned on its head and everything I knew to be true was disproven, but all in a good way.

In contrast to the Prime Minister, Jeremy Corbyn was looking very chipper at his count in Islington. He even attempted a high-five with Emily Thornbury MP, but at the crucial moment she took her hand away, so he ended up slapping his palm on to her right breast, which both of them tried to pretend hadn't just happened. He'd transformed the fortunes of the Labour Party and gained the greatest increase in vote share since 1945, so I think we can all forgive him one embarrassing faux-pas. There was no way that any of my preferred candidates for the Labour leadership would ever have mobilized the support Jeremy Corbyn had managed, and I had never been so pleased to be so wrong. This humble pie is delicious, cut me another large slice, but leave enough for all those Labour MPs, and nearly every columnist and commentator who said this could never happen.

I was all alone in front of the telly now, everyone else had gone to bed, except the dog, who kept looking up from her sleep as if to say, 'Are you still here? This is weird.' I wandered into the kitchen and was surprised to see it filled with daylight – dawn had come after a very long night (2010–17). At half past five I thought perhaps I should go to bed; it seemed like there weren't many surprises left for them to throw at us now, unless Theresa May suddenly pulled off her wig, like Dustin Hoffman in *Tootsie*, and declared in a deep, man's voice, 'I'm Edward Kimberly, the reclusive brother of my sister Theresa.' Actually, that would explain quite a lot.

Then there's that moment when you wake up the next morning and for a split second you don't remember that something wonderful has happened until it suddenly washes over you and your excitement leapfrogs all the usual drowsy stages of the morning and you are immediately wide awake like a child on Christmas morning. I rushed to turn on the radio news, just as they were attempting to explain the election result. The Conservative Party had won, but it had lost. The Labour Party had lost, but it had won. In Scotland, the SNP had won but lost, and the Conservatives had lost but won. The Liberals had slightly increased its number of MPs by slightly reducing its vote share. Having doubled their number of leaders, the Greens had managed to halve their number of voters. UKIP had . . . oh, they're not even worth talking about any more. Northern Ireland still liked to do things differently to the rest of the country; over there, it's impossible to get elected unless you *are* accused of being connected to terrorists. All the more moderate parties were wiped out, leaving the province divided right down the middle, but offering a possible lifeline to Theresa May. There were now ten MPs from the Democratic Unionist Party, so she could form an alliance with them, if she didn't mind their rather out-of-date social policies, which had yet to catch up with the publication of the New Testament. So the Conservative Party could continue in government with its well-known manifesto promises: to maintain current tax levels, to proceed with Brexit negotiations and to smite the antichrist who doth spill his seed upon the soil. In 2015, they had told us 'Don't let Scotland pull the strings,' and in 2016 they had told us, 'Don't let Brussels pull the strings,' and then in 2017 they tied us to the DUP. I wonder if Philip May said to his wife, 'It's quite ironic, isn't it, you warning about "a coalition of chaos", and then having to . . . what? Why are you looking at me like that?'

So the Nasty Party carried on with the help of the Even Nastier Party, and Theresa May stayed on in 10 Downing Street. We didn't want her there, the Tory Party no longer wanted her there, but there was just no way of getting rid of her; Theresa May was like that U2 album on your iTunes. But although nothing had changed, it felt like everything had changed. Because one day we had looked like we were out of power for a generation and still rushing down the path of political obscurity and the next, we had deprived the Tories of a working majority and turned the established orthodoxy upside down. The old rules of story-telling came in to play: now that Theresa May had shown herself to be a loser, everything she did was seen through that prism. Her speech outside Downing Street was wrong, her attempt to make amends for it was wrong, her attempt to soldier on and form a government was wrong, but if she had resigned the Tory leadership, that would have been wrong, too. Frankly, it was nice to see it happening to someone else for a change. Some might call it *Schadenfreude*, but I didn't think my joy was shameful; for me it was 'completely justified and long overdue joy', it was *Längstfälligevölligberechtigtefreude*.

The received wisdom was that it was the increased turnout from young people which had swung this election, but this verdict came with a slightly patronizing subtext that it was just those idealistic students who had voted for Jeremy's 'magic-money tree' and they'd soon learn life wasn't that simple. In fact, the greatest swing was among thirty-five to forty-four-year-olds: people struggling with job insecurity and the cost of housing, worried about their elderly parents and their kids' education;

the victims of in-work poverty, constantly being pushed to work longer hours for less money. Millions of ordinary people of all ages voted Labour for very good reasons, so stop interviewing that white rasta with all the massive nose piercings, as if to say, 'It was all these guys who supported Corbyn.' I supported Corbyn, the Parliamentary Labour Party supported Corbyn, millions of us suddenly became lifelong Corbyn supporters at 10 p.m. on 8 June. I mean, there may have been a bloke who looked just like me going around saying we were going to lose fifty seats, but he knows nothing about politics, you should never listen to him. Oh, and that foolish person may have also given the impression he thought Corbyn preferred the purity of permanent opposition and was incapable of the compromise needed to lead a party and a country – but I'm sure this was just affectionate banter.

I would never call myself a Corbynista; if I was forced to define my politics by one individual, well, I don't know, I aspire to George Bailey in *It's a Wonderful Life* but probably come over more like Rik from *The Young Ones*. I had thought his contempt for successive Labour leaders made Jeremy Corbyn unsuitable to be Labour leader. But my biggest problem had always been that I'd thought that he could never appeal beyond the people at his rallies. And then it turned out that there must have been 12,874,985 people at his rallies.

Of course, some people had voted Labour despite its leader, not because of him, but that's always the case. Those of us who thought we had it all figured out were the last to see how much things had changed. There were one or two New Labour throwbacks still trying to claim that a more centrist leader could have got that extra 3 per cent that Tony Blair had won in 1997, but nobody was buying it. Tony Blair had had the good fortune to face an utterly divided and discredited Tory Party, and that's where our opponents were heading right now. If Corbyn became Prime Minister, I am sure he would do things I disagreed with, but probably not as big as invading Iraq or causing Brexit, so perhaps all those people who were still so sure he'd be a disaster might try showing a little bit of humility for a while. We had just added three and a half million votes to our total from two years earlier, and that doesn't happen because you've changed the font on the leaflets.

If I met that man by the river in Oxfordshire again, I might have to correct him. I'm not *very* left wing, I'm just a supporter of the Labour Party, that stuff's all quite mainstream now. Abolishing tuition fees, building social housing, taking key utilities under state control, banning unpaid internships, a minimum wage of £10 an hour, that's all just common sense, aimed at making you live in a happier, less divided country. I'd urge him to vote for Corbyn just as, once, I would have urged him to vote for Blair.

When Labour came to power back in 1997, I'd thought my politics had finally come of age; we had found the route to power for the left, even if it wasn't quite the left I'd originally signed up for. But nothing stays the same. Now it was two decades on from that great watershed, my children had become adults, my parents had died, but my political family, the Labour Party, well, somehow it got younger.

What I had thought was naïve was actually bold; what I thought was self-indulgent was actually reaching out. For years, I'd wanted people on the left to compromise, in order to appeal to the wider electorate. But 8 June 2017 showed that it was me who had to compromise; the opposite route was also possible. This is a new type of Labour Party now, maybe Jeremy Corbyn should mark it with a new name. I'm trying to think of a new-sounding word that you could put in front of 'Labour' to signify this.

Hope – that's the precious fuel of progress that was coursing through our veins once again. Finally, enough people had faith in the modest notion that everything didn't always have to be so shitty. Obama had called his book *The Audacity of Hope*, which was exactly how progressive politics felt right now (and was probably a better book title than *Everything Doesn't Always Have to Be So Shitty*). I'd sensed the infectious hope in those Labour Party activists striding out ahead of me, I had seen it in seventeen-year-old Malika, who'd come canvassing with us for the very first time and I'd felt it from seventy-year-old Tom, who'd been fighting the Tories for half a century, through the good times and the bad. I had felt hope emanating from those thousands of people all around me on the demonstration against Trump's state visit, and I had felt it sitting all alone in the dead of night, watching the last few election results being declared.

Thank God for those optimists and the activists who kept on going when I didn't, for the people who never stopped knocking on doors for Labour or volunteering for charities to help those in greatest need, for those who sit in long meetings to make sure it all happens and the thousands of people on the marches who make a stand for what is right and do it with far wittier signs than we ever had when I was young. 'Melania; Blink Twice If You Want Us to Rescue You' or 'I'm Not Normally a Sign Guy, but Jeez'. Whenever I see how many people care, it fills my heart with pride and faith that the left will prevail in the end, because I know that we are right and they are wrong. Societies can only function if we do things for each other and not just for ourselves. It is the basis of every religion, it is the central lesson of history, the message of all the fables told down the centuries: selfishness leaves you with less, altruism makes you richer; we are all happier when we help each other, we are all of us diminished when we abandon anyone. So, we will prevail if we can be constructive, strategic and optimistic.

'The arc of the moral universe is long, but it bends towards justice' – Martin Luther King
'May your choices reflect your hopes, not your fears' – Nelson Mandela
'Just try not to be a twat' – John O'Farrell

Above my desk are pictures of my mum and dad from the mid-1940s, my dad still in his army uniform, and I think of the massive obstacles their generation had to overcome to create the caring, inclusive society they brought me into. And now my children are the age my parents were in those photos, and the political battles have morphed and reinvented themselves, but each generation of activists rises to the challenge. One of my grown-up kids is a party member, the other isn't; but far more importantly, both of them will help make the world a better place on various fronts, like so many of their generation. And my political education continues from them, and from Jackie, and from all the other thoughtful people I know who do so much more than me. I'm still learning the best way to be left wing, I'm still trying to find out how we can effect positive change, all I know for sure is that it won't happen if I do nothing and that none of us can do it on our own.

And my son has just invited me to a talk on child refugees that he is going to with his girlfriend. The speaker is Alf Dubs.

'You know I used to work for him when I was exactly your age?'

'Yeah, I know – that's why I thought you might like to join us.'

We go for a drink afterwards, and I watch Alf chatting away with my son, and I feel like I am staring down from above, watching these two meet for the first time, an eighty-four-year-old Labour Lord and a twenty-four-year-old charity worker; they speak the same political language, share so many presumptions and values. And later, my daughter rings up and tells us all about the Women's March and she's not seeing that new bloke again, he told her he never voted. They are just two of the millions of young people who turned out for Labour at this election, part of the highest youth turnout for decades that proved that voting really does make a difference and they make me feel optimistic about the years ahead as the baton is passed from one generation to the next.

And I think back to when my daughter was six years old and she joined the local Brownies and I helped her learn her Brownie-Guide promise. In her sweet little voice, she recited the sacred pledge to her mum: 'I promise to love my god, to serve my queen, to help other people *and smash the Tories*!' Jackie turned to me and said, 'What the hell! What if she says that in the church hall?'

'Well, it might liven things up a bit.' Every time she practised it to her grandmother or family friends, her angelic voice always promised to smash the Tories, she was enjoying getting huge laughs, but even I was becoming paranoid that she really might say that in front of Brown Owl and all the other mums and dads. Then the moment came. She stepped up in her new uniform, raised her three fingers in the Brownie salute and did the pledge perfectly, for the first time leaving out the promise to smash the Tories. She just looked across at her dad and gave me a little wink instead.

That wink said so much. It said, 'Don't worry, Dad – we will . . .'

Acknowledgements

Enormous thanks are due to everyone who read earlier drafts of this book and suggested improvements, large and small: John McNally, Pete Sinclair, Bill Scott-Kerr, Darcy Nicholson, Georgia Garrett and most of all Jackie, Freddie and Lily. And if you ever so much as delivered one bunch of leaflets for the right side – then thank you.

J O'F, July 2017

John O'Farrell's first book was a bestselling memoir, *Things Can Only Get Better*. Since then he has published five novels: *The Man Who Forgot His Wife*, *May Contain Nuts*, *This Is Your Life*, *The Best a Man Can Get* and, most recently, *There's Only Two David Beckhams*. He has also written two bestselling history books: *An Utterly Impartial History of Britain* and *An Utterly Exasperated History of Modern Britain*, as well as three collections of journalism from his *Guardian* columns. His books have been translated into thirty languages and have been adapted for radio and television. A former comedy scriptwriter for such productions as *Spitting Image, Room 101, Have I Got News For You, Murder Most Horrid* and *Chicken Run*, he recently co-wrote the Broadway musical *Something Rotten!*

@mrjohnofarrell